The Changing Face of Religion

The Changing Face of Religion

Edited by

James A. Beckford and
Thomas Luckmann

 SAGE Studies in International Sociology 37
sponsored by the International Sociological Association/ISA

First published 1989, first paperback edition 1991

SAGE Publications Ltd
6 Bonhill Street
London EC2A 4PU

SAGE Publications Inc
2455 Teller Road
Newbury Park, California 91320

SAGE Publications India Pvt Ltd
32, M-Block Market
Greater Kailash – I
New Delhi 110 048

British Library Cataloguing in Publication data

The changing face of religion. – (Sage studies
   in international sociology; 37)
   1. Society. Role of religion
   I. Beckford, James A. (James Arthur), *1942*
   II. Luckmann, Thomas
   306'.6

   ISBN 0-8039-8211-9
   ISBN 0-8039-8592-4 pbk

Library of Congress catalog card number 89–060459

Typeset by Photoprint, Torquay, Devon
Printed in Great Britain by Billing and Sons Ltd, Worcester

Contents

Introduction

James A. Beckford and *Thomas Luckmann*

This collection of papers has two main objectives. The first is to account for the changing meaning and form of religion in the modern and modernizing worlds. The second is to discuss the challenge that changes in religion are continually presenting to social scientists. In combination, these twin objectives are at the very core of the sociology of religion.

The birth of the social and human sciences coincided with the dawn of what came to be known as industrial society, and religion was of central importance to most commentators on the nature of the industrial society which was emerging in Europe and North America in the nineteenth century. For some, religion was expected to continue to contribute towards the stability of the new type of society even if it had to assume heavily modified or disguised forms. For others, religion in all forms would have to be swept away if the potential benefits of the new social order were ever to be realized. Still others refrained from such long-term speculation, preferring instead to examine in detail the shifting and possibly unpredictable relationships between religion and political forces, economic affairs, moral values, education, and the practical affairs of everyday life.

The thread which runs through studies of religion by the first generations of social scientists was a strong concern with the place of religion in rapidly changing societies. The changing face of religion was regarded both as a symptom of social change and as a source of change in itself. The dominant questions were therefore about the fate of religion in an increasingly urbanized world of formal organizations, rational work disciplines, impersonal market forces, and centralized state administration. This was the situation at the dawn of industrial society, and disagreement about the overall meaning or direction of religious changes is still rife.

The chapters in this volume illustrate the complexity of, and the subtle shades of meaning associated with, concepts of religious change. None of the contributions gives credence to the kind of triumphalism which might suggest that religious change was necessarily tending in a certain direction. There is no 'master' theory of religious change here. Three particular themes emerge most strongly. First, many contributions have a bearing on the concept of secularization, with the majority of them rejecting vulgar or mechanical applications of it to their particular topics. Evidence of its applicability is certainly presented, but in each case authors have also found it necessary to emphasize its occasionally contradictory and paradoxical features. No support is given to the triumphalist scenario of secularization, according to which the declining significance of religion is a necessary feature of modernizing and modern societies.

A second focus of many chapters is the argument that the functional differentiation of religion from other social institutions has banished it from the public domain and has relegated it to a private sphere of life. There is some support for the idea that religion is no longer the principal agent of societal integration in many societies, and its declining salience in public life is acknowledged in several chapters. Yet, it is also argued that the declining power of formal religious organizations in many western societies should not be allowed to hide the fact that purely voluntary and relatively specialized expressions of religiosity remain important.

Thirdly, several chapters actually challenge the functional differentiation thesis by focusing on the capacity of religion in some modernizing societies to re-draw or blur the boundaries between the public and the private realms. Evidence is discussed of religious symbolism and ideology which have the effect of re-framing supposedly private matters in terms of their public significance, and vice versa. It is even suggested that some religious movements are conveying new images of the global dimension of human life in the late twentieth century.

This collection does not set out to be comparative or exhaustive. Instead, authors were encouraged to write about the changing face of religion in the countries of their choice in the terms which were considered most appropriate to the situation. But there is a common focus on the changing position and significance of religion in society. The result is a unique set of chapters reflecting a balance between western and non-western countries. All the contributors are specialists in the study of religion in the countries about which they are writing.

*   *   *

The collection begins with a wide-ranging chapter in which Roland Robertson calls in question two things. The first is the uncritical use that sociologists have often made of 'secularization' in their attempts to identify trends in religious change. The second is the practice of thinking about religion exclusively in relation to the nation state. Robertson argues for the need to take into account the uniquely modern 'process of globalization', that is, 'the making of the world into a single sociocultural place'. In this perspective, separate states are said to be subject to pressures arising from the world-wide system of states. One early effect was to foster the idea that states were normally secular and that religion was a private concern. But, the argument continues, the tendency towards a western-led separation of religion from politics began to be reversed in the mid-1970s. States became more involved in regulating 'deep' issues of human life, and religious groups in turn took a greater interest in regulating political matters. The recent politicization of religion and religionization of politics are both interpreted by Robertson as responses to globalization at the level of societies, individuals, international relations, and mankind. As the apparatuses of government and economics have increasingly converged on a common (secular) model, there is evidence of a growing diversity of claims to distinctive cultural identity. Heightened awareness of the possibility of global annihilation by warfare or disease also strengthens the search for meaning and identity in a world that may appear to be 'dangerously' small. None of this, of course, denies the fact that politics and religion have been intertwined in various and varying ways at virtually all periods of human history. Robertson's argument about *recent* increases in politicized religion and religionized politics is set firmly against a background of the genuinely unprecedented circumstance of intense preoccupation with globalization. One of the major implications of this approach is that it runs counter to many expectations of secularization. Another is the demonstration that religious change must be situated in the context of wider social changes.

Robertson is careful to make it clear that the process of globalization is not simply confined to the level of states and systems of international relations. In fact, it is said to have a formative influence on present-day conceptualizations of the individual person as a relatively autonomous actor who is increasingly subject to pressures to identify selfhood with universal norms of 'mankind-ness'. This type of identity is very different, then, from the kind of *privatized* meanings which are widely believed to characterize culture in the modern and post-modern worlds. There is considerable tension, therefore, between the thesis of globalization and the thesis that Luckmann expounded in his book, *The Invisible Religion* (1967). Both theses are, in turn, in tension with yet another account of the changing face of religion, namely, Cipriani's thesis of 'diffused religion'.

The basis of Cipriani's argument for the importance of diffused religion in modern Italy lies in the recent improvement in the quality of relations between the Vatican and the Italian state. They agree to operate in separate spheres, but it is also acknowledged that many areas of public life remain open to Catholic influence. This means that, although many Italian Catholics depart from the codes of conduct that are explicitly enjoined on them by their church, they nevertheless continue to act partially in accordance with values acquired during religious socialization. Diffused religion represents a sediment of religious faith which is, on occasion, stirred up in day-to-day decision-making and may therefore exert an influence even on those outside the ranks of active church-goers and voters for the Christian Democrat party. Cipriani goes further and suggests that as Italian Catholics emerge from 'their ghetto of religious structures', they are consequently more likely to bring their basically Christian values to bear on issues in the public sphere. This suggestion could be construed, then, as a direct contradiction of the widespread view that the public realm has become sharply separated from, and immune to, the influence of 'privatized' religion.

The conclusion of Lambert's chapter on the religious changes that have taken place in a small Breton village during the twentieth century suggests that the notion of 'privatization' does indeed help to make good sense of them – but not on its own. The 'parochial civilization', in which the Roman Catholic church and its associated organizations played the central role, has gradually lost its capacity to structure the lives of parishioners and the activities of the community. Instead, religious practice has become largely a matter of personal choice and private conscience, especially in the post-Second World War period. There is still respect for some religiously celebrated rites of passage, but religious feasts and saints' days have been either abandoned or modified to suit the convenience of a more mobile, leisure-oriented population. The overall picture is therefore one of declining levels of religious practice in public and of rising levels of indifference towards religion in cognitive, moral, and spiritual terms. Yet, Roman Catholicism remains the only ordered system of beliefs and values to which most villagers still subscribe – however weakly. They have moved away from ideas about hell and they tend to be critical of some of the church's teachings; but religion has not disappeared entirely. Instead, Lambert insists that the villagers have evolved a new type of religiosity, 'transcendent humanism', which prizes the achievement of various humanistic ideals on earth such as love, justice, peace, human rights, and solidarity. There are various contradictions at work, then, between the forces secularizing formal religion and sacralizing aspects of everyday life. In part, this unquestionably conforms with the expectations of the privatization thesis. But, on the other hand, there is also scope for the application of transcendent humanism to matters in the public domain. It might be concluded that the analytical separation of public from private is not as clear-cut as some theories of secularization suggest.

A further refinement of the notion of secularization is made by Hill and Zwaga in their chapter on the changing face of religion in New Zealand. By contrast with the formerly hegemonic position of Roman Catholicism in the kind of French village where transcendent humanism has recently evolved, the religious situation in New Zealand has always been more diverse. Data from the New Zealand census, beginning in the mid-nineteenth century, show that rates of church participation have been considerably lower than in the UK and that 'nominal' membership of various Christian denominations has been the norm for a long time. Alongside the Christian churches a number of Maori movements of resistance and rebellion have added to the complexity at various times. Moreover, the pluralism in the sphere of religion has been matched by a largely secular political constitution for New Zealand. There was, then, no 'golden age' of religion in the country's modern history, but religious change has nevertheless been pronounced in several respects. The extent of nominal membership of churches has increased; the mainline denominations account for progressively smaller proportions of the total membership of all religious groups; the age-profile of mainline denominations shows a disproportionately small number of young adults and a high number of elderly people; but, by contrast, the fast-growing sectarian groups such as the Mormons, the Jehovah's Witnesses, and certain Pentecostals have an over-representation of young adults and an under-representation of the elderly. The major shifts therefore include the growing diversity of religious groups, the relative decline of membership of mainline denominations, the relative increase of membership of more specialized groups, and the swelling ranks of people who are not prepared to report any religious adherence on their census form.

To some extent, similar changes also form the backdrop to Maria Isaura Pereira de Queiroz's chapter on the growth of spiritism in modern Brazil. As the formerly hegemonic Roman Catholic church has moved into more specialized niches in Brazilian society, so the equally specialized spiritist movements have also proliferated. It is difficult to accommodate these changes within conventional accounts of secularization. The twentieth century has seen the proliferation of spiritist movements which combine, in varying combinations and proportions, ideas which originate in West Africa, pre-Columbian South America, and western Europe about the vital forces of the spirit world. As in the case of modern African religions, many Brazilian movements are syncretistic and focused mainly on the practical problems of life in Third World towns and cities. Their striking diversity is matched by the fluidity of their organizational forms and the continual mutation of their rituals. The result is a kaleidoscope of shifting images and practices which seem to fit well with the hectic pace of change in Brazilian society and culture. Indeed, Maria Isaura Pereira de Queiroz argues that the spiritist movements, *umbanda* in particular, having captured the emergent ethos of Brazil's rapidly modernizing cities – not just among oppressed and marginal people but also among the growing numbers of workers in service, white-collar, and technical occupations. Some movements, with distinctively ethnic or tribal origins, have actually helped to overcome profound social divisions and have contributed towards a genuinely national religious culture. The codification of beliefs, moral values, rituals, and organizational practices is inseparable from the transcendence of formerly tribal cultures and identities. Yet, other movements cling to their tribal origins and remain separate from the processes of homogenization and 'nationalization' which are characteristic of *umbanda*. The implication is that a notion like secularization would make very little sense of the changes that have taken place in Brazilian spiritism over the last hundred years. Nor would it throw much light on the growing salience of *umbanda*, in particular, within many sections of Brazilian society. Yet, this movement appears to be content to remain separate from the state although it nevertheless seems to contribute towards a kind of civil religion.

The same can definitely *not* be said about Islamic fundamentalism today. In fact, Arjomand's chapter shows that the fundamentalist ideologies which are gaining popularity in many Middle Eastern countries as well as, of course, guiding the Iranian revolution since 1979 are based on the assumption that Islam is a 'totally unified sociopolitical system and a total way of life'. But the idea of political ideologies is said to have spread to the Islamic countries of the Third World from the capitalist world as well as from state socialist countries. It was aided by migration from rural to urban areas and by the spread of literacy, and its principal protagonists in many countries have been journalists and university graduates opposed to the kinds of ideologies (such as liberalism, nationalism, and socialism) which had undergirded earlier movements of Islamic renewal in the modern era. Islamic fundamentalist ideologies are especially opposed to the idea of separating religion from government, and their ideal of the Islamic state knows no geographical boundaries.

Although Ayatollah Khomeini's particular version of this ideological tendency differs in key respects from that of other fundamentalist ideologues such as Maulana Mawdudi and Hassan al-Banna, there is strong agreement on the necessity to develop a distinctively Islamic state. This ideological development makes sense in the context of forces currently leading many Islamic societies towards national integration, societalization, and entry into the world systems of economics and politics. It represents a type of modernization without secularization – at least, in the short term. This is not to deny, however, that the pattern of ideological, political, and religious developments is varied in other countries where Islam is the dominant religion. The diversity of Muslim responses to modernization in such countries as Egypt, Saudi Arabia, Pakistan, Algeria, and Libya serves as a warning against facile generalizations about the relationship between Islam and politics.

This warning is emphasized in Regan's chapter on the Malaysian state's response to resurgent Islamic movements such as the *dakwah*. He underscores the ambivalence that marks official views of the evangelistic and fundamentalist movements which have found an enthusiastic following among sections of Malaysian youth. On the one hand, the government is suspicious of resurgent Islam's potential for political mobilization; but on the other, it has occasionally acknowledged the ethical ideals and codes of Islam as its own. There is, in fact, competition between the state and the religious movements for leadership and control of Islamic initiatives. Rule by mullahs, for example, has been strongly criticized and disparaged as 'un-Islamic' by leading politicians, and 'religious extremism' has been identified as a threat to national security. The main reason is not so much fear of Islamic revolution as fear of a breakdown of the 'consociational' type of regime which depends on intercommunal consensus at the level of ethnic group leaders. In particular, it is feared that Islamic resurgence may generate disproportionate power and resources for the Malay–Muslim 'pillar' or bloc, thereby accentuating universal or global themes at the expense of local arrangements and balances. This has been a recurrent possibility in the history of Malaysian Islam but it has recently assumed special significance in the light of Islamic fundamentalism's resurgence in Western Asia and of increasingly global sensitivities in the world system of nation states.

New or insurgent movements of religion in the Third World are not confined to Islam, and, as Bennetta Jules-Rosette's chapter on parts of Africa shows, they present especially challenging questions to the sociologist of religion. In addition to emphasizing the complexity of processes of change in many African states, she argues that notions of secularization which originated in western theories of industrialization and modernization are largely irrelevant to a sound understanding of the current transformations of African religion. In particular, various new religious movements are shown to integrate novel ideas of the sacred into everyday life in such a way as to enhance feelings of personal and collective empowerment. New religious groups *and* nationalistic political movements are both said to be re-sacralizing African societies at the same time as they are adapting to modern social and economic institutions. The thrust of secularizing forces is thus countered by a variety of religious responses including neo-traditionalism, revitalization, syncretism, and millenarism. Each response runs into problems when it takes organizational form and when it confronts the power of the state apparatus, but leanings towards ecumenism, social welfare, and political sophistication may herald the long-term viability of some of the current experiments in African religion. In turn, the new religious movements can supply fresh symbols of moral integrity and spiritual vitality for whole societies in process of radical change. They therefore defy the conventional sociological wisdom which invariably ties secularization to the process of transformation from agrarian to industrial social orders.

Finally, Soumen Sen argues that the confrontation between the primal culture of the Khasi people of North-east India and the forces of British imperialism indirectly led to religious innovation of an unexpected kind. His chapter documents the strains that were experienced in a tribal society when Christian evangelism threatened the integrity of traditional Khasi culture. An opposition movement was created at the end of the nineteenth century for the purpose of reinvigorating indigenous rituals and values. But instead of simply rejecting Christianity, the movement's leaders selectively codified their beliefs and elaborated a system of ethics of their own. The subsequent response to Christianity has therefore been both critical and constructive; both traditional and adaptive. It is as if the perceived need to meet the challenge of Christianity in a colonial setting has elicited a movement of cultural independence which has, paradoxically, had to adopt some western criteria of theological and ethical consistency in order to assert its distinctiveness. The complex web of relations between a colonial power and a primal society, between a monotheistic world religion and an originally polytheistic tribal culture, and between an indigenous but educated elite of reformers and their relatively uneducated kinsfolk illustrates the complexity of religious change in ostensibly 'simple' societies.

*   *   *

Most of the chapters in this volume were contributed to a symposium on the Changing Face of Religion which formed part of the World Congress of Sociology in New Delhi, India, 1986. It is hard to think of a more appropriate place in which to consider this topic. The highly visible presence of ancient and modern religions there provided an excellent backdrop for the discussion of religious change. It was a fitting context for papers which all tended to call in question the assumptions underlying so much western thinking about secularization. It was also a salutary reminder that religion remains a controversial and powerful force in many parts of the world. The changing face of religion reflects the changing character of modern societies.

1

Globalization, Politics, and Religion

Roland Robertson

My primary concern in this discussion is with the virtually globe-wide politicization of religion in recent years. The sheer global scope of this development suggests that we need to attend directly to the global circumstance in order to account for it. Were we to attend to the phenomenon only on a comparative, society-by-society basis we would surely, at the outset, miss the significance of the fact that religion has become increasingly subject to political concerns – and vice versa – in a great *variety* of societies. In other words, seemingly problematic relationships and elisions between church and state, religious and political movements, theology and ideology, and so on, have occurred in societies and in regional and civilizational contexts which, in terms of conventional sociological criteria, often differ quite sharply. Thus, even though it is certainly *not* claimed here that one can ignore the internal characteristics of societies in order to comprehend the phenomenon of the recent politicization of religion (and the 'religionization' of politics), I do argue that one major thrust of our analysis of contemporary changes and trends in the modern world as they relate to religion – and most other sociocultural phenomena – has to be global in character. Ideally, comparative analysis should be combined with global analysis – preferably in historical perspective. Here, however, I am concerned primarily with discussing the relevance of the contemporary process of globalization to the phenomenon of the politicization of religion.

I want to make it clear that in adopting a global approach to the issue of religious change I am not employing the analytical tools of the school of thought called 'world-system theory' and evidently associated in the minds of most social scientists with the particular name of Wallerstein. In fact, the only analytical tendency which is common to my approach and that of Wallerstein is the insistence that all societies have become increasingly subject to global constraints. And even in that regard there is considerable divergence. For whereas the Wallersteinians and many other adherents to world-system and related approaches have maintained that the basic constraints are economic, at the most politico-economic (in spite of a rapidly increasing interest on the part of Wallerstein in cultural phenomena) and that the major unit of the world system is the economic role-playing nation state, I promote a more fluid, multifaceted conception of the making and operation of the modern global circumstance. In that regard I propose that there are four major dimensions of the global-human condition: namely, *societies*; *individuals*; *the system of societies*; and (in the generic sense) *mankind* (Robertson and Chirico, 1985).

Whereas world-system theory in its Wallersteinian manifestation considers the world almost entirely in the mode of the system-of-societies (specifically, in inter-national economic or politico-economic terms), I insist that that is only one of four basic, interrelated dimensions of globalization (the making of the world into 'a single sociocultural place'). Thus processes of *societaliz-ation* (the globe-wide making of the modern national society); *individuation* (the modern making of the individual as a person); *internationalization* (the expansion of the original European state system so as to include virtually all the societies of the modern world in a globe-wide 'international society'); and *humanization* (the thematization of man- and womankind) are what dynamically constitute the modern world-as-whole. Although the most forceful thrusts along all four of these trajectories have almost certainly originated in the west, they have in the twentieth century been increasingly sustained by globally diffused normative conceptions. By now there are globe-wide general conceptions of state-run societies, individuals, international relations, and (again, in the generic sense) mankind. That does *not*, however, mean that there is consensus on these matters. Each conception is open to a wide range of interpretation (indeed, resistance).

Religion and politics: general considerations

In using the term *politicization* I have primarily in mind, first, an increase in concern on the part of ostensibly religious collectivities with governmental issues and, secondly, an inflation of interest among those with declared religious commitments in coordinating the latter with secular-ideological perspectives and programmes. That, second, more diffuse strand of the politicization process involves, in effect, a denial of the autonomy of religious, as well as theological, commitment. For some that denial veers in the direction of grounding religious doctrine and practice in secular ideology or experience; for others it moves toward claiming that religious doctrine and practice must have ideological consequences.

The former case involves opting for a particular religious commitment *on the basis of* extra-religious ideology – or, at least, the interpretation of an already accepted doctrinal perspective according to political-ideological or political-experiential criteria. The latter case (emphasizing the ideological implications of doctrine) involves the search for policies and programmes for the organization of social life which appear to follow from religious commitment.

In considering why it is that there has been a recent politicization of religion in these two main respects – that is, emphasis upon the governmental relevance of religion and the close aligning or conflation of religion and ideology – it must be emphasized as strongly as possible that I am not thereby suggesting that this is an entirely new phenomenon. As Stackhouse has stated:

> [T]wentieth-century events – as well as modern historical and cross-cultural research – have begun to bring about a fresh recognition of what most civilizations and politicians have known all along: religion must be reckoned with in politics. What religion can crown it alone can dethrone: what it can legitimate it can delegitimate. What religion brings into conflict politics cannot easily reconcile; what religion unites politics cannot easily divide. (Stackhouse, 1987: 410)[1]

Undoubtedly, then, it would be fallacious to consider the contemporary politicization of religion as constituting a unique historical circumstance. To the contrary, what stands out as unique in historical and comparative perspectives is the strength of the processes of differentiation which yielded relatively separate spheres of politics and religion, as well as the force of the myths that have sustained these processes (Robertson, 1987b). As Stackhouse (1987: 408) notes, 'the ideas that religion is and should be "private" and "nonpolitical" and that the state is "public" and "secular" derive in large measure from the enormous impact that a specific religious tradition has had upon modern Western social life'. However, while there can be no doubt about the intra-western origins of these ideas, their impact has by no means been restricted to western societies (which category includes, of course, the societies of the old British Empire that are not geographically in the west and also, presumably, Latin American societies).

Among non-western societies which have specifically attempted to follow the western model are modern Turkey and independent India. Japan had the model imposed upon it by MacArthur's occupying administration following its military defeat in 1945 (Woodward, 1972), while under apparent American influence the 1972 constitution of South Korea stipulated simply that 'religion and politics shall be separated' (Wright, 1975: 360). In a more diffuse sense, however, *the idea of* the secular state spread across most of the world between the early nineteenth and early twentieth centuries. That development was closely related to the diffusion of the idea of revolution – in the sense that the conception of the state as being basically secular greatly encouraged aspirations concerning the remaking of society by human effort; while the idea of revolution itself enhanced the notion that the state *should* be secular (Robertson, 1985a).[2] As with so many of the appurtenances of contemporary national societies, a certain conception of the 'status' of religion was also widely diffused to various parts of world, the critical take-off period in that regard probably being the last twenty years or so of the nineteenth century. That was a crucial phase in the making of 'international society' (Bull and Watson, 1985; Barraclough, 1976) – when the standard of 'civilization' included emphasis upon at least a modicum of individual religious freedom (Gluck 1985; Gong, 1984).[3]

Thus the ideas concerning the distinctiveness of the private, non-political character of religion and the public, secular nature of the governmental apparatus (the state) which Stackhouse traces to a specific religious tradition in the west – although it has surely interpenetrated with relatively autonomous traditions of *Realpolitik* and secular-rational law (Garrett, 1987) – were globalized (or nearly so) by the mid-twentieth century; wherever the ideas spread, however, they clearly encountered indigenous civilizational conceptions of the relationship between what Weber called intramundane and supramundane spheres. I cannot explore the major civilizational varieties of that relationship – the most primordial forms of which were centred upon the problem of the connection between the sacred and the secular aspects of kingship (Bendix, 1978: 21–60).[4] What I seek to emphasize in the present context is that not merely have rather specific ideas concerning the state (as the central component of a modern, 'civilized' society) become a crucial ingredient of global political culture (Boli-Bennett, 1979, 1980; Meyer, 1980) but that the constraint on modern states to be essentially secular has been complemented by globally diffused ideas concerning the category of religion, on the one hand, and the individual, on the other.[5] Moreover, I suggest that to a significant extent even the idea of religion as being basically 'privatized' is in part a sociocultural 'product' of the modern global circumstance – an aspect of the ordering involved in the rendering of the world as a single place.[6]

Thus I am suggesting not that we have suddenly witnessed an historically unusual politicization of religion but rather that religion has been politicized quite drastically during the past fifteen years or so, following a period of diffusion of the idea of the separatedness of the spheres of religion and politics (most emphatically in the USA). *Re*-politicization has clearly occurred most forcefully (largely as an aspect of globalization) in the contexts where religion and government have historically been most intimately related – namely, Islamic societies. It is, however, the great extent and simultaneity of politicization in a variety of contexts in which I am interested here; the other side of the coin of the contemporary politicization of religion being the 'religionization' of government. Religionization refers, first, to the way in which the modern state has become involved in 'deep' issues of human life (such as the politico-legal definition of life itself with respect to the abortion controversy and advances in medical technology facilitating the prolongation of lives, as well as the enormous problems concerning privacy, sexuality, morality, and the fate of the human species raised by the spread of AIDS); and, second, to the Durkheimian theme concerning the ways in which the state-organized society has become, in varying degrees, an object of veneration and 'deep' identification (Robertson, 1979). The latter is, of course, an important aspect of national identity, a feature of the modern world which has also been promoted and sustained by globally diffused ideas (Gluck, 1985). To some extent politicization and religion- ization are mutually amplifying processes, in that the more 'religious' the state becomes the more it provokes expansion of the activities of ostensibly religious actors along political lines. (For example, leaders of the new politico-religious right in the USA often trace the recent politicization of evangelicals to the Supreme Court's decision to liberalize the law concerning abortion in the early 1970s; while the elevation by military regimes in Latin America of 'national security' to the status of a diffuse totalistic ideology is often said to have precipitated the rise of liberation theology.) By the same token, the politicization of religion may draw actors in the ostensibly secular political realm towards religious interpretations of 'affairs of state'.

Religion and politics: recent connections

I move now to an indication, in a diffusely empirical mode, of the kinds of trend and circumstance that appear to need the global treatment which I have advocated.[7] My intention is only to emphasize by way of a few skeletally described examples the extensiveness across the contemporary world of religion–politics connections. (A fully fledged analysis would require both greater empirical richness and an analytical sorting of the empirical cases.)

In eastern Europe Poland is the most conspicuous example of the recent thematization of church–state tension and the interpenetration of religious and political interests. I refer of course to the complex relationship between the Vatican, the Polish Catholic church, the Solidarity movement and the Communist government since the 'proto-revolution' of 1979. However, not merely has the Soviet regime experienced problems with respect to a number of its religious groupings (ranging from Baptist Christians to Muslims), but the regimes in East Germany, Hungary, and Czechoslovakia (as well, perhaps, as other east European societies) have also been faced recently with religious challenges to policies of 'atheization', some of them in the form of Christian 'basic communities'. Generally speaking, in eastern Europe religion has recently become an object of governmental-political concern and subject to internal politicization.

In western Europe the situation has been more subdued, with the striking exception of the Northern and Southern Irish circumstances. However, a number of west European societies have encountered predicaments which parallel – but which have taken different form from and have usually been more muted than – those in the USA with respect to new religious movements, such as the Unification church, Hare Krishna, and so on. Spain and France have recently confronted problems concerning church and state, notably with respect to the rival claims of public-secular and private-religious education of children; while in England the debate about the liturgy of the established church in the late 1970s raised significant questions about the relationship between religion and national identity. (Moreover, in western Europe, and elsewhere, there has emerged the 'Green phenomenon', which, while certainly not religious in a traditional sense, involves considerable concern with human-existential questions of a kind which is challenging to the modern secular state.) Generally speaking, there appears to have been a strong move towards political involvement among religious elites in western Europe, and elsewhere, in recent years (Hunter, 1987).

In the Middle East there has, of course, been considerable intensification of various forms of Islamic (particularly, but certainly not only, Shiite) fundamentalism, involving the conflation of religious and political themes. In Israel forms of Jewish fundamentalism – most acutely, ultra-Orthodoxy – have been posing major 'church–state' problems, centred particularly on Israel's national identity, its relations with neighbouring Muslim societies, and its 'own' Muslim population. Other religio-political problems raised in the Middle Eastern conflagration include those centred upon the status of Coptic Christians in Egypt, Maronite and other Christians and the Druze in Lebanon, and the Bahai in Iran. In some respects the complex interweaving of religion and politics in the Middle East constitutes the fulcrum – or the paradigmatic case – of the conflation of religion and politics in the modern world; partly because of the enormous strategic and material significance of the Middle East in international affairs and partly, on the other hand, because of the historic importance of the Abrahamic faiths and their crystallization of the theme of religious-salvational universalism.

Societies in Asia (here I exclude the Asiatic portion of the USSR) – notably, Pakistan, Indonesia, and the Philippines – have experienced waves of the Islamic politico-religious militancy which has been so conspicuous in the Middle East; while in the Philippines – and, to a lesser extent, South Korea – we have also witnessed trends which are concretely linked to the expansion of the Catholic liberationist movement in Latin America. In China the problem of the relationship between the Vatican and Chinese Catholicism has recently re-surfaced. In Japan the issue has been raised as to the relationship between the Roman papacy and the Japanese state. In the same society activities of the Soka Gakkai movement constitute a major manifestation of the increasing involvement of religious movements and organizations in political matters; while there has also been a revival of the more nationalistic side of Shintoism and controversy concerning the involvement in that revival of Japanese government officials. In South Korea religious segments appear to be playing an increasingly prominent role in the ongoing political-constitutional crisis. In India the violence centred upon the situation of the Sikhs, particularly in the Punjab, has dramatically focused problems concerning the relationships between political and religious activity and between religion and national allegiance – as have other conflicts in India and in Sri Lanka, where hostility between Buddhists and Hindus is a central ingredient of the civil war arising from Tamil–Hindu agitation for independent national status.

In Africa – leaving on one side predominantly Muslim North Africa, where Islamic fundamentalism has certainly made some political impact – it is clear that in recent years there has been an acceleration of interest in political activity within and among religious collectivities (much of it along Catholic or Protestant 'liberationist' lines), while specifically in South Africa politicization of religion has greatly increased as part of the turmoil attendant upon the problem of apartheid – on both the dominant Afrikaaner and anti-apartheid sides.

We have witnessed church–state tensions and politico-religious conflation in many Central and South American societies; much of that resulting from the growth of the liberation-theology movement and its reversal of Catholic political quiescence (but more-or-less silent support of the status quo) in most Latin American societies. In some of those same societies there has also developed a significant right-wing political presence – some of it calculatedly encouraged by right-wing regimes – on the part of Mormons, Protestant evangelicals, and Pentecostalists. Generally, since the mid-1960s there has been much explicit intermingling of religion and politics across most of South and much of Central America. In the USA there has been much activity on the church–state front in recent years. Protestant fundamentalism, mainly in the form of 'the New Religious Right', has become greatly politicized, with parallel developments in some liberal Protestant and Catholic circles.

Such events and circumstances have arisen during a period of considerable academic re-thinking of the political significance of religion. In particular, political theology and liberation theology – both basically left-wing in ideological flavour – have been much in evidence in Christian and some other cultural contexts. (In turn, those orientations have had quite an impact on the way in which some social scientists now analyse the relationship between religion and politics.)[8] The idea of political theology developed in the 1960s and 1970s partly as a way of dealing with the problem of the relativization of religious traditions and the growing sense in some theological circles that no doctrinal position could claim validity except in terms of its capacity to engage directly with and transform the world – an implementation of Marx's insistence on the redundancy of mere interpretation and the necessity for changing rather than reflecting upon life and history (Lawrence, 1987: 405). Although not explicitly concerned with the global situation and the specific contribution of the globalization process to the relativization of religious traditions, it would nevertheless seem that the latter was a significant background factor in the emergence of political and liberation theologies. At the same time, the relativization of religious traditions has helped to stimulate a parallel reaction in the form of what is often called 'fundamentalism' in a variety of societal and religious contexts. The fundamentalist response to relativization represents a rejection of the explicitly political theological or liberationist position in that, rather than seeking to transform the world and thus 'discover truth', it advocates a retreat to an ostensibly primordial 'truth', involving political mobilization and the use of governmental politics for the dissemination – even the enforcement – of that truth.

Globalization and contemporary religion

Some of the cases which I have just indicated involve tension between a national government (or the laws of a national society) and a religious organization or movement which *transcends* national boundaries. But even more important to note as I begin to sketch more precisely the way in which religion is bound up with globalization is that religious movements, in being increasingly constrained by the global-human condition, are required to attend to the world as a whole. This does not, however, mean that religious movements are directly engaged with the world. By comparison, the Catholic church's engagement with the world is direct, and its conspicuousness on the global scene has surely been greatly facilitated by the globalization process. All I am suggesting is that the making of the world into a single place constrains religious movements to offer interpretations of that development and of their own place in it – to give it religio-theological meaning, which may well be done in very negative terms. Thus some fundamentalist movements in the Middle East and the USA have sought by political means to reject the very idea of globality. (In some recent legal cases initiated by fundamentalist Christians in Southern states of the USA objections to 'one-worldism' has been an *explicit* basis for resistance to the 'secular humanism' of public education.) What I call globe-oriented religious and quasi-religious movements – ones which directly engage the world as a whole – are, in their different ways, addressing more or less explicitly the problem of *world order*. (Apart from the Catholic church and its very loosely confederated and partly internal rival, liberationism, I would mention here the Unification church and Soka Gakkai.) They seek to give *meaning* to – as well as political leverage over – *the entire concrete world* and its cosmic context. And in so doing they often capitalize upon the ways in which 'religion' has become a globalized, but also contested, category. They use 'religion' – as do many other movements that are not explicitly globe-oriented – and they are almost inevitably political because they have to contend with the realities of nation states and international relations (cf. Hanson, 1987).

In addition to the globalization process as such, the threats of virtually globe-wide annihilation of life as a result of nuclear war and AIDS exacerbate the tendency for politico-religious concern with the world as a whole. (It can also be argued that the former has itself sped the globalization process, while the AIDS phenomenon may well speed it even more.) However, the proliferation of religion–politics connections around the world cannot be fully understood, nor can it be accounted for, in sole reference to organizations or movements which are oriented positively or negatively to the global scene *per se*. In other words, many particular manifestations of church–state tension and religion–politics elision have – or at least appear, at first consideration, to have – a primarily *intra*-societal significance and do not involve an obvious degree of concern with the global circumstance. Nevertheless, I argue that most of those manifestations which do not involve overt concern on the religious side with global matters have arisen under essentially global-conditional constraints. One major aspect of the latter circumstances should be emphasized here – namely, the globalized structure of the modern state as a *relatively* autonomous actor – as should the closely related phenomenon of the individual in the contemporary world as a whole (also as a *relatively* autonomous actor).

Both themes may be considered with respect to the idea that globalization involves and promotes *the relativization* of societal and individual (as well as ethnic and civilizational) identities (Robertson, 1985b). As certain general conceptions of the state-run society and the modern individual have been globally generalized, so those very developments have facilitated – have, to a considerable extent, overtly encouraged – the search for *particularistic* identities (both collective and individual). Globalization, in fact, involves both *the particularization of universalism* (what is taken to be applicable to *all* is increasingly interpreted as referring to a particular *global* all) and *the universalization of particularism*.

As the world becomes a single place, various collectivities – but given the form in which the modern world 'system' has been made, societies or would-be societies, in particular – are, so to say, called upon to declare their identities. They are constrained to declare their *calling* in the global-human condition, in a world which is no longer, to use the Marxist terminology, simply 'in itself' but in a context where there is *a problem* of the world being *for* itself (Anisuzzaman and Abdel-Malek, 1984: 68). (The latter theme relates mainly to the mankind component of the global-human condition.) Given the historical significance of religion as the primal source of political legitimation (and delegitimation), it is not at all surprising that it plays a large part in the new circumstance and that, moreover, religious traditions themselves will be constrained to 'place themselves and their heritage somehow' (Smart, 1981: 43). As Smart also says, in the modern planetary situation 'it is not possible simply to put the religions in a kind of superior ghetto'. Societies, religions, secular ideologies, and, I argue, individuals must construct 'at least a sketch of a general theory of their and others' existence. In brief the global city is a place where each group must possess a map. There are no ghettoes left in that city, only enclaves'.

The nationally constituted society derives, as I have argued, much of its shape from globally established norms. It is supposed to be basically secular, but at the same time to have a distinctive identity. There is, in fact, much evidence to suggest that whereas, across the world, the constitutions of contemporary states are very similar in secular respects, they differ greatly with respect to their specification of religious identity (Markoff and Regan, 1987) – which confirms Baum's general argument that whereas there is global *convergence* with respect to societies' economic subsystems there is amplified (and increasingly explicit) *invariance* with respect to *their connecting* of cultural identity and political authority. Since states are called upon to have roughly similar organizational apparatuses, they must find their inter- and intra-societal identities in terms of *particularistic connections between* their cultural identity and their (more or less homogenized) political subsystems (Baum, 1980). (Baum plausibly argues that *the greatest* divergence between and among societies centres upon their 'systems of solidarities' – their styles of communal social interaction.) Generally speaking, then, in the present global circumstance religions and religious movements are constrained to relate to – their activities are skewed towards – the coordination of the 'callings' of particular societies with religious universalism. At the same time their appeals to *individuals* are constrained by both the (globally suggested) attachment of individuals, as citizens, to national societies and the (globally suggested) commitment of individuals to their own subjectivities (Meyer, 1984), which, at least, indirectly, enhances their sense of 'mankindness'.

All in all, the globalization of the modern world constrains and encourages religious traditions and concrete religious movements to orient themselves to the fourfold contingency of the global human condition (consisting of societies, individuals, the system of societies, and mankind) *and* to attend to that condition as a whole (even if that means trying to deny its salience or regarding only one, two, or three of those components as important).

Life has become politicized. In the process that which, according to Durkheim, is *most* concerned with life – namely, religion ('religion is the serious life') – itself acquires political significance. Meaning and power, primordially united, are reunited. Or, to make the point in another form, we are, I suggest, witnessing a confirmation on a global scale of Saint-Simon's claim that 'the religious institution – under whatever spirit one envisages it – is the principal political institution'.[9]

Notes

This is a revised version of a paper ('Accounting for the Global Politicization of Religion') given in Session 4 of Symposium V of the 11th World Congress of

Sociology, New Delhi in August 1986. In his role as discussant, Thomas Luckmann provided a long, critical commentary on my paper – which in Luckmann's absence was read aloud by the chair of the session. Rather than responding directly to that commentary I have attempted, in greatly revising my paper, to clarify my original statement with some of Luckmann's arguments in mind. I am grateful to Luckmann for his 'challenge'.

1 Dumont has written at considerable length about the problematic relationships between societal spheres in western civilization. See in particular, Dumont (1982), which deals specifically with the growth of church–state and religion–politics 'confusions'. Beckford (1987) discusses how sociologists of religion have suppressed the *power* component of religion, in favour of the *meaning* component – and advocates 'the restoration of power' to the study of religion. Much of the present chapter complements Beckford's argument and emphasizes the degree to which religion *has* become concerned with power in recent years. See also Bourg (1980).

2 This is not to say that all modern revolutions are secular. Perhaps the idea that they have been so has been considerably exaggerated. The Iranian revolution of 1979 constitutes, in Weber's terms, a traditionalist revolution rather than a modern one.

3 I have unavoidably had to use the term *civilization* in two rather different senses here. First, I use it to refer to *a standard social practice*; second, I employ it in reference to *a large-scale sociocultural entity* which has endured over many centuries. It should be obvious in the text which specific meaning is intended.

4 See Robertson (1987a and 1987b) for brief discussion of some of the relevant literature. See also Stackhouse (1987) for discussion of the major politico-religious differences between monotheistic (i.e. Abrahamic) and 'ontocratic' (i.e. Asian) faiths. The former 'understand transcendence to be unitary, beyond and over existence, personal and dynamically involved in change', while the latter 'tend to understand transcendence as a unitary reality to be found deep within the structures of existence, as impersonal in character, and as the source of constant stability amid the swirl of apparent change' (Stackhouse, 1987: 415).

5 For an excellent discussion of such themes with respect to their reception in one particular society – namely, Japan – see Gluck (1985).

6 Meyer (1984) cogently argues (as did Durkheim) that individualism is *an institution* and has an institutional history. The 'public institutionalization of the life course' constitutes one dimension of the modern individual, while the *publicly celebrated* 'private' or subjective individual constitutes a second dimension. The modern state (across the world) has been increasingly involved in the production of the individual life course and, indeed, greatly depends on it. At the same time what Meyer calls 'the expanded legitimation of the self' – which is 'celebrated in national constitutions and law, and in the international codes and agreements that constitute the United Nations system' – is facilitated by the organization of the life course. 'The modern self . . . is free and is expected to relativize its stance to the institutional context. It seeks to find meaning and value in comparison to the referential structures set by the rationalized environment'. I believe this circumstance to be a major source of modern religiosity and the (misleading) idea that it is privatized. It also produces, I suggest, a kind of politicization of individual religiosity. A published version of Meyer (1984) is to be found in Thomas *et al.* (1987).

7 This section draws on Robertson (1987c).

8 For discussion of the Latin American case, see Robertson (1986).

9 Quoted in Durkheim (1962: 223). This view was, of course, systematically implemented in the historical sociology of de Tocqueville, most notably in his work on the USA. See Goldstein (1975). See also my attempt (Robertson, 1985a) to link

the Saint-Simonian and Tocquevillian line of thought to Durkheim's ideas concerning societal regeneration.

References

Anisuzzaman and Anouar Abdel-Malek (eds) (1984) *Culture and Thought in the Transformation of the World.* New York: St Martin's Press.

Barraclough, Geoffrey (1976) *An Introduction to Contemporary History.* Baltimore: Penguin Books.

Baum, Rainer (1980) 'Authority and Identity: the Case for Evolutionary Invariance', pp. 61–118 in Roland Robertson and Burkart Holzner (eds), *Identity and Authority.* New York: St Martin's Press.

Beckford, James A. (1987) 'The Restoration of "Power" to the Sociology of Religion', pp. 13–37 in Thomas Robbins and Roland Robertson (eds), *Church–State Relations: Tensions and Transitions.* New Brunswick, NJ: Transaction Books.

Bendix, Reinhard (1978) *Kings or People: Power and the Mandate to Rule.* Berkeley: University of California Press.

Boli-Bennett, John (1979) 'The Ideology of Expanding State Authority in National Constitutions, 1870–1970', pp. 222–37 in John W. Meyer and Michael T. Hannan (eds), *National Development and the World System.* Chicago: Chicago University Press.

Boli-Bennett, John (1980) 'Global Integration and the Universal Increase of State Dominance, 1910–1970', pp. 77–107 in Albert Bergesen (ed.), *Studies of the Modern World-System.* New York: Academic Press, Inc.

Bourg, Carroll (1980) 'Politics and Religion', *Sociological Analysis*, 41: 297–315.

Bull, Hedley and Adam Watson (eds) (1985) *The Expansion of International Society.* New York: Oxford University Press.

Dumont, Louis (1982) 'A Modified View of Our Origins: the Christian Beginnings of Modern Individualism', *Religion*, 12: 1–17.

Durkheim, Emile (1962) *Socialism,* Alvin W. Gouldner (ed.) and Charlotte Sattler (trans.). New York: Collier Books.

Garrett, William R. (1987) 'Religion, Law and the Human Condition', *Sociological Analysis*, 47(S): 1–34.

Gluck, Carol (1985) *Japan's Modern Myths: Ideology in the Late Meiji Period.* Princeton, NJ: Princeton University Press.

Goldstein, Doris S. (1975) *Trial of Faith: Religion and Politics in Tocqueville's Thought.* New York and Amsterdam: Elsevier.

Gong, Gerrit W. (1984) *The Standard of 'Civilization' in International Society.* Oxford: Clarendon Press.

Hanson, Eric O. (1987) *The Catholic Church in World Politics.* Princeton, NJ: Princeton University Press.

Hunter, James Davison (1987) 'Religious Elites in Advanced Industrial Society', *Comparative Studies in Society and History*, 29(2): 360–74.

Lawrence, Frederick G. (1987) 'Political Theology', pp. 404–8 in Mircea Eliade (ed.), *The Encyclopedia of Religion*, vol. 11. New York: Macmillan.

Long, Charles H. (1987) 'Popular Religion', pp. 442–52 in Mircea Eliade (ed.), *The Encyclopedia of Religion*, vol. 11. New York: Macmillan.

Markoff, John and Daniel Regan (1987) 'Religion, the State and Political Legitimacy in the World's Constitutions', pp. 161–82 in Thomas Robbins and Roland

Robertson (eds), *Church–State Relations: Tensions and Transitions*. New Brunswick, NJ: Transaction Books.

Meyer, John W. (1980) 'The World Polity and the Authority of the Nation-state', pp. 77-137 in Albert Bergesen (ed.), *Studies of the Modern World-System*. New York: Academic Press.

Meyer, John W. (1984) 'Self and Life Course: Institutionalization and Its Effects', Mimeo.

Robertson, Roland (1979) 'Religious Movements and Modern Societies: Toward a Progressive Problemshift', *Sociological Analysis*, 40(4): 297–314.

Robertson, Roland (1985a) 'The Development and the Modern Implications of the Classical Sociological Perspective on Religion and Revolution'. pp. 236–65 in Bruce Lincoln (ed.), *Religion, Rebellion, Revolution*. London: Macmillan.

Robertson, Roland (1985b) 'The Relativization of Societies: Modern Religion and Globalization', pp. 31–42 in Thomas Robbins, William Shepherd and James McBride (eds), *Cults, Culture and the Law*. Chico, CA: Scholars Press.

Robertson, Roland (1986) 'Liberation Theology in Latin America: Sociological Problems of Interpretation and Explanation', pp. 107–39 in Jeffrey Hadden and Anson Shupe (eds), *Prophetic Religions and Politics*. New York: Paragon Press.

Robertson, Roland (1987a) 'Church–State Relations in Comparative Perspective', pp. 153–60 in Thomas Robbins and Roland Robertson (eds), *Church–State Relations: Tensions and Transitions*. New Brunswick, NJ: Transaction Books.

Robertson, Roland (1987b) 'General Considerations in the Study of Contemporary Church–State Relations', pp. 5–11 in Thomas Robbins and Roland Robertson (eds), *Church–State Relations: Tensions and Transitions*. New Brunswick, NJ: Transaction Books.

Robertson, Roland (1987c) 'Church–State Relations and the World System', pp. 39–51 in Thomas Robbins and Roland Robertson (eds), *Church–State Relations: Tensions and Transitions*. New Brunswick, NJ: Transaction Books.

Robertson, Roland and JoAnn Chirico (1985) 'Humanity, Globalization and Worldwide Religious Resurgence: a Theoretical Exploration', *Sociological Analysis*, 46: 219–42.

Smart, Ninian (1981) *Beyond Ideology: Religion and the Future of Western Civilization*. New York: Harper & Row.

Stackhouse, Max L. (1987) 'Politics and Religion', pp. 408–23 in Mircea Eliade (ed.), *The Encyclopedia of Religion*, vol. 11. New York: Macmillan.

Thomas, George E. et al. (1987) *Institutional Structure: Constituting State, Society and the Individual*. Beverly Hills, CA: Sage.

Woodward, William P. (1972) *The Allied Occupation of Japan 1945–1952 and Japanese Religions*. Leiden: E.J. Brill.

Wright, Edward Reynolds (ed.) (1975) *Korean Politics in Transition*. Seattle: University of Washington Press.

2

'Diffused Religion' and New Values in Italy

Roberto Cipriani

Church, state, and 'diffused religion'

Even for someone who has always kept his sociological interest in current events alive, it is not easy to disentangle the guiding threads of the social, political, and religious dynamics which have characterized Italy in the last two decades. The fact is that one finds oneself in the present situation almost naturally, as though it had been expected, without even letting questions, doubts, or scientific curiosity about what has been happening to more than 50 million citizens, from the mid-1960s to the threshold of the 1990s, break the surface.

To find one's way through this maze, one must discover a thread or some guiding principle which might provide some direction. In this case, it may be identified in the socio-political dialectic between church and state. In fact, this dialectic was not based exclusively on the will of the two parties involved, and definitely not on the impromptu decisions made by political and religious leaders. In reality, the revision of the Concordat between Italy and the Holy See closely reflected and followed the changing socio-political scenarios in the country. The complex course followed by this issue began at a time when the Italian Socialist party (PSI) was a simple ally in the Centre Left governments, and ended (although developments continued at an executive level) at a time when the same party found itself occupying the key position of the presidency of the Council of Ministers. The Ecumenical Council, Vatican II, had only just finished when the Chamber of Deputies asked the government to revise the Concordat in 1976. The revision was also rendered necessary by the new lines emerging from statements in the official documents of the Vatican Council, and especially in the Pastoral Constitution on the Church in the Contemporary World, better known as *Gaudium et Spes*. Its point 76 states that

> The political community and the Church are independent of each other and autonomous in their own fields. Both, even with different motivations, are in the service of the personal and social vocation of the same human persons. They will discharge this service to the advantage

of everyone more efficiently as they better cultivate a healthy collaboration with one another, following methods adapted to circumstances of place and time.

Article 7 of the Constitution of the Italian Republic, which had been in force since 1 January 1948, had taken over the old Lateran Pacts which, in turn, had been stipulated by the Catholic church in the far-off days of 1929 with the Fascist regime of Mussolini. The same article provided for the modification of the pacts and enunciated a basic principle that was subsequently repeated literally in the council text quoted above: 'The State and the Catholic Church are each, in their own sphere, independent and sovereign.' The reference to the Catholic mode of religious expression alone is not without sociological significance. This is a recognition of a dominant, more widespread form of religious belief and practice.

The new Concordat between the Italian state and the Catholic church was signed on 18 February 1984. But after this official act some problems relating to ecclesiastical organizations and to the maintenance of the active clergy remained unresolved. They were finally dealt with in a law of 20 May 1985. When certain executive applications were in turn instigated, questions of an ideological nature arose, especially in connection with the teaching of religion in schools. Unusually for Italy, it was a lay minister, the Republican Spadolini, who had earlier extended religious teaching (although it was 'autonomous') to the nursery schools where it had not previously been expected. Moreover, this was the same scholar of history who had often written of the need for 'widening the Tiber', meaning that the divisions between the Vatican and the Italian state, as symbolized by the course of the capital's river, should be strengthened with wider margins and embankments. Indeed, Spadolini wrote in the preface to the 1966 paperback edition of his *L'Opposizione cattolica, Da Porta Pia al '98*:

> This reprint ought to coincide with a wish rather than with a conclusion: the wish that the barriers that de Gasperi deplored so much between Church and State, citizen and believer, religion and freedom, should no longer stand. The wish that the wider Tiber, the great conquests of the last two pontificates, the great victory consecrated in the deliberations of the Council should become an everyday reality, a reality stronger than all political stratagems or tactical ploys – stronger than electoral fluctuations themselves and governing coalitions. (Spadolini, 1966: xi)

This brief passage brings together the essential points that also bear on 'diffused religion'. First, the existence of a long historical tradition which has kept the spheres of politics and religion separate was recognized. This had been accomplished in a predominantly anti-liberal, anti-Risorgimento, anti-unity sense through an explicit

'Catholic opposition' in the 'Opera dei congressi' which organized sixteen national assemblies of Italian Catholics between 1874 and 1899 with the participation of thousands of representatives.

This entailed the deployment of a whole series of defensive measures by the Catholic side against the new Italian state (indeed, the idea of a Catholic university, which was actually set up in Milan twenty-four years later, dates from 1897). It also meant a withdrawal from commitment to politics at least until the 'Gentiloni pact' of 1909. The complex, contradictory events which followed did not do much to help in clarifying the terms of an appropriate relationship between religion and politics. The negotiations with Fascism themselves complicated and blurred the outlines of a dialectic that was already difficult. In fact, the barriers persisted, but bridges which favoured misunderstandings and subterfuges were thrown between the two sides. The agreement with Catholic officialdom undoubtedly favoured Mussolini and his regime. Thus it gained, if not consensus, at least the assent of a mainly Catholic population. So, it can be said that the 1929 protocols legitimated the Italian Fascist state even more than did the role of Catholics in Italy. The transition from the monarchy to the Republic in the post-war period, and especially the voting on Article 7 of the new constitution, marked a new phase: the recognition that the spheres of church and state were separate but also that a large space was granted to the Catholic presence in Italy. The Left was also in agreement, with the Communist Togliatti in the forefront. This time, perhaps more clearly, the barriers remained in place – but with different functions: no longer opposition but mutual acceptance. It may be acceptable in this context to consider the Christian Democrat De Gasperi, the protagonist of the first years of republican government, as tending to favour laicization. There were still, however, many Catholic influences which were wedded to a conception of politics as a space to be conquered at any cost. Some currents in the Christian Democrat party could be identified with this tendency, along with supportive organizations, in particular the Civic Committees which revived the old 'parish committees' that had been organized by the 'Opera dei congressi'.

The advent of Vatican II and the broadening of Roman Catholic horizons undoubtedly helped to take the emphasis away from internal Italian affairs. Equally influential was the weight of the two Popes, John XXIII and Paul VI, who demonstrated great openness while conceding little to the old partnerships with Christian Democracy and giving their attention to the new political dynamics. When Roncalli was a cardinal in Venice, for example, he welcomed a socialist congress to the city and called it 'an event of great importance for the direction of the country'. That was in 1957. When Montini was Archbishop of Milan he also replied in the negative to a very close friend who had sought his political support for a Christian Democrat candidate: 'I cannot intervene in favour of a political candidacy. . . . It is my programme, my duty, to abstain from any step in that direction'.

The council's statement quoted above regarding the separateness of religion and politics helped to reinforce certain widespread convictions among Italian Catholics, whose voting in elections and referenda had been gradually showing greater deviations from the official directions issued by some exponents of the hierarchy. In this respect, major deviations can be found in the election results marking an increase in support for the parties of the Left, up to the historical high point of 1976 when the Italian Communist party (PCI) almost drew level with the Christian Democrats (DC).

Table 2.1   *Elections for the Chamber of Deputies (percentage of votes)*

	Christian Democracy	Communist party	Socialist party	Total Left vote
1948	48.5	31.0		31.0*
1953	40.1	22.6	12.7	35.3
1958	42.4	22.7	14.8	37.5
1963	38.3	25.3	13.8	39.1
1968	39.1	26.9	14.5†	41.4
1972	38.8	27.2	9.6	36.8
1976	38.7	34.4	9.6	44.0
1979	38.3	30.4	9.8	40.2
1983	32.9	29.9	11.4	41.3

*Joint PCI–PSI lists.
†Joint PSI–PSDI (Social Democrats) lists under the name of PSU (Unified Socialist party).

Table 2.1 shows that the Communist and Socialist Left (without) taking into account the Social Democrats and the extreme Left, for the sake of comparability in the statistics over time) gained 10 percentage points in the first twenty years of the Republic, but Christian Democracy lost almost as many in the same period. After the years of unrest among young people and the working class 'hot autumn', the Left, whose results remained more or less constant, experienced two leaps forward by the PCI and the PSI respectively in 1976 and 1983, whereas the DC suffered a sharp fall of about 5 percentage points in the latest political elections. The fact that many religious believers voted for the Left certainly had an effect, as is indirectly confirmed by numerous empirical studies. The result of the referenda is even more convincing. The law proposed by the Liberal Baslini and the Socialist Fortuna had, since 1970, governed the dissolution of marriage, not without conflicts in the Catholic world which referred to the dictates of the 1929 Concordat. The number of divorces rose to 17,164 in 1971 and then to 31,717 in 1972 (with many 'delayed' cases) but fell to 22,500 in 1973. The following year there was a referendum on the abrogation of this law. The result was 59.1 per cent in favour of keeping it, and 40.9 per cent for its abrogation. In practice, four out of ten voters sided with the official position of the Catholic church. Then, in 1978 the law 'de-criminalizing' abortion was passed. There was a double referendum on this in 1981 which precipitated a clash between two different arguments about the interruption of pregnancy. The Radical party's proposal, which favoured more permissive legislation, had 11.5 per cent in favour and 88.5 per cent against. The proposal for abrogation, which was backed by the Movimento per la Vita (Pro-life movement) and was in line with the directives of Catholic teaching, received support from 32.1 per cent of the voters. So, if we take all these results into account, we can argue that 'diffused religion' is responsible for approximately 56.4 per cent of the votes cast in the two referenda. 'Diffused religion' refers to the characteristic conduct of believers who have received at least a Catholic education and who relate to it in a general sense. In fact, it refers to citizens who appear to be less than completely obedient to the directives of the Catholic hierarchy but who, on the other hand, refuse to reject completely certain basic principles which form part of the set of values promoted by Catholicism.

The post-conciliar years

Spadolini's wish in 1966 was that 'nobody should still have to write in ten years' time what De Gasperi wrote to me twelve years ago, in August 1954: "how many, many barriers still have to be pulled down"' (Spadolini, 1966: xi). In fact, twice that number of years have already passed, and many barriers have really been lowered. However, we are dealing with a process which has primarily concerned believers themselves more obviously than it has affected the summits of Catholic institutions. Proof of this is the fact that the institutions still believe it useful to have recourse to diplomatic solutions and decrees, whereas the majority of Italian Catholics can accept other solutions which are less legalistic and more 'tolerant' with regard to the secular nature of the nation state. In other words, collaboration between church and state was practised by millions of citizens in their daily lives even before it occurred in the higher levels of their representative bodies. Where necessary, this collaboration discriminated between the religious and the political dimensions. This did not jeopardize a mainly favourable attitude towards religion *tout court*. Indeed, there was discussion not so much of the advisability of religious education in schools as of the mode of expressing this policy in terms which might seem compulsory. The barriers thus seem to have fallen primarily at the level of social coexistence where they serve as points of reference for the 'new' values shared by believers and practising Catholics as well as by others. These orienting principles definitely do not neglect the religious education that is received in the phases of primary and secondary socialization, but which, in fact, often arise from them. In this way, their capillary nature and their interrelatedness substantiate and testify to 'diffused religion'. It is not expressed in the familiar form of church religion but through the continual reorientation of attitudes and conduct which deal with everyday circumstances of various kinds: moral, political, economic, or juridical.

It may be hypothesized that while official religiosity, linked to models of stricter orthodox observance, seems more readily identifiable and open to investigation through the customary techniques of research with questionnaires, 'diffused religion', by contrast, is best approached by means of face-to-face interviews which can probe more deeply, in the manner of interviews which lead to the gathering of life histories.

A second hypothesis is that the characteristic factors in church religion seem more constant. The variables in 'diffused religion' are, by contrast, more changeable according to the syntheses which it produces from time to time. They are achieved on levels determined by the dialectic between the basic values of primary and secondary legitimation and the 'different' ones which appear on the horizon in the long confrontation with other ideological perspectives. The 'new' value is internalized but almost never taken up in a wholly pure form or according to a formula that could totally replace the previous perspective. The new way of seeing reality, the different *Weltanschauung*, is, however, the result of the collision-encounter between what already exists and what is still in the process of becoming. 'Diffused religion' therefore becomes dominant precisely where there is a pre-existing, dominant, fideistic form of religion. If this were not the case, the outcome of social interactions would produce quite different sedimentations which would be typical of multicultural, and therefore, pluri-confessional, situations.

It is undeniable that Vatican II had a resonance in the country where it was held which should not be overlooked. We can also say that intra- and extra-ecclesiastical movements themselves found points of departure in the spirit and documents of the council. In particular, the space accorded to areas of heterodoxy helped to deprovincialize Italian Catholicism, which had been rather tied to Vatican, curial, clerical, and institutional problems. Interest in emerging catholicisms reinforced certain indigenous positions which were already developing in Italy. There was a qualitative leap which subsequently favoured the series of striking results enjoyed by the new method of participating in religion, not simply with a traditional outlook on practice but with more flexible perspectives that were less indulgent towards the hierarchy and more sensitive to social dynamics. This took place at least in the vanguard of a new religious sentiment, but was not without influence on other people on the fringes of Italian society who had been socialized, at any event, in accordance with models of Catholic extraction. Thus, 'diffused religion' appears to be an original phenomenon, even if it is hard to deny that some of its characteristic elements had existed in other historical periods as well (including the period of Fascism).

The dynamic of 'diffused religion' in Italy

When Robert N. Bellah went to Italy in 1972 on a research visit he gathered information and developed interpretations predominantly on the basis of the contributions of various philosophers and historians of the past (Gramsci, Croce, Salvemini, and Salvatorelli) but completely neglected the noteworthy contributions that Italian sociology of religion had provided in terms of empirical study and scientific analysis. His 'Five Religions of Modern Italy' (Bellah, 1974) is thus the fruit of purely theoretical reflection which does not even examine the real influence exercised by Marxist and liberal thought. However, the Berkeley sociologist should be given credit for having perceptively identified the presence in Italy of a kind of constant underpinning, a 'religious ground bass', the incessant accompaniment of the alternating developments of melody and harmony which are represented in the dominant motif of the Catholic religion. If we wanted to transfer the metaphor from the musical field to that of painting we could say that there is a tendency in the Italian system of 'perspective' to reproduce the various *colours* of reality according to a chromatic dominance or 'contrast' which brings out with greater emphasis the Catholic model with its higher wavelength (and scope of influence). The other, added, filters of Marxism and liberalism cannot 'correct' the dominant dimension, and they even become determined by it without being able to offer a 'neutral contrast' which would avoid the prevailing register.

The function of a dominant religion is not, however, confined to the prescription of conduct. The relevant sociological problems cannot be solved by merely asking whether orthodox beliefs and practices are accepted. In fact, the very rejection of a church's official teachings might have obvious foundations in its basic doctrinal contents. Therefore, the role of a dominant religion cannot be said to be fulfilled from an heuristic, cognitive viewpoint by simply noting that the Catholic church (or other religious institutions pre-eminent in different contexts) produces integration (Dobbelaere, 1985). Above all, the vast expanse pervaded by an active, ordered presence producing what might be called 'the mainstream effect' has never been investigated. It is also true that other counter-currents may be counterposed to this. Yet, they cannot fail to refer to the mainstream, and even use its support, in order to reverse the flow. Other solutions, similar to those of the so-called 'upwelling currents', also flow into the same environment created by the principal stream.

The 'mainstream effect' thus affects the secular religions of Italian Marxism and liberalism as well as the area defined as 'lay' (in the broad sense not restricted to the small parties which are often identified as belonging to it: Republicans, Liberals, and so on). Paradoxically, it could also be maintained that the very dynamics of secularization – even though they are recognizable as such – are to some extent fleshed out and moulded by some characteristics of more diffused religion such as dogmatism, ideologism, militantism, proselytism, and so forth.

It is as well to distinguish clearly and cleanly between 'diffused religion' and what Bellah has in mind with his 'religious ground bass' which has the appearance of a kind of 'real religion' as distinct from the 'official' and 'legal' religion of the institution. The latter is characterized by a profound loyalty towards the highest leaders of the religious hierarchy, observance with no breaks in continuity, and a strong sense of social reality in a predominantly religious mode. This concerns a cultural habit acquired in the specific Italian context, and it concedes little to the sentiments of an inner and wholly experiential faith. A lack of full awareness is common among Italian Catholics, who are defenders of a rather generic practice and are not accustomed to letting themselves be swept away by grand ideals or enthusiastic movements and thus to being disposed towards basic changes of direction. The data from the referendum on divorce refute the interpretation made by Bellah, who thought that Italian women would not welcome the law on divorce.

In fact, it is precisely the hypothesis of 'diffused religion' which helps to explain the Italian case differently (R. Cipriani, 1983, 1984). The Catholicism of Italians is crisscrossed horizontally and vertically by quite heterogeneous strands which reflect regional and territorial backgrounds, social stratification, and contingent historical events. Hence it is impossible to simplify matters, as Bellah would have us believe, by referring to Gramsci, by describing the structure of the Italian church as basically linked to two contrasting classes: on the one hand, an elite of the clergy with intellectual functions; and, on the other, the common people. In reality, the history of Italian Catholicism bears witness to somewhat deeper and often pronounced differences within both the clergy and the rest of the population. Bellah's quite open intention is to include Italian Catholics in the North American schemas of his 'civil religion'.

Bellah describes Italy's five religions as: 'real' religion (the 'religious ground bass'); 'legal' religion (Catholicism); liberalism; activism; and socialism. They are all supposed to be 'civil religions'. Catholicism is, and has also in the past been, a 'civil religion'. All this conceptual forcing reveals its underlying purpose if one moves on to observations of an empirical nature. Thus, it is hard to see how activism could substantiate its 'religious' nature. But, above all, the hypothesis of an experiential religion which leaves to one side the more formal theologies expressed by Catholicism and which proceeds on its own account, without being in tune (or in harmony) with developments in institutionalized religion, does not stand up. Catholicism still remains a constant measure of comparison, even if a conflictual one. Although the 'religious ground bass' originally had pre-Christian or, better, pre-Catholic characteristics, it has undoubtedly drawn values, orientations, models, and practices from the dominant Catholicism as well. In this way, instead of remaining pre-Catholic, it has gradually imbibed Catholicism to the point where it is hard to perceive the ground bass as a form autonomous from Catholicism except in moments of special divergence and open difference, above all in the field of political and moral choices (the latter especially at the level of private life). Rather than a sharp contrast between 'real' and 'legal' religion, it is perhaps more correct to speak of a basic parallelism which from time to time can also give rise to digressions, diversions, and even (rarely head-on) clashes.

Bellah is aware of these various possibilities, but not adequately. The space-time differences are noteworthy and certainly not generic in character. Furthermore, the weight of the formal Catholic religion is not secondary and does not slide away on the smooth, waterproof surface of Italian society. Rather, it impregnates it thoroughly to the point of influencing its declared opponents, Marxist or lay. Nor is this a matter only of an elitist Catholicism, since broad strata of the population feel the Catholic influence in many basic structures at the legitimating and socializing level, from educational institutions (not only confessional ones, now that teaching of the Catholic religion is also carried on in state schools) to institutions and organizations for welfare and leisure – with services and resources often beyond comparison in quantity or quality with those administered by the Italian state.

The fusion of political and religious values of which Bellah speaks in connection with the part played by the Christian Democrat party, of clearly Catholic inspiration, does not on closer inspection operate only in the particular milieu of that Catholic party *par excellence*. In fact, the fusion can also be found elsewhere, on the Left as well as on the Right. This is yet another effect of 'diffused religion', and indeed is one of its main indicators.

Nor can one say that there was only a perfect agreement between the Christian Democrat party, the church, and the state before John XXIII. This would be an injustice to the tendential 'layness' expressed on many occasions by the leaders of Christian Democracy themselves who have refused to take orders or to accept suggestions from the Vatican. The case of De Gasperi stands for them all: it represents devotion more on the level of faith than at the institutional level, a kind of 'upright' obedience which was intended to confirm the autonomy of the state *vis-à-vis* the church.

The post-conciliar period has offered the religious believer more possibilities for militancy and for voting outside the Christian Democrat framework. This diaspora situation might appear to be damaging for the destiny of Catholicism. The historical record shows, however, that the phenomenon of distancing themselves from the ecclesiastical centre, from the summits of the hierarchy, from orthodox teaching, and from the practice of obedience has reinforced, rather than weakened, the active presence of Catholics in various sectors, including politics, the economy, the press, radio and TV, teaching, and welfare. Instead of remaining in their ghetto of religious structures, believers have found a way of inserting themselves at various levels in the public sphere.

At the same time, the fear that the institutional leaders of Catholicism, above all the Pope, would lose all credibility has not been confirmed. The erosion of authority has not led to a serious danger. In fact, in the succession of various papal figures the leadership has remained almost intact, to the extent that there has been an evident recovery of features which had appeared confined to memories of the past (that is to say, the days of the Pacelli Pope, Pius XII).

It is no accident that the Communist party in Italy has never confronted the Catholic church in decisive and hostile forms. Nor is this to be explained in exclusively tactical and/or strategic terms. Clearly, there are quite different explanations for such a model of behaviour. In reality, the largest party of the Italian Left cannot help but take account of the fact that a good proportion of its members and militants do not by any means look down on a degree of respect for the religious mode of living, which is felt and experienced by them consciously as well as by many of their comrades and friends.

The Italian state itself, as Bellah also correctly observes, has not become a persecutor of the Catholic church but has, rather, come to its defence on many occasions, starting with the confirmation of the agreements made in the Fascist era on questions of a political and religious nature, in terms broadly favourable to Catholicism. This attitude of tolerant benevolence did not even decline after Vatican II. The separation between church and state has certainly been proclaimed and put into practice more frequently since the church and the Christian Democrat party distanced themselves from each other. These innovations also allowed a greater range of inter-institutional relations between religious and lay structures. After the hot phase of clashes in the immediate post-war period (excommunication for Communists, the anti-materialist battles, and so on) Italian Catholicism, both at the level of the hierarchy and at the popular level, to some extent re-entered the kind of wide-ranging collaboration that had taken place in the years of the Resistance and anti-fascism. (It should not be forgotten that many Catholics fought in partisan formations and that the meeting places of Catholic Action were closed during Mussolini's regime.) The responsiveness to the Left under the pontificates of John XXIII and Paul VI, as well as during the Aldo Moro governments, did not therefore appear as a completely new phenomenon. Historical experiences had made such an outcome likely because Catholics were not in fact indifferent to the creation of the new republican state which was founded on the values of democracy and social justice.

These preconditions helped Italian Catholics to contribute to the experience of the Centre Left in the 1960s and 1970s. They shared certain basic political and social demands, and they worked for their realization. The years of the opposing fronts were followed by those of loyal solidarity, albeit with various difficulties. It even happened that many Catholics chose firm commitment to the parties of the Left. This caused some embarrassment to the ecclesiastical establishment, but this phenomenon eventually faded from the news. A priest-intellectual even sided openly with the Socialist party, for which he addressed meetings without taking off his clerical garb.

In this perspective of shared orientations which outstripped ideological orientations, 'new' values emerged and became determining although they were no longer typically Catholic, Marxist, or liberal. This phenomenon confirms the influence of socialization which is normally and mainly inspired by Catholicism and by structures of a Catholic stamp. However, the final mixture was particularly varied and does not at all correspond to the canons of the 'religious ground bass'. Concrete forms of attitudes and conduct were defined according to circumstances, and did not always support those who considered that Italy was inveterately corrupt, inept, and lacking a legitimate succession (cf. Bellah, 1980: 115).

The empirical consequences of the new values

The sociology of religion developed most fully in Italy in the years following Vatican II. The first inquiry that provided information about the religious conduct of Italians dates in fact from 1968. The author, Silvano Burgalassi (1968), had his book presented publicly by a protagonist of the council, the Cardinal of Bologna, Giacomo Lercaro. Among the many data cited by Burgalassi, who tended to favour the prevailing use of empirical indicators of religious practice, special mention may be made of the link between church attendance and membership of the Christian Democrats or PCI. In particular, even frequency of attendance at Catholic worship was not always associated with a vote for the Catholic party. Many of the 'indifferent' voted Christian Democrat. Moreover, even where the PCI obtained most votes, church attendance stayed quite high and did not fall below 21 per cent of the population. In essence, political choice was connected with religious conduct, but no choice, not even that of the Left, completely cancelled out the existence of religious practice.

Gian Enrico Rusconi's (1969) study of secularization among young people had a different import. It made use of research among Milan University students between 1966 and 1968, from which a detailed picture of the confrontation between religiosity and atheism emerged. Between 15 and 17 per cent of young people (especially males) declared themselves in favour of atheism. However, there was a conspicuous percentage of regular church-goers (about 50 per cent). The percentage of those who believed that religion was necessary (74 per cent) was also high. Further-more, 68 per cent considered the church to be made up of everybody who had been baptized, but 54 per cent accused it of not heeding the voice of ordinary believers. Finally, it was the workers who, above all, showed themselves to be opposed to the church.

A later study by Burgalassi (1970) has come to represent an essential point of reference for understanding post-conciliar Catho-licism in Italy. The author asked where Italian Christianity was going, and above all posed the problem of change by secularization. He managed to identify five specific realities: atheistic belief (5 per cent); indifference (55 per cent); the official model of the church (15 per cent); the sacro-magical world (20 per cent); and prophetic innovators (5 per cent). So, in fairly precise terms, *Le cristianità nascoste* showed who composed the nucleus (15 per cent) of 'obedience' to the church's teachings. It was able to reach almost 35 per cent of the Italian population if one also takes into consideration the basic impulses of those belonging to the sacro-magical branch (20 per cent). This global percentage was exactly confirmed years later at the time of the referenda. In fact, the percentage of Italians who follow the teachings of the church, without raising many problems about controversial aspects, is even nowadays about 30–35 per cent. This does not mean, however, that there are no other 'faithful' Catholics, especially among those classified as 'indifferent', 'prophetic', or otherwise. In reality, the Catholic model itself influences many more people than can be identified by counting how many go to mass on Sunday or vote for the Christian Democrat party, or even those who in many cases accept socio-political instructions from the church. It is in this more obvious area, where people who are less indulgent towards church orientations belong, that 'diffused religion' is thriving: the influ-ence, that is, deriving from the clear dominance of Catholicism, thanks to its structures and unceasing capillary activities which guarantee continuity and flexibility in such a way as to leave an unmistakable mark on the years following contact with the church structure. A proof of this is the sensitivity encountered by Burgalassi even among those 'indifferent' towards the figures of the Madonna and the saints. There is a tendency to place God himself on a lower plane among other subjects of the world of the sacred (Burgalassi, 1970: 250).

As it is impossible to refer in detail to the conclusions of many other studies conducted in Italy after the Vatican Council, I restrict myself here simply to some of the most significant and to those referring to the specific object framed by the hypothesis of 'diffused religion'. This hypothesis is presented here for the first time for a preliminary examination while awaiting the more exhaustive study which is presently being conducted.

Among the authors deserving special attention, the Salesian Giancarlo Milanesi should be cited. He has for many years been considering the lives of Italian youth and its contact with Catholicism. Since 1971 he has been dealing with a central point of the 'Catholic question' in Italy; namely, the teaching of religion in state schools (Milanesi, 1971: 137–41).

This subject, which has recently returned to the fore after the revision of the Concordat between the Italian state and the Catholic church, is hotly contested not only from the lay side but also in Catholic circles. Apart from this, however, a rather favourable attitude, at least in principle, to the teaching of the Catholic religion has been recorded even in a region such as Umbria, which is quite famous for its clear orientation towards left-wing political preferences (especially the PCI). This attitude is dictated by interests of a formative-educational kind rather than by purely religious motives, but it is still sufficiently strongly determined to include even the retention and compulsoriness of Catholic teaching in public schools despite the deficiencies in content and methods that have been frequently cited (Milanesi, 1971).

The commitment of many distinguished exponents of Catholic dissent who are connected with 'base communities' has been focused on the teaching of religion. They have raised their voices on many occasions to deny the Catholic church the right to dominate in the educational field. Their many contributions have led to meetings, conferences, publications, and research which have all stimulated the parties of the Left, especially, to take clearer positions on the issue. The preferred approach has been confined to the level of the leadership, however, where diplomatic rather than openly conflictual choices have been made. In other words, the party secretaries have not allowed the dissenting Catholics much room, and have 'dialogued' with the Catholic church on general, theoretical levels. Some official declarations, especially from the Communist party, have been published only in response to requests that were felt to be too meaningful to be ignored (note, for example, Bishop Bettazzi who wrote to Berlinguer, head of the PCI). So, a line of interest has been maintained, with the intention of not upsetting the susceptibilities either of Catholic teaching or of the numerous believers who are either party militants or simply voters.

As far as young people are concerned, students of both sexes showed no tendency in the period of contestation around 1968 to spark conflict between politics and religion. Of young people surveyed in a study of an area in the South 36 per cent accepted that political choices and religious convictions could be harmonized. It is true that 60 per cent insisted on the independence of the two spheres, but only 3 per cent were agreed on the possibility of an opposition between political choice and religious belief (M. Cipriani, 1971: 105). This is evidence that influences of a confessional type are not wholly absent even in a purely worldly context. Another study carried out in the south in 1971 on the young in Naples revealed a largely favourable attitude towards religion as a value (Caporale, 1972: 26).

D'Ascenzi's (1973) study of peasants and religion deserves separate discussion. It has some methodological failings and some rather comforting data for the Catholic religion, but this is understandable in view of the fact that the interviews were conducted by clergy. However, one should not overlook the fact that it is in the peasant context that the religion diffused from Catholicism has worked long and deep, trying to defeat the ancient rites and cults that were still active until recently. Yet, there is some basic change here as well – for example, in relation to divorce and in anticipation of the referenda: 'one recognizes the tendency towards a greater liberality on the subject, in harmony with the tendency to give more importance to the happiness of the spouse and his or her agreement than to the maintenance of the bond at all costs' (D'Ascenzi, 1973: 105). It is on the basis of this and other similar considerations that growing numbers of Catholics are becoming more favourable to the institution of divorce.

On the subject of secularization in urban areas, the research by Pin (1975) on the people of Rome is fundamental. It is the only study so far which examines the religious attitudes and conduct in the capital of world Catholicism. The author outlines fifteen sociological types of religiosity; 26 per cent of Romans were 'remote' from Catholicism in the period 1968–70; 46.6 per cent were 'cultural Catholics' (traditional occasional, conforming, 'intra-worldly'); 13.4 per cent were 'most observant'; and the most committed amounted to 13.3 per cent. In all, 73.3 per cent of Roman citizens showed some measure of belonging to Catholicism. It is not easy to trace the characteristics of 'diffused religion' in the complexity of the indicators that were used. The strongest indication is provided by the 39.1 per cent of the sample who displayed Catholic religiosity of a cultural kind (with the exception of a special type of traditionalist). To this central core of 'diffused religion' should be added two categories of observing, practising (but not faithful) Catholics, and Catholics involved in 'spontaneous groups' (but not of the Azione Cattolica type) who accounted for, respectively, 7.2 and 4.6 per cent of the sample. The universe of 'diffused religion' seems to involve basically 50.9 per cent of Romans. Moreover, the cultural religiosity of Catholic descent is pervasive to the point of involving almost all the 'remote' Catholics with the sole exception of the atheists (Pin, 1975: 117, 332).

The 'hot' years of ecclesiastical dispute also favoured the development of a new phenomenology of youth which was linked to the birth of the Comunione e Liberazione (CL) movement. This is currently defined as Catholic neo-integralism because of its ideological content of confessional and Christian Democrat militancy. It is no accident that CL is rooted precisely in the Catholic University of Milan, even physically occupying the sites of earlier disputes and conflict which had been removed at the end of 1969. CL's 'revolution' uses values broadly shared by the young: fellowship, solidarity, innovation, and fantasy. Results have been achieved, and increases have occurred in the amount of support and the number of members. Over the years, the movement reached a certain plateau of young followers (as well as some adults, especially among young families). It is really its striking activism which draws attention to this new element in Italian Catholicism (the previous experiment of Gioventù Studentesca [GS] in Milan never actually attained national importance). Exaggerated personalism means that CL is especially visible in places like the university where the activity of Catholics has not generally borne much fruit in the past. This makes the activity of CL appear worthwhile to the point of convincing an impressive group of Italian bishops unconditionally to support the initiatives sponsored by the leader, don Giussani, a lecturer in 'Introduction to Theology' in the Political Science Faculty of the Università Cattolica del Sacro Cuore in Milan.

Meanwhile, considerable changes have taken place in the reality of Catholicism, as is shown by a questionnaire survey carried out at Lucca in Tuscany in the spring of 1976 (Scarvaglieri, 1978). Of the respondents 90 per cent believed in God, but 'only' 63 per cent had a 'theological conception of the church'. This indicates how the formerly homogeneous Catholicism has lost ground and become latent, mixed up, and fragmented into disparate forms in the folds of the sociocultural scene. The attitude towards the possibility of being Christian and Communist is especially instructive for questions about relations between politics and religion. Of those who saw an evangelical value in love for others 48.1 per cent were in agreement on such a possibility, and 33.9 per cent were opposed. However, the distinction between ideology (Christianity versus Marxism) and political choice (to be a Christian versus being a Communist) should not be overlooked. The same 'nominalistic' distinction between Marxism and being Communist is significant almost to the point of inverting the relative strengths of agreements and disagreements. In fact, if there is a certain preference for being both Christian and Communist, there is an almost equally unfavourable attitude towards Marxism as a theory. This indicates a distinction between a more lenient, orthodox religiosity and a 'diffused religion' which arises from an evangelical value (love for one's neighbour) and considers the double religious-political alignment practicable (Scarvaglieri, 1978: 113, 154). A further confirmation of this comes from the fact that 54 per cent of the sample perceived opposition between Christianity and Marxism, but only 20.2 per cent between Christianity and Communism (Scarvaglieri, 1978: 164). However, one must stress the detail that the area of Lucca is one of the least 'red' in Tuscany and the one which has the highest rate of religious practice.

A typical case of the relations between Communism and Catholicism in the years from 1959 to 1979 is examined in a study by Liliano Faenza (1979). It examined a parish of the Romagna countryside in a region celebrated for the strength of the Communist party's presence. In the twenty years under consideration, many events changed the religious, rather than the political, dimension. The most important was undoubtedly the Vatican Council, followed by two different pontificates. The impact of the liturgical innovations created some problems of adaptation at San Lorenzo a Monte, but as for the rest, there were no wholly new elements. There was no religious dissent, although this could have found fertile ground. Instead, the Jehovah's Witnesses began to exercise some influence, and by playing on the residues of 'diffused religion' they have been able to scatter their seed and gather some of its fruit. The element of socialization (including religious socialization) seems to be the sole constant in the church's practice. By 1979, however, different meeting places had taken the place of, and outclassed, the centrality formerly represented by the parish. The association with the church had not been completely severed, however. There was no lack of occasions of a cultural and personal order, especially associated with the figure of the parish priest, to re-tie old bonds which were all the more effective for having been formed in a highly receptive period which affects the formation of the personality.

Vito Orlando's (1979) research also involved a parish in the south at Potenza in Lucania between 1977 and 1978. The results of his questionnaire survey show that 90.06 per cent of the sample broadly accept the church as a source of 'support in the difficulties and sufferings of life'. The presence of a more autonomous world-view is equally conspicuous: 83.1 per cent thought that 'to have a religion does not mean going to church and doing various things, but doing what you believe to be right in your conscience'. However, one must ask what the source of this 'conscience' is, what principles inspire it, and what inputs it has received. Undoubtedly, this is the specific field of 'diffused religion'. Yet, the readiness to follow the ecclesiastical hierarchy is greatly reduced; for it is confined to only 45.03 per cent of respondents. On the specific subjects of contraception, abortion, and divorce the rate drops to 30.79 per cent (Orlando, 1979: 121, 199, 203).

The tendency towards heterodox responses to the dictates of Catholicism is also reflected in the increase of marriages that are celebrated with a civil rather than a religious ceremony:

> In 1964 civil weddings were 1.33 per cent of religious ones, and were carried out in 76 per cent of the regional capitals, mainly in the north. In 1977 civil marriages had reached 10.52 per cent. . . . It is estimated that by the 1990s, if the same growth rate is maintained, civil weddings could reach rates of 20 per cent and even higher, and that, together with *de facto* unions, they could exceed 30 per cent annually. (Burgalassi, 1980: 235)

Even if these forecasts are confirmed, they would in any case demonstrate the Catholic religion's strong capacity for resistance.

The future of Italian Catholicism is clearly linked to developments in the dynamics that are already in operation. This is why studies of the young attract much interest. The best-documented study was conducted by Giancarlo Milanesi, who concluded: 'It is the religion of a generation, rather weak in historical memory, which finds itself managing a complex and contradictory daily existence without firm points of reference, and which cannot or does not wish to run too many risks in trusting itself to overall projects of improbable utopias' (Milanesi, 1981, vol. I: 395). Youth therefore finds itself faced with a provisional religiosity which is weak and disconnected. The implication is that this situation of stasis does not render the efforts of the Catholic church wholly useless, especially the catechism preparatory to the sacraments of intitiation (Communion and Confirmation) and family teaching where the Catholic tradition prevails. Yet, the temporary uncertainty may also flow back into the channel of fideistic reassurance, however generic and unsustained it may be by cultural practice. Not even in the case of total 'abandonment' does it seem possible to obliterate completely the strategic role of Catholic socialization in Italy. Even in the working class there are significant indications such as 'a deep and continuous membership of an ecclesiastically oriented religion and/or of an alternative ideology of a strong kind' (Cipolla, 1981: 213–14). Religion and politics thus seem to be joined, or separated, but like links in the same cultural chain. They are even organized according to different parameters, but with an afflatus which remains 'religious' even when it cancels Catholic affiliation.

Nesti comes to a fairly similar conclusion at the end of his work on the working class: 'One notes a withdrawal of the religious category from the totalizing exclusivism of ecclesiastical "specialization". The Church is conceived of within social values and processes which are experienced critically' (Nesti, 1982: 207). The religious is not essentially identified with the ecclesiastical and, thus, with Catholicism.

Ampola defines the framework of Catholicism in quite explicit terms which can be extrapolated from the context of Leghorn, to which his investigation refers, and applied to the wider Italian situation:

> The religious typology which emerges clearly designates a *secular area which is trying to take on religious shapes*: in it, certain values of religious origins are revealed as secular values oriented towards a totalizing, legitimatory meaning. The central channel of change is aimed at an exchange of the type of religion – that is, at the anthropological rather than the social type of value, which is its characteristic feature. (Ampola, 1983: 108)

This, then, is the novelty at the level of values: religious elements are being taken up within new social, political, and lay functions.

Another commentator has spoken of 'latent' religion at the conclusion of a study of shop stewards in the south. Their attitudes are said to be divided between the model of church religion and that of a search for certainty and identity without having recourse to a demand for religion *in its totality* (Conte et al., 1983: 143).

Popular religion is another vast and only partly explored area where 'diffused religion' is broadly channelled and is directed particularly towards the saints and the Virgin (Giurati, 1983). The extent of the phenomenon is only suggested by the number of annual visitors to sanctuaries – almost a third of the entire population of Italy, according to very reliable estimates.

Furthermore, alongside this form of 'popularized' religion there is a kind of 'new morality' of a lay type which appears permissive but not destructive (Lanzetti and Mauri, 1983: 286). It is among young people above all that 'one meets basically with a refusal to channel the religious values of Christianity (which very many of them accept as a whole) in the direction of church religion' (Emma, 1984: 196).

The Italian Catholic church sought to inform itself about the effects of the Vatican Council by setting up a special study of liturgical reform. The latest findings bring out the hiatus between ceremonial intention and the participation of the faithful, in the sense that many services do not adequately transmit explicit contents and even become an obstacle to communication (Visentin, 1984: 166–7). This does not happen everywhere, however, as contexts are also to be found where innovation in the liturgy has produced good results (Pelaratti, 1985: 88).

The 'new values' according to the latest research

If the vote for the 'religious party', Christian Democracy, has remained *almost* unchanged in the last twenty years, it is clear that the capillary action of Catholicism is continuing to be somewhat effective. The decline in religious practice, which is now decelerating, does not suggest that there will be a decline at the level of 'diffused religion'. Rather, it is this mode which is increasing and fully substantiates one of the trends stressed by Ronald Inglehart (1977); that is, the persistence of a closer correlation between religious belief and voting. The variable of religious confession is so frequently transmitted in relations between the generations that it comes second only to racial and linguistic factors. In particular, the correlation between religion and party political preference is more significant than that between social class and party (Inglehart, 1983: 255–6).

This correlation is no accident in a country such as Italy. A recent survey by the weekly *Famiglia Cristiana* (1 January 1985) painted a complete picture of Italian Catholicism in a sample of 1,000 men and women: 32.1 per cent believed and practised; 36.1 per cent believed but rarely practised; and 17.3 per cent believed but did not practise. The last two figures can *as a general rule* be understood in terms of 'diffused religion'. The most advanced position in this sociological context is captured in the concept of 'implicit religion', which is without specifically confessional characteristics, identifiable in the most diverse areas, not codified but centred on certain 'basic' ideas relative to existence (Nesti, 1985: 15). On the other hand, the net of Italian Catholicism is so inclusive and structured as to occupy wide areas of the social world. It is worth dwelling on the fact that a fifth of the whole Italian press is explicitly Catholic (2,000 titles out of 10,000), including 125 diocesan weeklies with a print-run of 1.4 million copies and a readership of 5 million, as well as a weekly like *Famiglia Cristiana* with a very wide circulation in excess of 1.3 million, not to mention the non-periodical press, the cultural journals, the publications of Catholic associations, and the Catholic dailies (especially *Avvenire* and *L'Eco di Bergamo*).

Finally, mention should be made of the vital activity of the many thousands of groups of Catholic volunteers who are concerned with social services, civil defence, services in the home, blood donation, after-school activities, and transport of the sick and handicapped. There is a pullulation of initiatives which legitimate the credibility of Catholicism. This situation has only recently developed in the country and is also a consequence of the crisis of traditional associations (primarily of *Azione Cattolica*) which has now been overcome, and in the application of certain guiding principles which sprang from the two conferences of the Italian church held in Rome in 1976 and Loreto in 1985. To some extent, the growth of Catholic voluntary services has performed functions which are an alternative to the anti-institutional dissent expressed by the 'base communities' and the movement of Christians for Socialism – the last two phenomena marking time after an enthusiastic start. Moreover, the result of voluntary service has provided some people with a way out of the diatribes between the two 'contestants' among Catholic laity; CL, with its active presence in the social sphere; and Azione Cattolica, with its 'religious preference'.

No doubt, the recent vicissitudes in Italian Catholicism appear to be simultaneously contradictory and dynamic (Martin, 1978: 124–6). An explanation for them lies mainly in considering religion as a cultural system which gives expression to the ethos of a people, its quality of life, its moral inclinations, its world-view, and its basic ideas, in a synthesis (Geertz, 1973). Its values, in particular, contain traces of religiosity even among those who never attend religious services. According to the findings of the European Value Systems Study Group, 36 per cent of people who never attend religious services attribute importance to God in their own life, 40 per cent pray or do something similar, and 24 per cent find comfort and strength in religion (Calvaruso and Abbruzzese, 1985: 47). Of those who do not believe in God 25 per cent call themselves religious. If one then moves on to examine the moral aspect, the same international study by Jean Stoetzel shows that

> ethical values [in Italy], whilst not being the faithful reproduction of ecclesiastical teaching in their social dimension, do not thereby lose their intensity. On the contrary, they find their compatibility in a dimension of religiosity which can be understood as the search for a meaning in life rather than for adaptation to the rules of moral teaching. The fragmented ethic does not turn into immorality but, on the contrary, seeks new elements on which to base itself. (Calvaruso and Abbruzzese, 1985: 57)

It is no accident that certain principles remain fundamental for Italian Catholics: not to kill (97 per cent), not to steal (94 per cent), and to honour one's father and mother (93 per cent).

On the other hand, according to the authors of the research report on Italy,

> Diffused religiosity then becomes the dominant religious dimension for all those who, immersed in the secular reality of contemporary society, though not managing to accept those dimensions of the sacred cosmos which are more remote and provocative compared with the rational vision of the world, do not thereby abandon their need for meaningfulness. In the immanent dimension of individual everyday existence, diffused religiosity, rather than bearing witness to the presence of a process of laicization in a religiously oriented society, seems to enhance the permanence of the sacred in the secularized society. (Calvaruso and Abbruzzese, 1985: 79)

And, continuing to refer to my theory of 'diffused religion' Calvaruso and Abbruzzese added that

> while diffused religion persists in the context of a secularized society, the sound and dimensions of such an echo are so much greater because growing institutional differentiation, delegating the problem of meaning to specific institutions, reveals that it is impotent to define conceptions of the world and of life which are not directly pragmatico-utilitarian. But the basic resonance of diffused religion is even stronger as the church institution recovers its own role as producer of meaning and brings back to light even the more specific elements of its own vision of the world and of life (elements which are more provocative, however, *vis-à-vis* the bureaucratic-rational ideology of the surrounding society). Diffused religiosity is located in an intermediate area between a secular society in crisis and a resumption of the ecclesiastical administration of the sacred. It remains too 'lay' to accept the more specific elements of church doctrine and too much in need of meaning to survive in an epoch which is 'without God and without prophets'. (Calvaruso and Abbruzzese, 1985: 79–80)

Finally it should be said that the phenomenon does not seem destined to fade away if 89 per cent of Italians between the ages of eighteen and twenty-four say that they are Catholic and if 77 per cent of them believe in God.

Garelli's inquiry among 1,737 workers in Piedmont confirms the hypotheses associated with 'diffused religion' at many points. Old and new interact in the cultural dynamics of Italian Catholicism: the workers are not '"disaffected" from a religious referent nor from church religion' (Garelli, 1986: 21). Religion always offers a meaning for life. There is likewise a potential in the dominant Catholic religion to help 71.4 per cent of the sample to find a meaning for their own existence (that also holds good in the main for workers who are politically oriented towards the Left). About 80 per cent of respondents said that they prayed in some way. The partaking of sacraments such as First Communion and Confirmation is a widely observable constant. Many take an interest in the Christian education of their children, as well as in the promotion of peace and the struggle against injustice. Moreover, having a religious belief is considered one of the most important values (seventh in a total of sixteen levels of importance). Essentially, 'all this indicates that amidst a general transiency of religious referents in the population as a whole, some models of religiosity which are characterized by a peculiar internal organic character are encountered and are particularly capable of influencing the conditions of life' (Garelli, 1986: 304). At any rate, this would seem to involve too ephemeral a referent: everyday reality would leave it out of consideration, with the result that religion would remain nothing but a backdrop or the scenery of daily existence. This reduction to the cultural level does not, however, mean the disappearance of the dominant religion nor does it reduce it to being 'invisible'. Rather, it is precisely its function as scenery which enhances its meaning and which offers a context and contents.

In other words, the stage is basic for understanding the action. However fragmentary, disconnected, evanescent, and sketchy, the scenery remains permanently discernible. Essentially, it is possible to talk in terms of 'diffused religion' in Italy rather than of a blacked-out, pulverized, or annihilated religion. Diffused religion lacks the kind of clear-cut characteristics which would be visible in, for example, church attendance, but it works through long-range conditioning, which is due, above all, to mass religious socialization, and to which there is a corresponding kind of 'mass loyalty' of a new type (R. Cipriani, 1978).

References

Ampola, M. (1983) *Mondi vitali, religiosi e secolari in transizione: la morfologia sociale livornese* (Life-worlds, religious and secular worlds in transition: the social morphology of Leghorn). Pisa: Giardini Editori.

Bellah, R.N. (1974) 'Le cinque religioni dell'Italia moderna', pp. 439–68 in F.L. Cavazza and S.R. Gaubard (eds), *Il caso italiano*. Milano: Garzanti; published in translation as 'The five religions of modern Italy', pp. 86–118 in R.N. Bellah and P.E. Hammond (eds), *Varieties of Civil Religion*. San Francisco: Harper & Row, 1980.

Burgalassi, S. (1968) *Il comportamento religioso degli italiani* (The religious behaviour of Italians). Florence: Vallecchi.

Burgalassi, S. (1970) *Le cristianità nascoste* (The hidden Christianities). Bologna: Edizioni Dehoniane.

Burgalassi, S. (1980) *Uno spiraglio sul futuro. Interpretazione sociologica del cambiamento sociale in atto* (A glimpse of the future. A sociological interpretation of current social change). Pisa: Giardini Editori.

Calvaruso, C. and S. Abbruzzese (1985) *Indagine sui valori in Italia. Dai post-materialismi alla ricerca di senso* (An inquiry into values in Italy. From post-materialisms to the quest for meaning). Turin: SEI.

Caporale, V. (1972) *Cosa pensano i giovani della religione?* (What do young people think of religion?) Naples: Edizioni Dehoniane.

Cipolla, C. (1981) *Religione e cultura operaia* (Religion and working class culture). Brescia: Morcelliana.

Cipriani, M. (1971) *I giovani del Sud e la Chiesa* (Southern youth and the church). Cassano-Bari: Edizioni del Circito.

Cipriani, R. (1978) *Dalla teoria alla verifica: indagine sui valori in mutamento* (From theory to validation. An inquiry into changing values). Rome: Goliardica Editrice.

Cipriani, R. (1983) 'Religione e politica. Il caso italiano: la religione diffusa', *Studi di Sociologia*, 21(3): 245–71; published in translation as 'Religion and politics. The Italian case: "diffused religion"', *Archives de Sciences sociales des Religions*, 58(1) 1984: 29–51.

Conte, G. Di Gennaro, D. Pizzuti, and R. Russo (1983) *Cultura operaia nel mezzogiorno. Sindacato dei consigli e modelli culturali: una ricerca sui delegati di fabbrica* (Working class culture in the South. Council-based unions and cultural patterns. An inquiry into shop stewards). Rome: Edizioni Lavoro.

D'Ascenzi, G. (1973) *Coltivatori e religione* (Farmers and religion). Bologna: Edagricole.

Dobbelaere, Karel (1985) 'La dominante catholique', *Recherches sociologiques*, 16(3): 193–220.

Emma, M. (1984) *I giovani e la fede oggi. Ricerca longitudinale socio-psicologica sulla religiosità dei giovani* (Youth and faith today. A longitudinal socio-psychological study of young people and religion). Naples: Edizioni Dehoniane.

Faenza, L. (1979) *Comunismo e cattolicesimo in una parrocchia di campagna. Vent'anni dopo (1959–1979)* (Communism and Catholicism in a country parish. Twenty years after). Bologna: Cappelli.

Garelli, F. (1986) *La religione dello scenario. La persistenza della religione tra i lavoratori* (The religion of scenario. The persistence of religion among workers). Bologna: Il Mulino.

Geertz, C. (1973) *The Interpretation of Cultures*. New York: Basic Books.

Giurati, P. (1983) *Devozione a S. Antonio. Ricognizione socio-culturale* (The cult of St Anthony. A socio-cultural inquiry). Padua: Edizioni Messaggero.

Inglehart, R. (1977) *The Silent Revolution*. Princeton, NJ: Princeton University Press; published in translation as *La rivoluzione silenziosa*. Milan: Rizzoli Editore, 1983.

Lanzetti, C. and L. Mauri (eds) (1983) *Famiglia e religione. Aspetti di una transizione difficile. Ricerca sociologica su un'area italo-meridionale* (Family and religion. Aspects of a difficult transition. A sociological study of a southern Italian area). Milan: Vita e Pensiero.

Martin, D.A. (1978) *A General Theory of Secularization*. Oxford: Blackwell.

Milanesi, G. (1971) *Religione e liberazione. Ricerca sull'insegnamento della religione in Umbria* (Religion and liberation. A study of the teaching of religion in Umbria). Turin: SEI.

Milanesi, G. (ed.) (1981) *Oggi credono così. Indagine multidisciplinare sulla domanda religiosa dei giovani italiani* (This is the way they believe. An interdisciplinary inquiry into religious demand among Italian young people). vol. I. Turin: Editrice Elle Di Ci.

Nesti, A. (1982) *Le fontane e il borgo. Il fattore religione nella società italiana contemporanea* (The fountains and the village. The religious factor in contemporary Italian society). Rome: Editrice Ianua.

Nesti A. (1985) *Il religioso implicito* (Implicit religion). Rome: Editrice Ianua.

Orlando, V. (1979) *Religione e cambio sociale. Indagine socio-religiosa in una parrocchia meridionale* (Religion and social change. An inquiry into a southern parish from the standpoint of the sociology of religion). Bari: Ecumenica Editrice.

Pelaratti, C. (1985) *La liturgia eucaristica nella parrocchia di S. Basilio in Roma* (The eucharistic liturgy in St Basil's parish in Rome). Rome: Pontificia Universita Lateranense.

Pin, E. (1975) *La religiosità dei romani. Indagine sociologica con nota metodologica di Sergio Bolasco* (Religion and Romans. A sociological inquiry with a methodological comment by Sergio Bolasco). Bologna: Edizioni Dehoniane.

Rusconi, G.E. (1969) *Giovani e secolarizzazione* (Youth and secularization). Florence: Vallecchi.

Scarvaglieri, G. (1978) *La religione in una società in transformazione* (Religion in a changing society). Lucca: Maria Pacini Fazzi.

Spadolini, G. (1966) *L'opposizione cattolica. Da Porta Pia al '98* (The Catholic opposition. From Porta Pia to 1898). 2nd edn. Florence: Vallecchi.

Visentin, P. (ed.) (1984) *La riforma liturgica in Italia. Realtà e speranze* (Liturgical reform in Italy. Reality and hopes). Padua: Edizioni Messaggero.

3

From Parish to Transcendent Humanism in France

Yves Lambert

The purpose of this chapter is to outline the main conclusions of a study of the changes which have occurred in a rural French parish from the beginning of this century to the present day (Lambert, 1985, 1986). The distinguishing feature of this parish is that it is located in a part of Brittany which remained firmly a part of Christendom until the 1950s (Isambert and Terrenoire, 1980; Le Bras, 1976). Its evolution since then has been very striking: a fall-off in religious practice, a halt in vocations, a crisis in belief as well as the ascendancy of a new form of Catholicism. The situation provides the opportunity to reveal in a very clear manner what happens when a traditional rural society is violently thrust into the modern, even post-modern, world. In this regard, Limerzel is representative of something which has also occurred in Quebec, the north of Portugal, the Castilian region of Spain, the north of Italy, Limbourg in Belgium, Ireland, or Poland, even though, in these last two countries, the religious influence has remained very strong for the special reasons of nationalism and communism.[1]

The aim of this study is first to recreate this parochial civilization, which was an achievement of the Catholicism of the Counter-Reformation, and then to describe step by step the recent shifts in an effort to explain them. The research was based on historical, ethnographical, and sociological methods, with the primary emphasis on belief. The problem of secularization remained in the background in the form of this question: was it only a decline in the social influence of religion, or was it also a loss of belief? Two conclusions will be drawn. A shift has taken place from one historical form of Catholicism to another, which is better adapted to modernity, and there has been an increase in indifference and unbelief. These two phenomena have not previously been sufficiently distinguished, but they have different implications for 'secularization'. After a comparison between the parochial life of long ago and of today (taking a typical year), I shall propose an interpretation of these changes.

The parochial civilization

Let us go back fifty years to Limerzel in the Department of Morbihan (in the south of Brittany), a parish with 1,600 inhabitants. The big granite church overlooking the houses was built at the end of the nineteenth century in the aftermath of the Catholic Restoration and the agricultural revolution. Electricity has only just come to the village (1931); travel is by means of bicycle or by horse and cart (there are no more than ten cars); oxen are used for working the land; and most people live in a house with only one or two uncomfortable rooms, although families have an average of six children. The parish has three priests, one of them a teacher and principal of the boys' Catholic primary school, and eight nuns, one of them being the principal of the girls' school. No more than 2 per cent of local children attend the state school, although 84 per cent of all French children are in state schools.

'In this first Sunday of Advent . . .', in the words of the priest at the mass which marks the start of the liturgical year at the beginning of December, all the villagers apart from a handful come to mass, as they do every Sunday. To miss mass would be very serious: it is a 'mortal sin' punishable by hell (unlike 'venial' sins which only lead to purgatory). With the gentry in front and the less well-off (or the half-hearted) behind where the seats are cheaper, the church is packed and resounds with Latin. After mass there is plenty of life in the shops, in the cafés, on the square, and everybody catches up on the week's news. Half of the congregation return in the afternoon for vespers, and afterwards there are meetings for apostolic groups, Children of Mary, advowsons and movements for Catholic Action or for Catholic schools. The parish has also encouraged the creation of a Catholic agricultural union and cooperative, and the curate is in charge of a credit union. Most of these organizations have been formed since the beginning of the century in order to combat laicization – republicanization, at the beginning – and urban influences. It should be made clear that this parish was *'chouan'* (insurgent royalist) during the French revolution and was opposed to the separation of church and state in 1905.

The first Friday of the month is devoted to the Eucharist: many women, children and young people come to mass to receive Communion, having been to confession the night before. The Catholic church encourages Communion while enforcing certain precautions such as fasting and confession, so much so that it is mainly received only at Christmas, Easter, and All Saints, as well as on the feast of Perpetual Adoration which was specially instituted for that purpose. On 8 December, the feast of the Immaculate

Conception, the faithful of the Virgin Mary come to worship, and many light candles (for health, the family, and success), just as on every feast of Our Lady. Then there is Christmas, with the huge crib in the church already full of offerings, the three midnight masses, the presents brought to the children by the baby Jesus and the play put on after vespers by the girls who also play male parts because it would be unthinkable for the group to be mixed. Guess what is the traditional wish on New Year's Day, which is observed like a Sunday? 'Happy New Year, good health, and heaven at the end of your days' or '. . . at the end of the year' is what the well-wishers say.

The feast of Perpetual Adoration, so called because it is celebrated every day of the year in a different parish of the diocese, is celebrated in Limerzel on 26 January. This is as important as the Easter celebration and it is a bank holiday (the Catholic-owned saw mills are closed, and the pupils at the *école publique* are allowed by their parents to take part). After two days of religious instruction and confession, with men and women taking part separately, the whole parish receives Holy Communion and many of them take their turn in adoring the Blessed Sacrament for one hour at a time.

Lent begins shortly afterwards. During Holy Week there are no processions in Limerzel, unlike in southern Europe, but almost everyone participates in the services on Maundy Thursday and Good Friday, when the atmosphere in the village is full of solemnity. On Good Friday life is practically suspended, the farmers do not harness the cows and horses, the villagers eat only one main meal, even the bells are not rung ('they have gone to Rome', as the saying goes), the tabernacle on the altar is empty, and the statues are covered. Until Saturday night, however, the church is a hive of activity with the penitents coming to do their Easter duty. Since this obligation is the most pressing (decreed by the Lateran Council in 1215), only about a dozen parishioners fail to attend. Easter: flowers, decorations, alleluias, bells (which bring the children their eggs), everything celebrates Christ's triumph; and, in the afternoon, the men stage their play. On Easter Monday there is mass again, just as on a Sunday. During Lent, the congregation do the Stations of the Cross every evening, and there are even more who say the rosary during May (Our Lady's month) and in October (the month of the rosary) when prayers are said at home in more than half of these rural households and where crosses and statues are adorned with flowers.

There is a feast day in May which has been a major event since the beginning of the twentieth century: the feast of Joan of Arc who symbolizes the Catholic vocation of France – the eldest daughter of the church – in opposition to the secular republic and which, since the First World War, is the Catholics' way of expressing their patriotism. It should be made clear that there were *chouans* here who voted in favour of the Royalists until the Christian Democrat victory of 1928, and that believing in God, protecting the family, respecting property (a natural and divine right), being patriotic, following the path of righteousness, all amounted to just one thing – that is, opposition to the 'godless society', socialism, and communism. 'If religion went, everything would disappear', it was said, because 'there is no morality without religion, and no order without morality'. Even the war was seen by the clergy as a divine punishment, and the victory as a favour: 'the soldiers fight, but it is God who gives victory', in the words of Joan of Arc. This goes back to the basic political rift in the west of France since the French revolution, setting apart *chouans* and republicans, those in favour of the church and those against the church, the right and the left (Siegfried, 1913; Berger, 1972).

Limerzel belongs to a part of the country characterized by the 'accepted hierarchy', to quote André Siegfried, where the church legitimated social status by means of segregation between the pews, different classes of services and honours, the ideology of the acceptance of the social condition; an acceptance which is resigned and which leads to redemption (the most virtuous people will be the first to enter Paradise). However, faced with the challenges made by school, democracy, and progress, the clergy is progressively becoming more mindful of encouraging promotion and modernization, especially for the 'Young Catholic Farmers' (founded in 1930) which was to become the popular elite of the future.

The three days leading up to the Ascension begin early in the morning with the Rogation procession where the people ask God to bless the earth's produce as if to remind the Lord, before his ascension into heaven, that human beings must remain on earth. These processions across the countryside are a very ancient type of Christianization of past rites and are well attended, as are the other agrarian rites for St Antoine (for pigs), St Jean Cornely (horned beasts), and so on, and the masses where rain is prayed for. This Catholicism is deeply rooted in the life of the farming community. There is a correlation between the liturgical cycle and the agricultural cycle; for example, Easter coincides with the rebirth of nature, and All Saints with death. This correlation is reinforced by the fact that the Christian calendar serves as a temporal landmark for many sayings and customs: 'on the feast of St Catherine all the trees take root' (25 November); the farmers' leases are renewed on the feast of St Michael; the weather vane on the bell-tower (the

Gallic cock) is supposed to indicate the direction of the prevailing winds of the year during the procession on Palm Sunday; and so on. Agrarian rites and annual feasts are celebrated in the chapels in the outlying parts of the parish (the 'frairies' or 'brotherhoods' which were subdivisions of the parish in the Old Regime that originated in Celtic clans); and the bell is tolled at the chapel before being tolled at the church.

Coming a short time after the Solemn Communion and just before the beginning of the main work on the farms (hay-making and harvest), the feast of Corpus Christi is the chief event of the liturgical year and of the parish: the streets are richly adorned, three majestic altars are erected, and the Blessed Sacrament is there in all its glory in the middle of a magnificent procession. This feast overshadows Pentecost, which never enjoyed such popular attention because the Holy Spirit is a more abstract concept apart from that one day, every four years, when the Bishop comes to administer Confirmation in great solemnity. In fact, for the parishioners, the real Trinity is made up of the Father, the Son and . . . the Mother, who is considered by the Catholic church to be the Mother of God and the privileged intercessor close to heaven. This is the impression given by the feast of the Blessed Virgin on 15 August (the feast of the Assumption) with its well-attended procession. The clergy are mindful of the fact that it was the wish of Louis XIII that the feast should be celebrated since he had implored the Blessed Virgin to bring victory against the besieged Protestants in La Rochelle. If nothing else, this acts as a confirmation of the protective and intercessory powers of Mary. Everybody goes on pilgrimage to Lourdes at least once in his lifetime (this is the only major trip for the majority). On the feast of the patron saint of the village there is also a final procession and the village kermesse. The final procession is in October in honour of St Clair who was the first missionary to go there, and whose fountain is well known for predicting the future even in affairs of the heart; the procession goes from the fountain to the St Clair chapel along a beautiful path which is said to be the Roman path that he himself had taken.

Autumn is the season for weddings, where two or three hundred people come together. For young people, this is the main opportunity for meeting and dancing. Dance halls are forbidden by many parents and strongly condemned by the clergy, who are vainly opposed to the new type of dances such as the tango and the waltz that are accused of being indecent. There is no need to stress the fact that marriage is for life. 'Purity beforehand, fidelity during', is how Catholic morality may be summarized; and 'fertility but no pleasure' because the church treats procreation as the main purpose of marriage and the only excuse for sexuality which is considered, outside this purpose, as a sin to be confessed. The church manages to curb the spread of birth control but it has no influence on divorce, which is also very foreign to the secular rural mentality.

The last major feast of the liturgical year, All Saints, brings everyone to face the most important thing of all: the hereafter. In fact, saving one's soul is considered by the church to be the main objective of life; life on earth is seen as no more than a place for passing through, full of trials, where misery and suffering are providential means of atoning for one's sins. Every ten years, there is a parish mission which stresses this fact for two or three weeks. This is accompanied by spectacular ceremonies. In 1922, for example, there was a ceremony which enacted the final destiny of souls in the next world. The number of children equalled the number of people who had died in the parish in the preceding year and whose names had been called back. Thus, some arrived dressed in black representing those souls which were condemned to hell for eternity. Meanwhile, the preacher listed from the pulpit the most common mortal sins in the parish and the horrors of hell. Then other children came forward, also dressed in black but tending gradually towards the other side, the white side, as they atoned for their sins and gained indulgences ('for the souls in purgatory'). Others, who had lived a life of virtue, piety, and devotion and who had accepted their trials with faith, were dressed entirely in white and went straight to heaven.

Although the parishioners have one eye on heaven, they also have their feet firmly on the ground. The concept of salvation held by the masses gives priority to earthly life (moral guidance, supernatural assurances, solemnization of rites of passage, legitimation of the social and political order), and it sees in the hereafter, above all, a means of compensating for injustices, gaining credit for good deeds, punishing the wrong-doers and for obtaining one's final happiness. Everyone knows that he must bear his cross on earth ('the more unhappy you are here, the happier you'll be above'), yet thinking that 'God did not make good things for nothing'. There is a great fear of hell, but everyone thinks that there are ways of avoiding it. And, after all, 'We are as he made us', 'Surely, God isn't as bad as all that', 'You do your purgatory on earth', and 'We're not Communists' not forgetting the fact that confession 'gives you a clean slate'. Thus, the logic of salvation of the church and that of the masses go hand in hand, based on a close integration of ordinary living with the religious life; that is, a close association between belief and practice.

A new world

Streets filled with cars, tarmac on all roads even in the smallest hamlet, television in all houses, every type of comfort, central heating even in the church, tractors and farm machinery, an increase in the number of waged labourers to about half the working population – all show that times have changed in Limerzel. Its population has now shrunk to 1,200 inhabitants because of rural depopulation. These changes have taken place mainly since the 1950s. All that has already been said about the difference between traditional society and modern society is also valid here. But of course we must avoid making too neat a distinction between 'long ago' and 'today': modernity was already beginning to appear in the nineteenth century, and certain aspects of post-modernity are present, whereas certain traditions are still retained or adapted. What has become of religious life? 'Will Limerzel be able to keep its reputation for being a good parish for much longer? . . . The sense of God and the sense of sin are weakening in our modern society.' This was the observation made by the parish priest in 1957.

The church seems disproportionately large and is now attended by no more than one-third of parishioners; more women than men, more old people (half of them over sixty-five) than young (20 per cent). The rate of decline is more striking than for France as a whole, yet the level of practice is still clearly higher than the French level of regular (and quasi-regular) practice: 15 per cent (but 10 per cent in the 18–24 age group). Mass is no longer felt to be a basic obligation but rather a matter for personal choice. The parish priest himself stopped issuing the threat of hell in 1965, but even by that time a certain number of people no longer believed in it. This great Sunday meeting-place has lost its social function. Neither the introduction of mass on Saturday evening in 1969, nor the liturgical reforms brought about by the Second Vatican Council (1962–5), including the mass in French in 1967, could halt the decline that was taking place so rapidly in the 1970s. Vespers were the first casualty in 1963 of the competing attractions of fairs, football, and free time. The parish now has only two elderly nuns and one priest who will not be replaced when he leaves. All the teachers in the Catholic school, which has been co-educational since 1972, are lay, and one-third of the schoolchildren now attend the state school.

Most of the guilds and committees of long ago have disappeared one after the other. The apostolic groups and devotional groups have seen their numbers decrease, and those who remain active in them are growing older. The young girls have left the Children of Mary behind them in the aftermath of the Second World War because it was considered 'old-fashioned'. The young people then began to enjoy local entertainment events and public dances. To combat this, the clergy introduced football, which had been brought to the area by refugees from the north of France in 1943, and Catholic Action. The latter was at its peak between approximately 1946 and 1960, because it seemed to answer the new demand for leisure while keeping parents happy at the same time. Then the young people started to free themselves completely from the church when they entered secondary school, started going to dances, discovered sexual freedom, and became sceptical about religion. The parish has not had a single 'vocation' since 1968, and the last ordination was in 1972. Other activities have been secularized because they had lost their *raison d'être*: this was the case with the agricultural union in 1946, the Christian workers' union in 1966, and the Crédit Mutuel in 1972. The football club is still a parish organization, using the name of St Clair, while retaining its function as a community club. On the other hand, new activities have been set up to cater for new needs: a group for the elderly called '*vie montante*' ('rising life'), a catechetics group, and, since 1985, twelve liturgical teams which participate in the services and are preparing the way for a parish without a resident priest. Finally, the schools protection movement still remains very active, as can be seen by the fierce opposition to the bill for the nationalization of the Catholic schools proposed by the Left in 1984.

The first Friday of the month is no longer observed since the church has had to do away with everything which made Communion seem like a series of obstacles (an image of life on earth?). As for the feast of the Immaculate Conception on 8 December, it is now observed by only a handful of parishioners, and this is also true for all the other Marian feasts apart from the feast of the Assumption on 15 August. At Christmas, the tradition of the crib has been retained, and attendance at mass is 50 per cent higher, but Santa Claus has replaced the baby Jesus when it comes to presents. On New Year's Day the greeting has changed significantly: instead of wishing Paradise for one's neighbour, it is rather 'hoping that you will have everything that you could wish for'. Only those who practise regularly go to mass on this day. As for the feast of Perpetual Adoration, it was first of all compressed into a single day to make it easier for schoolchildren and farmers to attend; then it was done away with completely. Now Lent seems no different from any other time of the year since the church dropped the obligations for fasting and abstinence, leaving it to everyone's discretion except for Good Friday. The times of the services during the week have had to be changed due to the demands of secular life such as work, school transport, and television. The daily Stations of the Cross were abandoned due to lack of participants, and a similar fate befell the May devotions and the rosary. Finally, confession began to disappear. Easter still remains an important feast, even though the famous Easter duty of long ago is no longer fulfilled by more than half of the parishioners.

All the spring processions had to be dropped, despite the parish priest's wish to keep them, because there were fewer and fewer parishioners to take part and to prepare for them. Even though the decline in processions had begun before the Second Vatican Council, it accelerated from then on, as if the wind of change gave an extra reason for them to be abandoned. The parish priest decided to drop the processions of St Sixte in 1968, 15 August procession in 1970, Rogations in 1971, St Clair in 1973, and Corpus Christi in 1974. The only ones to remain were the procession for Solemn Communion (around the church) and All Saints (to the cemetery). Traffic has certainly interfered with these processions but it has not prevented marches or cycle races.

The feast of Joan of Arc was the first to disappear because the providentialist conception of France's destiny was unable to withstand the test of the Second World War: liberation by foreign countries, the decisive role of technical expertise, and a discrediting of the Pétain government. Paradoxically, it was under Gaullism that the local socio-political life was fully secularized, for the Fifth Republic strengthened Catholic forces and formally integrated Catholic education into the national educational system at the cost of an internal secularization of time-tables, curricula, and teachers. The final step was taken when the Left withdrew its decision to nationalize education. The socialist Left, which appeared in Limerzel in 1946 and today represents 25–30 per cent of the voters, coexists harmoniously with the Centre (one-third) and the Right (one-third). The parish priest no longer instructs people how to vote and strives to be parish priest to everyone. Similarly, the social functions of the parish have, to a large extent, lost their importance since social class divisions no longer operate in the context of religious services, and so on. However, the traces of former class divisions may be seen in the fact that so few workers and small farmers now practise their religion.

The most important practices in the church now are those relating to local life, prayers of intercession, and family occasions. The chapels in the 'frairies' or subdivisions of the parish are well maintained, their services are well attended, and the young seem to show a degree of involvement in them. The parish and the school kermesses are still very popular and always finish up with a big meal just like the celebrations of long ago in the very famous Gallic village of Asterix, especially since a *'coq au vin'* is made in huge cauldrons. Most of the parishioners continue to go on pilgrimage occasionally, if only for the sake of a journey, and the parish priest was able to re-establish the pardon of St Clair in 1986. The major rites of passage such as baptisms, Solemn Communion, marriages, and funerals persist as the most important church events with a participation rate of around 90 per cent. The rate for funerals is 99 per cent. The Solemn Communion, re-defined as a profession of faith by the church, remains an important feast with many gifts and with a big meal in a restaurant; but it also marks the final stage of compulsory catechism and the beginning of non-attendance at mass. The church has not been able to preserve the importance of Confirmation. Death remains the strongest link between the villagers and religion: All Saints is the only occasion on which the church is full. The vigil in the house of a deceased person is the only new practice to have been introduced in the recent past. And on 11 November and 8 May, armistices of the First and Second World Wars, it is quite normal in Limerzel for all the ex-servicemen to join in a mass offered for those who died in both wars, followed by a visit to the war memorial and a reception.

The example of the new catechism introduced between 1965 and 1966 is a clear sign of the changes that the church wishes to promote in religious attitudes. Formerly Catholics had to learn the questions in the catechism off by heart, literally, and the church inculcated a morality based on what was permitted and what was forbidden in fear of the life hereafter. But since then it has been a question of interiorizing a personal progression in one's faith in the hope of developing one's relationship with Our Lord – a God who is a friend, a God of love – and with one's neighbours, all of this occurring with a conception of a hugely de-mythologized world. This change is also the result of a necessity because the former conception was no longer credible ('a lot of drivel', for example), and faith was no longer automatic, even here, because of the rise in scepticism and unbelief. Religiosity has evolved towards a more personal type of faith, less ritualistic and less conformist, with a certain autonomy in relation to the church – religion which is *'à la carte'* and a rejection of the doctrine of guilt. Practising young couples want to make up their own minds about contraception, and the average number of children per household has fallen to less than three.

This is a break from the Catholicism of the Counter-Reformation. The Second Vatican Council speeded up this evolution and lessened the apathy of the young, but at the same time it shocked a certain sector of parishioners by weakening the whole fabric of the church by the way in which it changed things that had formerly been presented as unalterable. Old people in particular were confused by the changes in the liturgy and felt that in the past they had laboured for nothing as the church was now watering down its demands and its threats, some of which had already been rejected by other people. Nowadays, salvation in the hereafter is no longer the objective of the parishioners. And, in so far as it does remain an objective, it is no longer conceived of as the end of a difficult road, with purgatory on one side and hell on the other, except for a few people. In the eyes of some inhabitants, especially the young, morality, order, and values are based on the commonly accepted necessities of society and not of religion.

Two fundamental tendencies: renewal and indifference

It is clear that the basic characteristics of these changes are not exclusive to the parish of Limerzel. We can try to explain them by examining what was, and what has become of, the role of Catholicism in the following domains: cognitive, material, ethical, social, political, and spiritual. Religion used to fulfil important functions in each of them as follows:

1 Cognitive functions, by the global world-view and the time patterns that it sustained, by the education and the knowledge that were controlled by the church.
2 Material functions, by the providentialism or by the different misfortunes in which the wrath of God was felt, or simply by the parish organizations like the savings bank, agricultural union, or youth movement.
3 Ethical functions, because it was believed that there could be no morality without religion. And for some, religion was nothing but morals. It is this consciousness about which Emile Durkheim wrote, 'If ever the common man has a slightly distinct idea, it was only with the help of religious symbols' (Durkheim, 1968: 302).
4 Social functions, mainly for the benefit of the privileged classes, by the legitimation and the consecration of the social order (each in his or her place and all together, services according to status, compensation in the future for the under-privileged). This order was accepted by the majority in Limerzel.
5 Political functions, by the religious opposition between two sides, the good and the bad, the latter being represented by the Republic at the beginning of the century and subsequently by the non-religious, Socialist, or Communist forces; 90 per cent voted for the Catholic Right.

6 And spiritual functions concerning the meaning of life, the supernatural, the communion, relations with the divine and the beyond, the symbolic transcendence of the human condition.

Today, the evidence of religion is dispersed, indifference is increasing especially among 'youth, and religious practice has declined. This evolution can be analysed at first as a relative weakness or rejection of religion, as follows:

1 In the cognitive domain, by the penetration of external influences and modern, technical rationality: a kind of delayed Enlightenment is taking place. The God who ruled nature is becoming more and more alienated.
2 In the material domain, by the discrediting of providentialism (at least in part) and, above all, by an unprecedented improvement in the conditions of life, and this is not due to religion, except to a minor extent, but to the new rationality, to new technologies, and to money.
3 In the ethical domain, because God has more or less lost his significance as the voice of conscience; and it is the same with the wrath of God or with hell. This is also the result of the rejection of certain principles, especially among youth (for example, conjugal morals), or because of the desire for ethical autonomy even among the parishioners.
4 In the socio-political domain, by the secularization of trade unions, political life, social insurance, and the legitimation of status (for example, by educational qualifications).
5 In the spiritual domain, by the relative loss of credibility of the notion of salvation, by doubts about the existence of God and life after death, and so on, for a significant number of villagers.

On the other hand, Catholicism continues to play a role in a new manner for all or for some of the parishioners, as follows:

1 In its cognitive role, at the cost of a certain amount of de-mythologization. Unlike religion, modern rationality does not supply the meaning of life, and this rationality may have been itself induced by the church in, for example, the agricultural youth movement.
2 In material functions, at least by the desire which more or less persists, to be blessed when things are beyond one's control, especially for health, family life, and examinations (even the driving test) – as well as by ethical rationalization.
3 (Above all) in ethical and affective functions, given this desire for self-determination: here Catholicism remains the only explicit moral system, and it plays a role as a means of personal and familial achievement.

4 In its social role, at least by the religious community, the parish fetes and the services. But this Catholicism seems to be seeking its role in the local society now that social life is largely autonomous.

5 In political functions: those who practise continue to support the Right – more precisely, the Centre Right – with only a few of them being Socialist. If socialism is tolerated, communism, by contrast, remains the enemy.

6 In its spiritual function, in the form of a more personal faith for those who still believe. As for the hereafter, they still believe in heaven but rarely in hell (or, at least, they live as if this was their belief). It is mainly the younger generation which has rejected most of the idea of hell unless it is potentially a nuclear war.

This Catholicism may be defined as a *transcendent humanism*, oriented towards achievement in this world while still entertaining the idea of an undramatized afterlife. One wonders if the success of Pope John Paul II might not be partly due to the fact that he goes along with this implicit re-definition of Catholicism, which is not exclusive to Limerzel. In fact, the Pope's popularity does not rest on his attitude towards the salvation of the soul in the hereafter, but rather on his treatment of love, justice, peace, solidarity, and human rights, basing them on the Christian revelation. The main change in the modern world is that people want heaven on earth in some ways because they have greater means to be satisfied and happy. Then, either religion contributes to happiness or achievement, or it is useless. Anyway, as it is impossible to be fully contented, it is always possible to desire something transcendent or absolute that religion can always supply. Furthermore, to quote Durkheim's conclusion of *The Elementary Forms of the Religious Life*, 'a society can neither be created nor recreated without creating an ideal at the same time' (Durkheim, 1968: 603). Thus, religion remains one of the main 'store-houses' of ideals. If we consider the fact that other-worldly ultimate purpose (and world-rejection) was a feature of the major religions, as stressed by Max Weber (1971), this constitutes a basic change which confirms certain investigations by R.N. Bellah (1976): this (and the greater autonomy of the self) is possibly the principal means of adapting religion to modernity which, according to him, appears with the rise of Protestantism.

Regarding the approach to secularization which was worked out in those countries where Protestantism was the main religion, the example of this Catholic region of France can help us to distinguish between two phenomena which are often confused, as was stated on page 49. This is because the adaptation of religion to modernity and the rise of religious indifference are more easily identifiable here. My claim is that those who are indifferent to religion and those who are completely 'without religion' are in favour of the complete autonomy of social life (in the broadest sense) from religion, while still acknowledging the church's right to express itself, and that most of these people consider that the services (rites of passage) are part of life just as the church is part of the countryside. Perhaps this is merely a legacy of rural Christianity? For their part, those who practise are torn between their desire for the relative autonomy of behaviour in the Catholic church and their anxiety to have their aspirations recognized by society, in, for example, the sphere of education.

It is as if most of the villagers have tried to combine the advantages of religion (guidance, assurance, ceremonies, life after death, and so forth) with those of secularization (including autonomy, this-wordly happiness) while avoiding their negative features such as strictness, the fear of hell, and disenchantment. The degree of secularization is therefore the result of various factors with contradictory meanings. I would also like to stress that it is the same factors which lead to this new Catholicism or to this indifference and unbelief: rationalization, autonomization, individualization – in a word, modernization. The approach to secularization has probably underestimated both the limits of modern rationality (relating to values, affectivity, and so on) and the adaptive capacity of religion and even its productive capacity, linked to modernity, as suggested by Max Weber and confirmed by the research done on new religious movements (Wilson, 1981; Beckford, 1986).[2]

In conclusion, the usefulness of the fact that people contribute to the reinterpretation of religion has led me to the notion of a common 'theoretical sense' (different from the scientific one, of course, and complementary to the 'practical sense' as defined by Pierre Bourdieu [1980]) as a means of taking into account the explicit and systematic part of these symbolic changes.[3] Bourdieu's model of sociological explanation is based upon the theory of 'habitus', the dialectic between 'objective structures' (social class conditions, institutions) and 'embodied structures'. Since the habitus is a system of 'schemes of thought, of judgements and of action' which is the interiorization of objective structures and which produces practices tending to reproduce these structures (of which it is the embodied and usually unconscious form), this theory cannot adequately take into account the role of beliefs, concepts, consciousness, ideology, or symbolic changes. I have therefore proposed the concept of 'referential' to designate these symbolic realities. Just as 'practical sense' corresponds with the practical control brought about by habitus, this 'theoretical sense' designates the symbolic control brought about by the referentials or systems of reference.

Notes

1 See Moreux, 1969; Voyé, 1973; Boulard and Rémy, 1968; Ferreira de Almeida, 1986; Breslin and Weafer, 1986; and Sac, 1983.
2 This point has also been developed by Hervieu-Léger, 1986.
3 I have elaborated on this point in Lambert, 1987.

References

Beckford, J.A. (ed.) (1986) *New Religious Movements and Rapid Social Change.* London: Sage; Paris: Unesco.

Bellah, R.N. (1976) *Beyond Belief: Essays on Religion in a Post-Modern World.* New York: Harper & Row.

Berger, S. (1972) *Peasants against Politics. Rural Organization in Brittany 1911–1967.* Cambridge, MA: Harvard University Press.

Boulard, F. and J. Rémy (1968) *Pratique religieuse urbaine et régions culturelles.* Paris: Editions Ouvrières.

Bourdieu, P. (1980) *Le sens pratique.* Paris: Editions du Minuit.

Breslin, A. and J. Weafer (1986) *Religious Belief, Practice and Moral Values in Ireland: a Comparison of Two National Surveys, 1974 and 1984.* Maynooth.

Durkheim, E. (1968) *Les formes élémentaires de la vie religieuse.* Paris: PUF.

Ferreira de Almeida (1986) *Classes sociais nos campos.* Lisbon: Instituto de Ciências Sociais.

Hervieu-Léger, D. (1986) *Vers un nouveau christianisme?* Paris: Editions du Cerf.

Isambert, F.A. and J.P. Terrenoire (1980) *Atlas de la pratique religieuse des catholiques en France.* Paris: Presses de la FNSP et Editions du CNRS.

Lambert, Y. (1985) *Dieu change en Bretagne. La religion à Limerzel de 1900 à nos jours.* Paris: Editions du Cerf.

Lambert, Y. (1986) 'Un paradigme inspiré de Weber. Pour contribuer à renouveler le débat sur la sécularisation', *Archives de Sciences sociales des Religions*, 61(1) 153–65.

Lambert, Y. (1987) 'L'art d'accommoder et de transformer la religion: le sens théorique populaire', *Recherches Sociologiques*, 2.

Le Bras, G. (1976) *L'Eglise et le village.* Paris: Flammarion.

Moreux, C. (1969) *Fin d'une religion?* Montréal: Presses de l'Université de Montréal.

Sac, W.Z. (ed.) (1983) 'Religion and Social Life', *Religious Sociological Studies*, 6.

Siegfried, A. (1913) *Tableau politique de la France de l'Ouest sous la IIIè République.* Paris: A. Colin.

Voyé, L. (1973) *Sociologie du geste religieux.* Brussels: La Vie Ouvrière.

Weber, M. (1971) *Economie et Société.* Paris: Plon.

Wilson, B.R. (ed.) (1981) *The Social Impact of New Religious Movements.* New York: The Rose of Sharon Press.

4

Religion in New Zealand: Change and Comparison

Michael Hill and *Wiebe Zwaga*

The study of change in New Zealand religion reveals a number of processes which have been identified in other western societies. In particular, the process of secularization in New Zealand contains a number of features which have been traced in societies such as Britain, Canada, and Australia. In this chapter we shall set these general trends against the particular historical and cultural background of New Zealand; we shall show how the historical setting of New Zealand religion had specific implications for the secularization process; we shall examine the impact of Maori religious movements in the nineteenth and early twentieth centuries; and we shall then look at the state of collective religiosity in contemporary New Zealand. The context of this comparative analysis is set by David Martin's outline of a general theory of secularization (Martin, 1978) in which New Zealand is grouped together with Canada and Australia as having a somewhat more pluralistic religious situation than that of Britain: we find in a comparison of New Zealand with its Commonwealth partners that religion has maintained a somewhat lower social profile, and that the level of current religious activity is also somewhat lower.

Indeed, there are statements by a number of contemporary observers which confirm the generally low profile of New Zealand religion. Compare the following three appraisals:

> In social terms a religion can be seen to have two particularly important functions – to express in a ritual and symbolic way the identity of the community it serves and to validate and perpetuate a system of morality. In neither of these activities is the Christian Church in New Zealand very effective. (Jackson and Harre, 1969: 131–2)

> It would . . . be misleading to imply that the New Zealanders are a very religious people – some of them go to church when they are christened, many when they marry and more when they die. The prevailing religion is a simple materialism. The pursuit of health and possessions fills more minds than thoughts of salvation. (Sinclair, 1969: 288)

> Tangible evidences of religion in New Zealand are unspectacular enough

to be taken for granted most of the time. We have no holy cities and few sacred shrines . . . religious buildings signify nothing much to us, empty and closed as they generally appear to be. (Colless and Donovan, 1985: 9–10)

These are all contemporary assessments and they raise an important question. Are they evidence of substantial decline in religiosity within the last 100 years in New Zealand, or has this society always been characterized by low levels of religious adherence and practice? An historical benchmark is needed in making such assessments; otherwise we are in danger of assuming some mythical 'golden age' of religion (Hill, 1973: 232–4) which is often attributed to the Victorian era. In the next section we look at the historical evidence.

The historical dimension

There is considerable disagreement among observers of New Zealand religion in the nineteenth and early twentieth centuries. A number of writers have quoted with approval the statement of André Siegfried, who visited New Zealand in 1904 and found that 'no tradition remained so strong as the religious one' (McLeod, 1968: 160; Mol, 1972: 365). There is certainly evidence that in the nineteenth century the church occupied a central social role in small-town New Zealand: 'Many of the communal leisure events in the district focused on the school and the church, and these buildings served as multi-functional centres for social intermixing' (Pearson, 1980: 23). In contrast, we find evidence of low levels of religious activity from early in the nineteenth century. Sinclair suggests that although Protestant denominations in New Zealand were very active and vocal, 'whether, as is often supposed, the general population was in any sense more religious is doubtful. In Auckland in the late forties only a quarter or less of the population attended church – rather less than in England. In Canterbury a settler remarked in 1863 that a labourer was almost never seen in church: churchgoers were "mostly the upper and middle classes and women and children of the lower"' (Sinclair, 1969: 105). Two comments can be added to this statement. Firstly, an attendance rate of 25 per cent or less of the population was very much lower than that of England in the same period, where an attendance level of between 47 per cent and 51 per cent of the population over ten years of age was estimated (Pickering, 1967: 394). Secondly, the social groups which in England had the most firmly entrenched religious 'habits' – the middle and upper classes – were notably under-represented among migrants to New Zealand. Migration itself, followed by high geographical mobility within New Zealand, weakened the cohesiveness of church congregations and reduced the social pressures in favour of attendance.

A comparison of 'actual' church attenders with 'nominal' adherents to the different denominations is made possible by the fact that from the middle of the nineteenth century the New Zealand Census included a question on religious adherence, and between 1874 and 1926 attempted to estimate religious attendance on an average Sunday. The figures for 1889–91 show high levels of nominalism in some of the major denominations.

Table 4.1   *'Usual attenders'** as a percentage of Census adherents, selected denominations, New Zealand, 1889–91*

Church of England	15
Presbyterian	29
Methodist	56
Roman Catholic	35
Congregational	55
Baptist	34

*This was not strictly defined by Census enumerators and should only be regarded as showing trends.

Source: Jackson, 1983b

In one respect the religious situation in New Zealand has been remarkably stable, and that is the large percentage of New Zealanders which has always been prepared to adopt a nominal religious identity while being otherwise inactive. Religious practice in the form of church attendance has been characteristic of a markedly smaller percentage of the population. Furthermore, there is evidence of a decline in church-going in later Victorian New Zealand similar to that noted by McLeod (1974) in England from the 1880s (Jackson, 1983b). Again using the loose definition of 'usual attenders' as a percentage of the New Zealand population 15 years and over, the figures decline from a high point of 48.3 per cent in 1886, to 36.2 per cent in 1906, and to 27.0 per cent in 1926. The decline was primarily a Protestant one, with the Anglican and Presbyterian churches accounting for the bulk of the decline. Equivalent Catholic figures for 1886, 1906, and 1926 were 54.7, 44.7, and 46.9 per cent respectively. Jackson also contends that in New Zealand, as in Britain, the growth in leisure activities was a consequence rather than a cause of church decline (Jackson, 1983a: 103).

The connection between pluralism and the secularization process has been controversial in the wider sociology of religion, and is equally so in the context of New Zealand. On the one hand it has been argued that religious pluralism is a central component of secularization because, when a shared moral universe becomes fragmented among distinct social constituencies, its plausibility is undermined (MacIntyre, 1967: 30). Against this, Martin has argued that monopoly, not pluralism, is associated with high levels of secularization in Protestant societies (Martin, 1978: 27–36).

There are two competing accounts of the impact of pluralism in New Zealand. The first bases its analysis on the observation that by the middle of the nineteenth century, when migration to New Zealand was rapidly increasing, the religious situation in Britain was already pluralistic, with the Church of England maintaining a decreasing monopoly. However, the transposition of traditional religious institutions into a New Zealand environment had the effect of heightening this pluralism because, thinks Geering:

> The migration to New Zealand by settlers from all parts of the British Isles had the effect of throwing together Christian denominations which had, to some extent, been geographically separated in the homeland. Thus New Zealand became somewhat more pluralistic than had been the case in Britain. (Geering, 1985: 217)

However, an entirely different interpretation is given by Jackson, who thinks that:

> the greater homogeneity of the people in New Zealand weakened religious belonging. At home social divisions went deep and political and religious allegiances reinforced one another. A Tory found it natural to belong to the established church, a chapel-goer to vote for Gladstone, so that attendance at worship was higher than if it had been a more purely religious act. The boundary between the two socio-religious communities became ever less sharply drawn in England from mid-century, but in New Zealand they had had only a vestigial existence from the beginning. (Jackson, 1983b: 55)

These competing accounts can in part be reconciled by noting that from the outset religious denominations competed on a more equal basis than they had done in Britain – so that, for example, groups like the Methodists were relatively more central in New Zealand religious life – but that there was not the same cleavage along religious/social/political lines as there had been in the homeland. While the Church of England made some early attempts to replicate the established status it had enjoyed in England, these were decisively rejected by proponents of freedom of religion (Wood, 1975).

It was partly because of the competing claims of different Christian denominations in the nineteenth century that the sphere of official, and especially governmental, activity rapidly came to be defined in neutral, secular terms: the 1877 Education Act is a prominent illustration of the process (Breward, 1967). This assumption of secular neutrality also helps to explain why it is difficult to find evidence of 'civil religion' in a New Zealand context. The two annual national observances of Anzac Day and Waitangi Day have coexisted uneasily with Christian input. 'The strands of New Zealand nationalism, of pride in a military achievement, interwoven with those of mourning, prevented Anzac Day from being associated totally with the Christian God of Peace' (Sharpe, 1981: 109). Waitangi Day, commemorating the signing in 1840 of a treaty between the Maori chiefs and the British Crown, has become a potent focus of conflict over the Maori rights issue, with Christian representatives often at the forefront of protest.

We may summarize the historical situation as follows. Despite some early attempts to introduce religious uniformity on a regional basis in New Zealand – Free Church of Scotland in Otago, Church of England in Canterbury, traces of which can still be found in the regional distribution of denominational adherence – New Zealand society was pluralistic and had a firmly secular constitution at a very early stage. Together with evidence of high nominalism and comparatively low rates of attendance, the notion of a 'golden age' of religiosity seems singularly inappropriate to New Zealand. This historical background should be borne in mind when examining the contemporary evidence of secularization.

Maori religious movements

No account of change within New Zealand religion would be complete without an account of the succession of prophetic and millennial movements among the indigenous Maori population which began in the first years of contact with the Europeans and reached a highly politicized stage in the 1920s. Since then there have been no major new religious movements, but the impact of the earlier wave can still be traced both in the formal political context and in a recent adoption of Rastafarianism by some younger Maoris. In its New Zealand variant, the latter has clear links with earlier movements of religious protest. Indeed, these movements provide impressive evidence of the impact of Christianity on the Maori and of its capacity for syncretism with traditional beliefs, and its has been suggested that they arose out of 'the conviction that Christianity was too good to be left to the Pakeha [European]'

(Oliver, 1966: 13). While being on the one hand unique to their historical and cultural location, these movements also have characteristics which are shared by a vast number of movements in Third World and colonial situations (Lanternari, 1965).

A theme which emerged at the point of first contact with European Christianity was the idea of the Maori as a 'lost tribe of Israel'. In 1833 the prophet Te Atua Wera identified the Maoris with the *Hurai*, the Jews, claiming that they were a chosen people who were to be given the particular protection and love of *Ihowa* (Jehovah) (De Bres, 1985: 31). This has remained a persistent theme in Maori religious movements and finds its contemporary equivalent in the significant percentage of Maoris attracted to Mormonism (around 50 per cent in 1981) as well as in the 'Babylon' motif of Rastafarians: one should note that the latter have been especially active on the east coast of the North Island, a region with a large Maori population which has been a fertile source of earlier millennial movements.

A highly dynamic period of Maori religious and political activity occurred in the 1860s when the Land Wars hardened both social cleavage and ideology. The tendency of radical movements to oscillate between pacifist and militarist poles of social action (Martin, 1965: 221) was evident in the movement begun by the Maori prophet Te Ua Hau Haumene. He occupied the traditional priestly role of *Tohunga* and had also studied under Wesleyan missionaries; out of these two sources he syncretized a new movement which he named *Pai Marire*. Although this translates as 'good and peaceful/quiet', the movement soon incorporated military drill and developed an increasingly aggressive stance towards the colonists. In a rich amalgam the movement's ritual combined traditional Maori, Christian, and British military elements (Wilson, 1973: 249). The Hau Hau movement was both religious and political; it supported the Maori King movement and it also identified with the lost tribe of Israel. Between 1864 and 1866 when the movement was finally suppressed its members engaged in a number of military exploits.

After defeat, the Hau Hau members were deported to the Chatham Islands, and deported with them (though he had not been one of the rebel fighters) was the man who led the next major Maori religious movement, Te Kooti Rikirangi. His contact with Christianity came through his education in a mission station, and while he was on the Chathams he laid the basis for a new Maori religion, Ringatu. Once again the syncretic element was evident, since Ringatu represented a bridge 'between traditional Maori and Christian ideas and belief' (Nichol and Veitch, 1980: 61). Furthermore, the movement represented a strong oscillation away from the militarism of Hau Hau towards a religion which was pacifist, introverted, and represented a form of solace in defeat. The movement reinterpreted remnants of Hau Hauism – or as Wilson (1973: 399) puts it, 'it was a working out or tidying up' – so that, for example, the upraised hand which Hau Hau saw as a way of warding off bullets was reinterpreted as a gesture of homage to God. The charismatic basis of Te Kooti's leadership was established when in 1868 he made a dramatic escape from the Chathams with many of his followers. A more aggressive phase of his movement saw raids against both settlers and Maoris loyal to the government, but eventually it stabilized and became a distinct and withdrawn ethnic remnant.

Charisma is strikingly evident in the movement led by Rua Kénana Hepetika, which emerged in the early years of this century. Rua had already established himself as a faith healer and claimed charismatic succession when he stated that 'he was the man prophesied by Te Kooti to be the new leader of the Maori people' (Webster, 1979: 158). Having successfully established his charismatic pedigree and leadership, Rua built his own movement on a reinterpretation of the beliefs and the structure of Ringatu. His followers called themselves *Iharaira*, or Israelites, and keenly anticipated the expulsion of the Europeans and the return of New Zealand to the Maori people; this was to be accomplished through the intervention of King Edward VII. The movement was characterized mainly by non-violence and by the formation of a theocratic community under Rua's leadership – once again combining traditional Maori and biblical beliefs, for the community was both in structure and beliefs conceived as a new Jerusalem.

The capacity of Third World and nativistic movements to politicize in their later stages is an important part of Worsley's analysis of Cargo cults (Worsley, 1968: 254–6). The most recent Maori movement is also the most politically oriented: Ratana until very recently had a monopoly on the four Maori seats in Parliament, and its representatives formed an alliance with the New Zealand Labour party. The Ratana church was founded by Tahupotiki Wiremu Ratana, who was the nephew of a Maori prophetess and was himself a faith healer. He began his ministry in 1918 and his church was formally established in 1925. In contrast to Ringatu's very large component of traditional Maori beliefs, Ratana represents a movement with a considerably more substantial Judaeo-Christian element. One of the movement's major concerns – which has drawn it into the mainstream of New Zealand politics – has been the ratification of the Treaty of Waitangi. While the Ratana movement could claim the adherence of some 20 per cent of the total Maori population in the 1936 Census, that figure had dropped in 1981 to 11 per cent, and it has lost its monopoly on the Maori Parliamentary seats. Also in 1981, out of the 279,252 individuals recorded as Maori in the Census (just under 9 per cent of the total population) there were 5,769 Ringatu adherents, 21 adherents of the church of Te Kooti Rikirangi, and 108 Hau Hau: though the echoes of the turbulent days of New Zealand's early history are weak, they linger in these statistics of religious adherence.

Recent patterns of religious change

An analysis of religious change in New Zealand can be based on a variety of data. The richest source of such data is the five yearly Census of population, which since the middle of the nineteenth century has included a question on religious adherence. The Census also permits broad comparisons with religion in Australia and Canada, since these countries also include a question on religion in their own censuses, which are taken in the same year as that of New Zealand. While a number of denominations in New Zealand cite Census data as a general indicator of membership trends in their own organizations, they also maintain records of communicant membership and attendance which can usefully be compared with Census statistics. A further source of national data comes from a postal survey of some 2,000 Methodist and Presbyterian communicant members in 1982 (Hill and Bowman, 1983). Opinion poll and other general surveys of social participation provide broad estimates of church attendance (Social Indicators Survey, 1984; AGB: McNair, 1982; Heylen Research Centre, 1986). Additional material can be found in local surveys, which tend to be more detailed and therefore 'flesh out' the national data (Blaikie, 1969, 1972; Mol, 1982; Reynolds, 1972).

Some comment is needed on the use of the Census data on religion, since their very detail has lured some commentators into uncritical acceptance of the trends that they show. Firstly, the Census question asks respondents to state their 'Religion', and this is the only Census question which allows the reply 'Object to state'. The percentage of the population taking this latter option has doubled from 7 per cent to 15 per cent between 1951 and 1981, though it is important not to regard the 'Object' category as synonymous with 'No religion'. It will contain, for example, highly committed religious participants who for reasons of conscience refuse to state their allegiance on official documents, as well as children whose parents regard religious affiliation as a matter of choice and therefore decline to adopt a religious label for their children. Secondly, the extent of nominalism will be more evident in the larger religious professions such as Anglican, Presbyterian, and Roman Catholic; by contrast, there is a much closer correspondence between the Census adherence of a group such as the Seventh-Day Adventists and the statistics of membership kept by that organization (Jackson, 1985: 135). So long as it is remembered that Census data relate to adherence rather than to practice, however, an analysis of them reveals some significant trends.

Table 4.2   *Percentage adherence to selected religious professions, 1951–81*

	1951	1961	1971	1981
Total NZ population	1,939,472	2,414,984	2,862,631	3,175,737
% adherence:				
Anglican	37.5	34.6	31.3	25.6
Presbyterian	23.1	22.3	20.4	16.5
Object to state	7.1	8.4	8.6	14.9
Roman Catholic	13.6	15.1	15.7	14.4
No religion	0.6	0.7	2.0	5.3
Methodist	8.0	7.2	6.4	4.7
Not specified	0.5	0.6	3.6	3.4
Christian*	0.2	0.5	1.2	3.2
Baptist	1.6	1.7	1.7	1.6
Latter Day Saints	0.5	0.8	1.0	1.2
Ratana	0.9	1.0	1.1	1.1
Brethren	1.1	1.1	0.9	0.8
Agnostic	0.1	0.1	0.3	0.8
Atheist	0.1	0.1	0.3	0.7
Salvation Army	0.7	0.6	0.7	0.6
Protestant*	0.7	1.9	1.3	0.5
Jehovah's Witness	0.1	0.2	0.4	0.4
Assemblies of God	–	–	0.1	0.4
Seventh Day Adventist	0.3	0.3	0.4	0.4
Pentecostal*	–	–	0.1	0.2
Church of Christ	0.6	0.3	0.2	0.2
Ringatu	0.2	0.2	0.2	0.2
Hindu	–	0.1	0.1	0.2
Lutheran	0.2	0.2	0.2	0.2
Indigenous Pentecostal	–	–	–	0.2
Apostolic	–	0.1	0.1	0.1
Congregational	0.4	0.4	0.3	0.1
All other religions	1.9	1.5	1.4	2.1
	100.0	100.0	100.0	100.0

*No other designation.

Source: New Zealand Census of Population and Dwellings: 'Religious Professions', 1981

In New Zealand, as in other western societies, there is no evident reluctance to adopt a religious label. Around 75 per cent of the New Zealand population record a religious profession on their Census return; and while this is markedly lower than Canada's 93 per cent (Bibby, 1985: 288) and almost identical with Australia's 76 per cent (Wilson, 1983: 26), it nevertheless suggests a relatively high level of 'religious encasement' (Bibby, 1985). At the same time, there has been a marked erosion in the proportion of the total population adhering to the four mainline 'denominations'. For the past century the four main religious groups have been, in order, Anglican, Presbyterian, Roman Catholic, and Methodist. In 1921 these four categories incorporated 92.5 per cent of the population; by 1951 this had fallen to 82.2 per cent, to 79.2 per cent in 1961, 73.8 per cent in 1971, and by 1981 had reached 61.2 per cent. Furthermore, in 1981 the Catholic proportion (14 per cent) had been overtaken by the 'Object to state' category (15 per cent), while the Methodists, with 4.7 per cent of the total population, had been overtaken by those reporting 'No religion' (5.3 per cent). Additional evidence of the attenuation of mainline commitment can be seen in the growth in significance of the 'Christian' label, which increased twenty-fold between 1951 and 1981, and now accounts for 3.2 per cent of the total population. A summary of overall trends is given in Table 4.2.

A comparison of Census statistics with those collected by the larger Christian denominations reveals the extent of nominalism in each group as well as the differential decline in 'core' membership from the early 1970s to the early 1980s. Though the membership criteria of the denominations differ, there is a consistency in the comparisons they show which suggests that the bedrock of 'core' membership is being approached. Significantly, the denomination which has lost most in Census adherence between 1971 and 1981 –

Table 4.3 *'Core' Membership of mainline denominations, 1971 and 1981*

	1971 %	1981 %
Anglican	18	19
Presbyterian	22	18
Roman Catholic	42	35
Methodist	24	19

Explanation: Christmas communicants (Anglican) or communicant members (Presbyterian and Methodist) as percentage of Census adherence aged 15+; Roman Catholic mass count (all dioceses 1971, Wellington and Palmerston North 1984) as percentage of total Census Catholic population in the equivalent areas.

Anglicans, with a decline from 31 to 26 per cent of the total population – marginally improved its 'core' position, while Roman Catholics, whose Census level dropped by only 1.3 per cent of the total population, showed greatest 'core' attrition. Table 4.3 summarizes these data.

A comparison of Census data with those of our survey of Methodist and Presbyterian communicant members pinpoints the concentration of nominalism among young adult males. For these two churches at least, the Census understates the degree of female concentration and also understates the average age of adult members (Hill and Bowman, 1985: 105). Table 4.4 summarizes this evidence.

Table 4.4   *Census/sample comparisons of Presbyterians and Methodists*

		Presbyterians	Methodists
Census population age 15+	1981	397,773	112,434
Communicant membership	1982	68,766	21,784
Hill–Bowman sample	1982	919	908
Females–Census %	1981	54	55
Females–sample %	1982	70	67
Census mean age, age 15+	1981	45	45
Sample mean age,	1981	55	55
Standard error of sample %		1	1

Sources: New Zealand Census of Population and Dwellings: 'Religious Professions', 1981; Hill and Bowman, 1983

A comparison over time shows the extent to which this ageing process has brought about major changes in the demographic composition of the mainline Protestant denominations. For example, in the period before the Second World War the membership of the Church of England was broadly similar in its age composition to that of the total New Zealand population. Over recent years that situation has changed markedly, and now the Anglican church – and one might add the Presbyterian and Methodist churches too – is characterized by an under-representation of adherence in the younger age-groups, by an even more marked under-representation of twenty to forty-year-olds, and by a significant over-representation of those in the oldest age-groups. The change is graphically illustrated in Figure 4.1, where we have constructed age-profiles by indexing the proportion of each age-group within the religious category to the corresponding age-group proportion in the total

Figure 4.1 *Anglican age-profiles, 1921 and 1981*

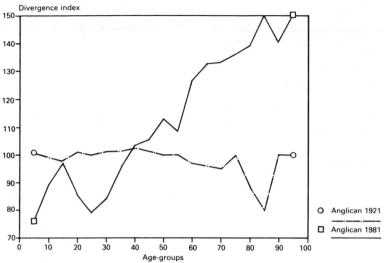

Source: New Zealand Census of Population and Dwellings, 1981: 'Religious professions'; Census of the Dominion of New Zealand, 1921, Part VII, 'Religions'

population, so that the latter is expressed as a constant of 100. This form of standardization permits comparison over time as well as cross-nationally.

In Figure 4.1 it can be seen that the Anglican age-profile has tipped from one which was broadly similar to that of the population as a whole to one which under-represents the youngest, and over-represents the oldest, groups of adherents. Nor is this a feature only of New Zealand Anglican adherents, for by comparing Australian and Canadian age-profiles in a similar way (that is, by indexing each age-group against the proportion of that age-group in the total population and superimposing the graphs for each country) we find a remarkably similar cross-national age-profile for Anglicans in all three countries (Figure 4.2).

Cross-national comparisons of Presbyterian and Methodist age-profiles are invalidated by ecumenical mergers in Canada and Australia, but a comparison of Roman Catholic age-profiles shows the same remarkable similarity of age-patterns in the three countries (see Figure 4.3). The Roman Catholic church has a more 'youthful' age-profile, but it shares with the mainline Protestant groups the same under-representation of the young adult age-groups.

Figure 4.2   *Anglican age-profiles, 1981, Canada, Australia, and New Zealand*

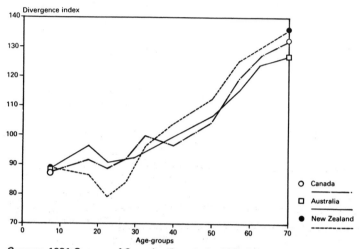

Source: 1981 Census of Canada, 'Population', 'Religion'; Census of Population and Housing, 1981, Australia, 'Religion'; New Zealand Census of Population and Dwellings, 1981, 'Religious Professions'

Figure 4.3   *Roman Catholic age-profiles, 1981, Canada, Australia, and New Zealand*

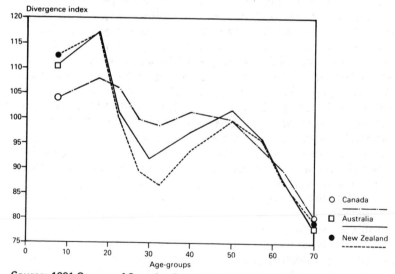

Source: 1981 Census of Canada, 'Population', 'Religion'; Census of Population and Housing, 1981, Australia, 'Religion'; New Zealand Census of Population and Dwellings, 1981, 'Religious Professions'

Figure 4.4 *Minor religious groups, New Zealand, 1951–81 (percentage of total population)*

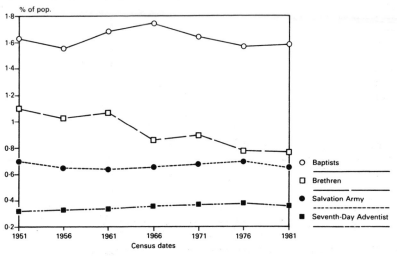

Source: New Zealand Census of Population and Dwellings, 1951–81, 'Religious Professions'

Turning to the smaller religious groups, especially those of a sectarian kind, we find in New Zealand evidence of selective sectarian growth. The groups which have shown most rapid growth are the Mormons, the Jehovah's Witnesses, and the Pentecostals. As a percentage of the total population, other conservative evangelical groups are either relatively static in membership or show evidence of decline. These changes are summarized in Figure 4.4, which shows religious groups that have been stable or have declined in the period 1951–81, and Figure 4.5, which identifies minor religious groups in a growth period.

Mormon growth has until relatively recently been associated with membership recruitment from the Maori population. Before the Second World War the Mormons were firmly established among the Maoris but it was not until the early 1950s (when the Mormon Temple in Hamilton was built) that the group embarked on a period of especially rapid growth: this coincided with a period of rapid urbanization and high fertility among the Maori population. More recent growth has been achieved by recruitment from the non-Maori population. Thus, whereas in 1926 85 per cent of Mormons were Maori, the figure in 1981 was 51 per cent. The Jehovah's Witnesses, who have also grown rapidly since the early 1950s, have a much lower proportion of Maoris among their adherents (15 per

Figure 4.5   *Minor religious groups, New Zealand, 1951–81 (percentage of total population)*

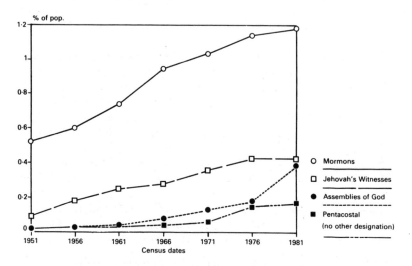

Source: New Zealand Census of Population and Dwellings, 1951–81, 'Religious Professions'

Figure 4.6   *Age-profiles, Mormons and Jehovah's Witnesses, New Zealand, 1981*

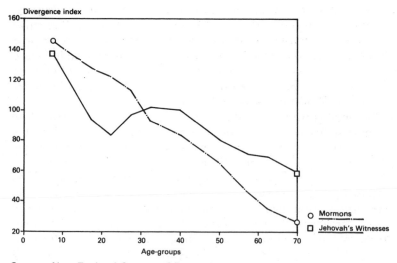

Source: New Zealand Census of Population and Dwellings, 1981, 'Religious Professions'

cent in 1981), but they share with Mormons the feature of an extremely 'youthful' age-profile. Compared with the mainline groups, Mormons and Jehovah's Witnesses have a substantial over-representation of adherents in the younger age-groups. Their age-profiles are compared in Figure 4.6.

The marked increase in Pentecostal adherence in the past decade is accounted for principally by those who label themselves simply 'Pentecostal' and those who adopt the label 'Assemblies of God'. Pentecostal adherents are characterized by a youthful age-profile and, in particular, by a peak in adherence within the twenty to forty age-group – in other words, the age at which mainline denominations appear to experience significant loss.

It was noted in the section detailing the historical background of New Zealand religion that the religious situation has always been strongly influenced by migration patterns. The recent migration of population from South-east Asia and India (Zodgekar, 1980) is evidenced by the growing proportion of Buddhists and Hindus. Conversely, the decline in Jewish and Eastern Orthodox adherents as a percentage of the total population results from a wave of post-war migration which is now receding. The arrival in New Zealand of Pacific Island migrants, especially Samoans, in the past decade has resulted in a growing number of Christian churches with a specific ethnic constituency. This is illustrated in Table 4.5.

The pluralism to which we have several times drawn attention can also be traced in the increase in sectarian and cultic adherence, which represents a growing percentage of the total population giving a religious response to the Census question. Until the Census of 1966 the published volumes reported every religious profession, even those which had only 1 adherent (this necessitated a category

Table 4.5 *Membership of selected migrant religious groups.*
1981 Census

	Number of adherents
Samoan Congregational	2,310
Samoan Christian church	258
Cook Islands Christian church	219
Samoan Methodist	111
Free church of Tonga	90
United church of Tonga	75
Cook Island Congregational	57
Cook Island church	33

Source: New Zealand Census of Population and Dwellings: 'Religious Professions', 1981

of 'facetious' – though how the decision was made to assign a response to this category, out of the enormous variety of responses accepted as legitimate, is difficult to comprehend). To give some indication of the range, in 1921 there were nearly 200 separately listed religious professions and of these one-third had only one adherent. By 1966 the total number of professions had increased to 400, and even in 1971, when a minimum requirement of five adherents was needed for a separate listing, the total number of professions was still 250. In 1981 the minimum requirement was fifty adherents and there were 126 listed professions. When all the larger religious professions have been listed in the Census, there is a residual category of 'All other religions', and this in 1981 contained a total of 15,500 respondents. Included in this total would be the adherents of more visible religious movements such as, for instance, the Unification church, which in 1981 had insufficient numbers of Census respondents to merit separate listing. The 'All other religions' group is more numerous in the larger urban centres, especially Auckland, and it is significant that the age-profile of this group closely resembles the age-profile of the Pentecostals and those who report 'No religion', with an over-representation of young adults and a marked under-representation of older age-groups.

Figure 4.7   *Weekly church attendance and percentage of Census Catholics, Canada, Australia, New Zealand, early 1980s*

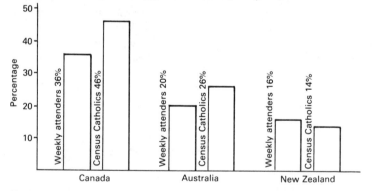

Explanation: 'weekly attenders' = percentage of population 15+ reporting church attendance once a week or more; 'Census Catholics' = percentage of total population so recorded 1981

Sources: Australia: Bouma and Dixon, 1986 (for 1983 poll), and Harris et al., 1982 (for 1980 poll), averaged;
Canada: Bibby, 1985 (for 1983 poll);
New Zealand: Social Indicators Survey, 1984 (for 1980–81 poll);
Heylen Research Centre, 1986 (for 1985 poll)

Having looked at the pattern of pluralism in New Zealand, we are now in a position to examine more closely the link between participation and pluralism which is proposed by David Martin. In his discussion of Protestant pluralism, Martin makes the following statement: 'If you take participation and pluralism they run in a direct positively correlated line from the USA to Canada and Australia, to England, to Scandinavia. Indeed figures are respectively about 40+ per cent, 25+ per cent, 10+ per cent and 5 per cent (or less) per Sunday' (Martin, 1978: 35). Canada, Australia, and New Zealand can indeed be located between the participation levels of the USA and England; moreover, they can be located in a precise and almost linear progression using the criterion of weekly church attendance. Figure 4.7 records the percentage weekly church attendance for adults in the three countries at various dates in the early 1980s, and compares these figures with the percentage of the total population which is Roman Catholic.

Although there is not a simple linear relationship between total weekly attendance and Catholic percentages in the overall population (such that we could, perhaps, speak of 'Martin's constant'!) it appears that Catholics make a crucial contribution to the level of religious participation. Australia's 'deviation' from Martin's constant might well be explained by the intervening variable of ethnicity. The post-war Catholic population of Australia has contained a substantial proportion of Italians (just under 8 per cent in 1976 (Harris, 1982: 278)), and, as Lewins (1976: 126–7) has shown, there is a tendency for this group of migrants to lack the kind of 'Italian' identity which might crystallize around religious participation. A similarly low level of religious participation among Italian Catholics has been found by Greeley in the United States (Greeley, 1979: 119).

A number of commentators have drawn attention to the importance of contextual and demographic factors in understanding church growth and decline (Roozen and Carroll, 1979; Hadaway, 1981). These factors have, moreover, been seen as *more* important than those of theology and belief in explaining certain types of religious change. Bibby, for example, is sharply critical of explanations of growth in conservative churches in terms of their theological appeal, pointing out that much of the supposed growth can be attributed to the recycling of members, as well as to recruitment from an affiliate pool of members' children which is proportionately larger than that of the mainline churches (Bibby, 1985; Bibby and Brinkerhoff, 1974). An analysis of the comparative fertility of New Zealand religious denominations provides substantial support for trends which have been noted in other western societies. Basically these can be summarized as a decline in fertility among mainline Protestant denominations, a 'regression to the mean' by Catholics from an earlier situation of significantly higher fertility, and a high level of fertility among sectarian and Pentecostal adherents. In Table 4.6, the child/woman ratios have been indexed to the ratio for the total population at each Census date.

Table 4.6   *Child/woman ratios (children 0–4 per thousand women 15–44), selected religious groups, 1961, 1971, 1981, as index of total population (= 100)*

	1961	1971	1981
Total population	100.0	100.0	100.0
Anglican	92.2	89.8	78.8
Presbyterian	94.1	88.7	76.8
Roman Catholic	121.4	117.6	100.3
Methodist	92.0	95.0	74.3
Christian*	94.4	77.8	144.1
Baptist	82.1	89.3	82.7
Latter Day Saints	145.8	130.3	127.4
Ratana	160.4	164.8	140.2
Brethren	85.6	93.3	105.0
Agnostic	24.4	15.7	40.2
Atheist	56.0	30.3	33.8
Salvation Army	93.6	110.0	97.2
Jehovah's Witness	100.0	99.6	122.3
Assemblies of God	97.8	101.5	129.1
Seventh-Day Adventist	90.0	109.4	114.0
No religious adherence	169.2	169.0	224.9

*No other designation

In predicting the future growth or decline of different religious groups in New Zealand, it is likely that their current age-profiles and levels of fertility will have a considerably more important impact than such factors as theological orientation or proselytizing.

Unlike other countries' Censuses, which tend to combine all expressions of religious disaffiliation ('Atheist'/'Agnostic'/ 'Humanist'/'No religion') into a single, almost residual category, that of New Zealand reports fully the different nuances of secularity. Perhaps this is evidence of the commitment to freedom of religious choice which has historically characterized New Zealand in contrast, say, to a country like Canada, where until recently Census enumerators would not take 'No' for an answer (Bibby, 1985: 295). In the light of this abundance of material it is surprising that so little attention has been paid to what have been called 'the religious "nones"' (Vernon, 1968).

As can be seen from Table 4.2, when the categories 'Atheist', 'Agnostic', and 'No Religion' are combined, they show a seven-fold growth from 1 per cent of the total population in 1951 to 6.8 per cent in 1981: as we have noted on p. 73, this group now out-numbers the traditionally fourth-placed denomination, Methodist. A brief composite profile based on the 1981 Census reveals that the religious 'nones' are characterized by some specific socio-demographic features. For instance, they are overwhelmingly clustered in the twenty to forty age-groups. Although the sex distribution in all three categories is weighted towards males (60 per cent of Agnostics, 66 per cent of Atheists, and 57 per cent of 'No religion' respondents), the percentage growth of female 'nones' is higher than that of males. They show an urban concentration, and have a tendency to cluster in inner-city areas, most specifically around universities. The latter may explain their substantially higher than average level of education, and while Agnostics and Atheists have very low child/woman ratios (see Table 4.6), those reporting 'No Religion' have a substantially higher than average ratio, suggesting that New Zealand parents are somewhat inclined to avoid religious ascription for their children. The finding that religious 'nones' have a higher concentration in the public sector of employment has some parallels with research on Australian secularists who, according to Hogan, 'are less satisfied with economic conditions than other Australians and more in favour of government intervention in the economy' (Hogan, 1979: 399–400).

Religious change: a concluding interpretation

New Zealand is fortunate in having an analysis of religious change which is possibly unique and which permits a detailed interpretation of patterns of religious change (Nolan et al., 1986). The analysis is based on a sample of 12,000 1981 Census returns which was matched with Census questionnaires completed by the same individuals in 1976, the purpose being to check the degree of consistency between the two sets of data. The matching ratio (number of respondents traced as a proportion of total sample) was 85 per cent, which is a highly favourable result, given the five-year lapse in time. The comparison of religious responses in the two Censuses provides a fascinating picture of short-term changes in self-reported religious affiliation.

The study found that fully 26 per cent of the sample changed their religious affiliation between 1976 and 1981. For those who retained the same religious designation, Table 4.7 shows the degree of 'stability' or 'encasement', for different groups, in ranked order.

Table 4.7   *Percentage of 1976 Census sample still retaining the same religious label in 1981*

	%
Roman Catholic	86
Ratana	84
Anglican	82
Presbyterian	80
Mormon	73
Methodist	72
Other religions	67
Baptist	66
Atheist/Agnostic	50
No religious adherence	49
Christian (no other designation)	48
Object to state	48
Not specified	26

Source: Computed from Nolan et al., 1986: 64

When we examine the main directions of change and the chief characteristics of changers, the following patterns emerge. Firstly, there is very little circulation among adherents to the mainline religious groups; for example, of the 18 per cent of Anglicans who changed allegiance between 1976 and 1981, only 1.2 per cent identified with the Presbyterian, Roman Catholic, and Methodist churches. The bulk of Anglican changers (7 per cent) objected to state, and the remainder either became religious 'nones' or failed to state a religion. The Anglican pattern also applies to Presbyterian, Roman Catholic, and Methodist adherents. Secondly, the major route of those adhering to a smaller religious group in 1976 was towards 'No religion' or 'Object to state'. Thirdly, the major route *into* the mainline religions was from those who in 1976 either belonged to the religious 'nones' or adopted the 'Christian' label.

The characteristics of changers are also revealed by the study using a step-wise ranking technique. This shows that the most significant feature of changers is that they belong to the age-group twenty to twenty-nine – precisely the group to which we have earlier drawn attention in our analysis of age-profiles. Within this volatile group the next most important characteristic is sex: males are significantly more likely than females to change their religious affiliation as young adults. In sum, the New Zealand data support a strikingly similar conclusion to that of Bibby (1985). Noting that most of the non-affiliated are under forty and that there is a tendency for mainline denominations to recruit from the non-affiliate pool, he says: 'For many and perhaps most of the Nones, then, non-affiliation is seemingly a temporary category adopted in early adulthood, yet foreign both to one's past and future' (Bibby, 1985: 295).

Returning to the broad context of Martin's general theory of secularization, we have shown that the New Zealand religious situation is both a product of, and a unique environment for, the interplay of the pluralist dynamic of western Christianity. The nature of New Zealand pluralism meant that the society was officially defined in secular terms at an early stage, yet the impact of religion has punctuated its subsequent development in important ways. The successive waves of Maori millennialism highlight the pluralist dynamic and express in a particularly vivid way the unique interplay of religion, ethnicity, and political articulation. While the mainline religious groups have always been typified by high levels of nominalism, they too appear to have experienced rapid change in the last two decades. Whether the trend from nominalism to non-affiliation is a transitional phenomenon or a more deeply embedded pattern for the future is an issue that requires further analysis. Part at least of this analysis will be based on the 1986 Census of religion taken in Canada, Australia, and New Zealand, and on more recent surveys which have provided as yet not fully analysed data for all these countries.

Acknowledgements

For help and ideas in the writing of this chapter we wish to thank our insightful colleagues, Drs Arvind Zodgekar and Kwen Fee Lian, our trans-Tasman source of inspiration, Tricia Blombery of the Christian Research Association, Sydney, and our remarkable typist, Helen Gillon.

The research on which this chapter is based was made possible by a grant from Victoria University's Internal Research Committee.

References

AGB: McNair (1982) 'Frequency of Church Attendance: 1982', Survey for Presbyterian Church of New Zealand, Wellington.

Bibby, R.W. (1985) 'Religious Encasement in Canada: an Argument for Protestant and Catholic Entrenchment', *Social Compass*, 32 (2–3): 287–303.

Bibby, R.W. and M.B. Brinkerhoff (1974) 'When Proselytizing Fails: an Organizational Analysis', *Sociological Analysis*, 35(2): 189–200.

Blaikie, N.W.H. (1969) 'Religion, Social Status, and Community Involvement: a Study in Christchurch', *Australian and New Zealand Journal of Sociology*, 5(1): 14–31.

Blaikie, N.W.H. (1972) 'What Motivates Church Participation? Review, Replication and Theoretical Reorientation in New Zealand', *Sociological Review*, 20(1): 39–58.

Bouma, G. and B.R. Dixon (1986) *The Religious Factor in Australian Life*. Melbourne: MARC Australia.

Breward, I. (1967) *Godless Schools*. Christchurch: Presbyterian Bookroom.

Colless, B. and P. Donovan (eds) (1985) *Religion in New Zealand Society*. Palmerston North: Dunmore Press (2nd edn).

De Bres, P.H. (1985) 'The Maori Contribution: Maori Religious Movements in Aotearoa', in B. Colless and P. Donovan (eds), *Religion in New Zealand Society*. Palmerston North: Dunmore Press (2nd edn).

Geering, L. (1985) 'The Pluralist Tendency. Pluralism and the Future of Religion in New Zealand', in B. Colless and P. Donovan (eds), *Religion in New Zealand Society*. Palmerston North: Dunmore Press (2nd edn).

Greeley, A.M. (1979) 'Ethnic Variations in Religious Commitment', in R. Wuthnow (ed.), *The Religious Dimension. New Directions in Quantitative Research*. New York: Academic Press.

Hadaway, C.K. (1981) 'The Demographic Environment and Church Membership Change', *Journal for the Scientific Study of Religion*, 20(1): 77–89.

Harris, D. (1982) 'Counting Christians', in D. Harris, D. Hynd, and D. Millikan (eds), *The Shape of Belief. Christianity in Australia Today*. Homebush, NSW: Lancer.

Heylen Research Centre (1986) 'New Zealand Values Study, 1986', Wellington.

Hill, M. (1973) *A Sociology of Religion*. London: Heinemann.

Hill, M. and R. Bowman (1983) 'Churches in a Changing World', in *Religions and Change*, Centre for Continuing Education, Victoria University of Wellington, International Religious Studies Conference, 22–25 Aug. 1983, Wellington, pp. 235–72.

Hill, M. and R. Bowman (1985) 'Religious Adherence and Religious Practice in Contemporary New Zealand: Census and Survey Evidence', *Archives de Sciences sociales des Religions*, 59(1): 91–105.

Hogan, M. (1979) 'Australian Secularists: the Disavowal of Denominational Allegiance', *Journal for the Scientific Study of Religion*, 18(4): 390–404.

Jackson, H. (1983a) 'The Late Victorian Decline in Churchgoing: Some New Zealand Evidence', *Archives de Sciences sociales des Religions*, 56(1): 97–106.

Jackson, H. (1983b) 'Churchgoing in Nineteenth-Century New Zealand', *New Zealand Journal of History*, 17(1): 43–59.

Jackson, K. and J. Harre (1969) *New Zealand*. London: Thames and Hudson.

Jackson, L.F. (1985) 'Seventh-Day Adventists in New Zealand: Towards a Demographic History', in Peter H. Ballis (ed.), *In and Out of the World. Seventh-Day Adventists in New Zealand*. Palmerston North: Dunmore Press.

Lanternari, V. (1965) *The Religions of the Oppressed*. New York: Mentor Books.

Lewins, F. (1976) 'Ethnic Diversity within Australian Catholicism: a Comparative and Theoretical Analysis', *Australian and New Zealand Journal of Sociology*, 12(2): 126–35.

MacIntyre, A. (1967) *Secularization and Moral Change*. London: Oxford University Press.

McLeod, A.L. (ed.) (1968) *The Pattern of New Zealand Culture*. Ithaca, NY: Cornell University Press.

McLeod, H. (1974) *Class and Religion in the Late Victorian City*. London: Croom Helm.

Martin, David A. (1965) *Pacifism: an Historical and Sociological Study*. London: Routledge & Kegan Paul.

Martin, D.A. (1978) *A General Theory of Secularization*. New York: Harper Colophon.

Mol, Hans (ed.) (1972) *Western Religion: a Country by Country Sociological Inquiry*. The Hague: Mouton.

Mol, Hans (1982) *The Fixed and the Fickle. Religion and Identity in New Zealand*. Waterloo, Ontario: Wilfrid Laurier University Press.

Nichol, C. and J. Veitch (1980) *Religion in New Zealand*. Wellington: Victoria University of Wellington Tertiary Christian Studies Programme.

Nolan, F., T. Moore, and S. Yetman (1986) *The 1976/81 Intercensal Consistency Study*. Christchurch: Mathematical Statistics Division, Department of Statistics.

Oliver, W.H. (1966) 'Christianity among the New Zealanders', *Landfall*, 20(1): 4–20.

Pearson, D.G. (1980) *Johnsonville*. Sydney: Allen & Unwin.

Pickering, W.S.F. (1967) 'The 1851 Religious Census – a Useless Experiment?', *British Journal of Sociology*, 18(4): 382–407.

Reynolds, P.L. (1972) 'Religion and Voting in Auckland', *Political Science*, 24(1): 34–48.

Roozen, D.A. and J.W. Carroll (1979) 'Recent Trends in Church Membership and Participation: an Introduction', in D.R. Hoge and D.A. Roozen, *Understanding Church Growth and Decline 1950–1978*. New York: The Pilgrim Press.

Sharpe, M.R. (1981) 'Anzac Day in New Zealand: 1916 to 1939', *New Zealand Journal of History*, 15(2): 97–114.

Sinclair, K. (1969) *A History of New Zealand*. Harmondsworth, Middx.: Penguin.

Social Indicators Survey (1984) *Report on the Social Indicators Survey 1980–81*. Wellington: Department of Statistics.

Vernon, G.M. (1968) 'The Religious "Nones": a Neglected Category', *Journal for the Scientific Study of Religion*, 7(2): 219–29.

Webster, P. (1979) *Rua and the Maori Millennium*. Wellington: Price Milburn/ Victoria University Press.

Wilson, B. (1983) *Can God Survive in Australia?* Sutherland, NSW: Albatross Books.

Wilson, B.R. (1973) *Magic and the Millennium*. London: Heinemann.

Wood, G.A. (1975) 'Church and State in New Zealand in the 1850s', *Journal of Religious History*, 8(3): 255–70.

Worsley, P. (1968) *The Trumpet Shall Sound*. London: MacGibbon & Kee.

Zodgekar, A.V. (1980) 'Demographic Aspects of Indians in New Zealand', in K.N. Tiwari (ed.), *Indians in New Zealand: Studies in a Sub-culture*. Wellington: Price Milburn: 183–98.

5
Afro-Brazilian Cults and Religious Change in Brazil

Maria Isaura Pereira de Queiroz

Old Afro-Brazilian cults

There was such variety among religious cults in Brazil at the end of the eighteenth and beginning of the nineteenth centuries that they could usefully have been indicated on a map of the country. The constant arrival of Portuguese colonists and African slaves, who served as their contacts with the native population ('Indians'), had resulted in cultural mixtures that were noticeable even in religious cults. In the cities that dominated the wealthy regions where products for export were cultivated, the combination of Christianity with African cults was renowned; in the northern part of the country, where the native population was abundant, Catholicism mingled with the Indian cults; and in the backlands, where farmers of European origin were more or less isolated, the rustic Catholicism of the Portuguese peasants was preserved almost intact (Calasans, 1952; Bastide, 1958, 1961, 1978; Pereira de Queiroz, 1965, 1968, 1972, 1976, 1981a).

The existence of all these religious mixtures was already known during the seventeenth and eighteenth centuries, for the Inquisitors who had been sent to Brazil between 1591 and the mid-eighteenth century denounced 'idolatrous cults' and accused slaves, freemen, and even large plantation owners of belonging to them.[1] The plantation owners had the important duty of assuring the salvation of their slaves' souls by baptizing them, so their first concern was to put an end to their barbaric practices. Nevertheless, only a few of them did anything about it, and the conversion of the Africans was not genuine. Catholicism with its numerous saints was employed as a screen to protect the 'barbaric' beliefs, and the slaves went on practising their rituals. All African groups – Yoruba, Genge, Nago, Bantu, and others – disguised their gods behind the mask of a Catholic divinity, and each African temple had an altar decorated with the image of a patron saint in addition to its *pegi*.

Brazilian researchers were aware of this phenomenon at the end of the nineteenth century and described it in their books and reports. It thoroughly intrigued them, and they wanted to discover how elements from such different origins could have become united in spite of their disparity. Their descriptions are excellent portrayals, showing that these 'cultural conglomerates' had a richness of content and meaning plus a capacity for renewal that has still not been exhaustively investigated even today (Ortiz, 1975a, 1975b; Negrão, 1986; Borges Pereira, 1986).

Coming from different African tribes, the cults did not mingle together: each religious group had its own priests, its various cult agents, its body of religious knowledge and traditions. Priests and other religious agents attained their position through a long process of initiation in which the transmission of knowledge was entirely oral and gestural. The faithful were thus integrated into a multi-level hierarchy. The rites, some of them very spectacular, reached their highest point in beautiful festivities in which the divinities were incarnated in their initiates and made them dance in different ways, each of which was specific to one divinity.

The cults inevitably underwent changes in time but none the less conserved the essence of their doctrine and ritual. The incessant flow of slaves from Africa to supply agricultural manpower[2] certainly contributed to the maintenance of the cults in a state similar to that in which they had existed in their countries of origin. Their hierarchical structure was an important factor in this continuity, and, from this point of view, towns and villages offered greater advantages than did the great estates and farms in rural regions.

In fact, conscious of the danger that they incurred by being isolated in the middle of a large black workforce, plantation owners and farmers bought slaves from different tribes, if possible enemy ones, and always speaking different languages. These circumstances did not make it easy for people from the same origins and who were faithful to the same gods to gather together. On the other hand, plantation slaves worked very hard and did not have time to undergo the long initiation processes to be a priest and attend to all the activities that this position required.

The situation was very different in towns and villages where a number of black freemen could be found and where slaves of the same tribe could come together during their work.[3] In fact, some of these slaves were employed in various trades and crafts, enjoying a certain liberty of movement. Regardless of whether they were free or slaves, therefore, blacks in these places had the possibility of organizing their religious practices in secluded locations and of assuring the perpetuation of their cults. The towns and big villages along the coast were the location for African religion, but they were not found in the backlands where the plantations were dominant. The cults, specific to African ethnic groups, were looked upon mainly by Catholic priests as superstitious beliefs that showed how ignorant and obtuse were people of lower social groups. Nevertheless, even some of the large plantation owners took part in these cults and had been faithful to their divinities since the earliest centuries of the colonial period. Some of them were denounced to the Inquisition and were condemned by it.

The cults were based on the African conception of several vital forces, each of which was incarnated by a particular deity. The adepts owed obedience to them, and through scrupulous observance of ritual practices they could hope that their demands would be favourably considered by the gods. The notions of sin, evil, and good had no place in their beliefs; all that mattered was the attentive execution of the rituals or the failure to perform them. The divinities would also be compelled to help the believers, provided that the latter obeyed the sacred injunctions revealed to them by the priests.

Various degrees of priesthood were organized around the sacred 'fathers' and 'mothers' of a temple (*pais* and *mãis de terreiro*). Entry to the priesthood was gradual, and only those showing their religious quality through a long process of initiation could aspire to this honour. All religious knowledge was orally transmitted: explanations of the universe; history of divinities and their interrelationships as well as their relations with humans; meaning of the various components of nature; and techniques for discovering and dealing with everything that is hidden in the world.

Each congregation formed a single unit, and rivalries between them frequently prevented them from coming together to form a federation under a central power because they were jealous of their independence. Each sect was strictly connected with an African tribe at first; but as time went by, each one sought less to preserve its tribal distinctiveness and more to enhance the common cultural attributes that demonstrated the specificity of all African people as distinct from white people. This situation persisted throughout the colonial period until the end of the Brazilian Empire.[4] The numerous temples that existed in different towns, especially in Salvador (Bahia), Recife (Pernambuco), S. Luiz (Maranhão) and Rio de Janeiro maintained very limited relationships with one another, and preserved their character as more or less isolated units with a purely local focus. This was reflected in the fact that their appellation varied from one town to another, but the name 'candomblé' became general and applied to all of them.

The priests tried to remain in constant contact with Africa in order to preserve the 'purity' of their cult, but the tribal implications were gradually lost. By the nineteenth century the fact of belonging to a congregation did not mean that one came from a specific tribe. The sects then relaxed their efforts to preserve their respective tribal inheritance and sought, rather, to conserve a religion that had become to the Africans and their descendants the only possible way of holding on to something from their native country, its way of life, its civilization and philosophy. The loss of tribal implications emphasized the religious functions of the cults and their symbolic character: they became the living image of an African cultural inheritance and not the particular image of a single tribe.

In spite of all efforts to maintain the purity of beliefs, the correspondence between Catholic saints and African *orixás* – a consequence of the adoption of Catholicism as a shield against persecution – could not help but eventually bring with it some changes, but they seemed limited to the level of ritual and did not attain the core of the faith. The changes were sufficient, nevertheless, to make the cults different in some respects from the ones that had existed in Africa and to become Afro-Brazilian cults. In losing their tribal character, they no longer incarnated a kinship of race, blood, or language but simply the spiritual kinship uniting those whom slavery had brought to an alien country to work as mere beasts of burden.

These new cults were born in a situation of subordination which went beyond the loss of freedom. They were not cults of slaves only; they were cults of people from the lower ranks in the social scale, and they were branded with the label of primitive savagery by the higher classes. In fact, the Afro-Brazilian cults remained associated with segments inside Brazilian society, and never reached large collectivities or a whole stratum. There were individuals in the lower classes who did not belong to *candomblé* and remained faithful Catholics; and, on the contrary, large plantation owners could be found among its adepts. But they were not linked to it in the same manner as the Africans and their descendants. Any identification with Africa was out of the question in the case of white people; in spite of their associations they remained white people who were mainly related to Europe. They were proud of their civilization and they considered it superior to any other. They were convinced that white people were also superior to any other ethnic groups, and they still believed that, after all, Catholicism was the only true religion. The fact that they went more or less frequently to the *terreiros* only showed that they accepted them as places where they could summon the magical forces that existed in the world. Their participation in the cults did not reflect deep involvement, nor did it have anything in common with the faith of the Africans and their descendants who belonged to the lowest ranks of the social hierarchy. For the latter, their strong links with *candomblé* were a clear consequence of the severe and unrestricted subjugation that they had to endure. The more ardent and zealous the process of subjugation, the more intense was the attachment of the followers. This is shown by the continuity of Afro-Brazilian cults throughout the centuries, their expansion, and even their modifications. The transformation from a tribal symbol to the symbol of Africa was a clear cause of this success.

The Afro-Brazilian cults that existed more or less peacefully during the colonial period were the victims of violent persecution after 1870. Brazilian authorities accused their ritual of being 'cruel' and 'bloody', and severe restrictive measures were taken against them, especially in Rio de Janeiro which was then the capital of the country. The abolition of slavery in 1888 aggravated this state of things. In fact, white people and the government feared the reactions of the black masses when they were transformed into free citizens. During this difficult period priests and temples found refuge in hidden places on the periphery of towns where rituals were carried out in secret. These difficult conditions brought about a considerable simplification of the ritual and favoured the emergence of new aspects of doctrine and ceremonies which were either born from imagination or copied from other religions.[5]

One of the modifications was the multiplication of divinities. Along with the gods and goddesses already existing and corresponding to Catholic saints, other sacred beings made their appearance: spirits of Indian origin (*caboclos*) as well as others of various (mainly European) sources (*encantados*). The number of African deities declined. They did not disappear, but their role underwent changes, their principal function remaining to help believers to overcome difficulties in their everyday life. The believer became much more a client than an adept, and the priest was more a healer than a mediator between man and God.

Some Manichaean concepts were introduced into doctrine, and Exú, the divinity of openings, became the incarnation of evil, with an intensification of its diabolical character. Ritual practices of different origins were also adopted and integrated into the ancient African ceremonies. Some were taken from the native Indians – the immoderate use of tobacco, for instance. Religious hierarchy also lost its neatness and became more or less fluid. But both doctrine and rituals increased in complexity, and with them the notions of the celestial hierarchy and the conception of the universe. One of the important effects of persecution was to shorten the period of initiation, and this had a major influence over the transmission of sacred knowledge, so that written transmission eventually came to complement the oral one (Bastide, 1961; Ortiz, 1975a, 1975b, 1979; Negrão, 1986).

The process of transformation could be seen most clearly in Rio de Janeiro and very quickly migrated to São Paulo where Afro-Brazilian cults had been almost non-existent until then. They attained what could be called their maturity in these two cities at the same time – that is, during the 1920s. Elements borrowed from the spiritism of Alain Kardec were mixed with the religious elements of Catholicism, African and native Indian rituals and beliefs, with the result that these combinations gave birth to a new Afro-Brazilian cult named *umbanda*.

A new cult: *umbanda*

The importance of *umbanda* has increased with time, and it is still spreading throughout the country and across all social classes. Its supreme god is surrounded by a first rank of deities, each of whom commands 'lines' or 'phalanges' of less important spirits. The sacred beings are either masculine or feminine, and all the human ages are also represented among them. Reincarnation has become one of the most important features of the new faith. Thus, if the believer obeys the injunctions of his divinity, it is believed that he would be reincarnated in a much better social and economic situation after his death. But if he chose to disobey, the belief is that he would be punished in a future existence.

The notion of sin is incorporated into *umbanda*, with the consequent belief that offences against divine and moral laws would certainly have unpleasant results in another life and would result in the deterioration of the believer's social and material situation. The prospect of having to answer for one's actions in another life is a sign that the notion of individual moral responsibility has been awakened: a person could choose to obey or disobey the orders of the sacred beings. In this way, concepts of good and evil which had not existed in the ancient African beliefs, but which are fundamental in all Christian philosophy, were also integrated into *umbanda*.

Some of the divine beings protect the believers and help them in their everyday life and difficulties. They are 'good' in the Christian sense of the word, and they are linked with everything that concerns the 'moral' domain. However, there are also spirits, masculine as well as feminine, that are vicious, wicked, harmful, and even 'amoral'. They are always seeking mischief and have to be placated by offerings in order to keep them away from temples during ceremonies or away from individuals in their everyday life. But these spirits have another function: payment of an appropriate recompense can even make them help believers to solve their problems and magically destroy their enemies on request. But the person who thus asks for their help will pay for it in another life. The evil spirits are fully recognized by the priests and theologians of *umbanda* to be indispensable for the equilibrium of the world, so that the individual may choose his preferred path. Those who have recourse to the forces of evil know, however, that in their reincarnation they will suffer a deterioration in their social and economic circumstances.

Attempts are constantly made in *umbanda* scientifically to prove its truthfulness – a cultural trait that was also borrowed from the spiritism of Alain Kardec. A large number of religious texts are continuously being published for that very purpose. Religious knowledge is transmitted both orally (during the process of initiation) and by means of religious texts. The adoption of the written word as a useful means of religious transmission helps *umbanda* to differentiate itself from the old Afro-Brazilian cults that were passed on by word of mouth only. It also favours the creation of a new level of 'sages' parallel to that of the priests. This 'intellectual caste' specializes in the study of religious dogma and rites, and its members have gradually acquired high esteem and a high position in the religious hierarchy. This gives them a power of decision without precedent in the history of Afro-Brazilian cults. *Umbanda* has thus become a religion of the book without abandoning the character of a religion of the spoken word.

Finally, *umbanda* was quick to develop a tendency to form a federation of congregations under the control of a central higher committee. This tendency sets it clearly apart from *candomblé*, whose units have continued zealously to defend their independence (Bastide, 1961; Ortiz, 1975a, 1975b, 1979; Fry, 1978; Negrão, 1986). The formation of federations and the organization of congresses would be impossible without the introduction of the written word as a major instrument for the transmission of know-ledge. Indeed, institutional and administrative structures are indis-pensable for their existence. This tendency attests to *umbanda*'s ambition to become a *national* religion, and its development in that direction is undeniable: it is spreading not only to all regions of the country but also to all its social strata. The written studies not only play 'an extremely important role in the diffusion and codification of the *umbanda* religion' but they also, with its codification, increase the tendency towards uniformity and homogeneity in doctrine and ritual.[6] All this is in sharp contrast to the old cults with their independent local units.

The religious beliefs and activities of *umbanda* come, then, from different civilizations and sources, and this feature is heavily emphasized by the priests, who attribute special importance to its triple origins: European, African, and Indian. From *candomblé, umbanda* has retained a sizeable body of African divinities, the importance of initiation, divination through shells (*'caoris'* or *'buzios'*) but above all its festive character and the religious trances that mark, with their dancing and singing, the commemorations. From the spiritism of Alain Kardec, *umbanda* has retained a conception of the world which is different from that of *candomblé*, and a different philosophy which is based on the belief in reincarnation. From the Indians, *umbanda* has taken some rituals and the utilization of herbs and tobacco. From Catholicism, *umbanda* has kept the correspondence between African *orixás* and the saints, as well as some ceremonies (masses). It could be said, then, that in the realm of the Afro-Brazilian cults 'African religious thought yields its place to Brazilian thought' in *umbanda* (Ortiz, 1979: 52–3) because the specific characteristic of Brazilian civilization is its syncretism.

Umbanda's first adepts were drawn from the lower strata of the cities of Rio de Janeiro and São Paulo and were mostly of African origin. It quickly spread, however, to European immigrants and their descendants in the same strata who had arrived in the country shortly beforehand (Bastide, 1961). Within a few years it had spread to people of the lower middle classes and went on climbing to higher strata. It has now reached the highest social, economic, and intellectual levels of the national status hierarchy. Its numerical strength showed corresponding growth, and recent assessments put it at more than 30 million adepts in a population of 130 million.[7] The importance acquired by the new cult parallels its rise in the social scale.

The rising socio-economic fortunes of *umbanda* in Brazilian society can also be gauged by the progressive 'whitening' of believers: the number of white people attending the rituals is growing steadily in a country where black people are still very much confined to the lower strata. This upward mobility has an influence over some of the new cult's characteristics when it is compared with the old *candomblé*. All the African features that could harm non-African sensibility – for example, the blood sacrifices of animals – have tended to disappear from the ritual. The prominent African elements that have been retained nevertheless emphasize *umbanda*'s non-European character: its varied rituals, the mystic trance and intitiation, and its different phases. The fact that they have been retained and are highly prized as extremely important conceals the loss of other very relevant African characteristics in the cult's doctrine and philosophy. The notions of individual responsibility and of sin, the importance of 'scientific' explanations of nature and of the world, and the place taken by the written texts are all features which did not exist in the old Afro-Brazilian cults, and they show that a very important part of the African heritage has been abandoned (Teixeira Monteiro, 1977).

Afro-Brazilian cults have always been urban cults. In the past, *candomblé* used to be the religion of slaves and poor citizens, almost all of them black or mulattos. Rich planters and merchants – that is, rich white people who financed the costly festivities – were more or less affiliated to the *terreiro*, but they were very few in number. *Umbanda*, on the contrary, acquired a very large following in all social classes and in all ethnic groups in all parts of the country.[8] It achieved the status of a legal religion and is considered to be on the same footing as the great western and Asian religions. It paved the way for legal status to be extended to the old Afro-Brazilian cults that had never benefited from this condition before and that were thus protected against official persecution.

The great success of *umbanda* in the urban society of Brazil seems all the more surprising as it has accompanied the accelerating economic and industrial development of the whole country and of its two biggest cities. In fact, São Paulo and Rio de Janeiro are the two poles of industrial expansion, and it is also in them that the cult has achieved its greatest increase. The success transformed *umbanda* into a political force which has to be reckoned with during elections. Political leaders and the government in general are well aware of it and seek more or less openly to support priests and 'sages'. It seems that urban growth in Brazil, based on industrial development, does not necessarily lead to an increase in secularization or in a materialistic interpretation of the world and daily life. At least, they have not prevented religious sects from flourishing.[9]

The birth of *umbanda* and its great success among almost all social classes and ethnic groups in Brazil must be examined sociologically at two different moments: the moment of its gestation and appearance – that is, the beginning of the twentieth century; and the moment of its expansion, which began in the 1930s. Much more research is still necessary to produce reliable answers to all the questions that arise from these observations, but some clues can perhaps be found in analysis of the historical and social circumstances in which they developed. Such clues may lead to a preliminary explanation.

Towards an explanation

The south-eastern region of Brazil entered a period of great change at the end of the nineteenth century, and the two cities that dominated the rural area became extremely rich and underwent internal transformations. The expansion of coffee plantations in the region after 1860 created a need for manual labour just at the moment when the slave trade was abolished.[10] A great wave of European immigrants then flowed in from Italy, Portugal, and Spain, while other immigrants arrived from Syria and Lebanon, and a little later from Japan. Most of them were peasants whom the large plantation owners attracted to their properties, but many left the plantations and, instead, went to work in the cities as soon as they could. During the First World War the two cities of São Paulo and Rio de Janeiro experienced their second industrial development. And São Paulo in particular then entered on an extraordinary transformation, with a rapid increase of tertiary employment which gave work opportunities to people of lower status: they could open a small shop or a craft workshop or find work as minor functionaries in some public or private enterprise.[11]

In the first twenty-five years of this century 'out of the 1,894,000 immigrants who came to Brazil, more than a million were attracted to the city of São Paulo' (Martin, 1966: 97). Immigrants and their descendants, former slaves and their descendants were all mingling in an urban society that was changing quickly. The creation of whole categories of new jobs in industry, commerce, administration, and business made it necessary to train workers of all types very quickly, and this included manual as well as white-collar workers. There was a sudden multiplication of what Roger Bastide called 'intermediary classes' (Bastide, 1954; see also Azevedo, 1953; Fernandes, 1978) that were produced by the advancement of all those who mastered any indispensable technique (primarily reading and writing), whether they were black people, former slaves, or immigrants. Immigrants and their descendants, who were already better adapted to industrialization, had more facilities for upward mobility in the social and economic scale than the descendants of Africans (Pereira de Queiroz, 1974; Fernandes, 1978).

The great influx of immigrants, most of them European, and their successful advancement threatened to submerge the national population and was somehow pushing it down to lower levels in the social hierarchy. The newcomers were accompanied by a great wave of occidental culture which could have destroyed the existing civilization that had emerged from the mixture of traits from three different origins. It dated from the colonial period and was characterized by a syncretic pattern which was already fully crystallized. The autochthones were conscious of the danger, and the result could have been a wide gulf between them and the immigrants, especially in the lower levels of the social hierarchy. In reality this did not occur, but, on the contrary, a new type of mixture took place then and there. The lower social ranks of São Paulo and Rio de Janeiro acted as an excellent milieu for the interpenetration of the old and the new collectivities. And it was there that the new Afro-Brazilian cult was created.[12]

It seemed that Brazilians felt at that time that their peculiar civilization was in danger of disappearing since it could have been weakened by the avalanche of alien cultural traits. Faced with an overwhelming demographic and cultural flood that came first of all from Europe, but also from the Middle and Far East, the Brazilians seemed to attach themselves firmly to everything that would give special prominence to the original character of their culture. And its syncretic character, which had been observed since the end of the nineteenth century, was readily apparent. The creation of a new cult was probably one of the ways for the autochthones to prevent their cultural heritage from being destroyed. This also explains why the *umbanda* priests placed such emphasis on the fact that their religion came from three different origins – the same three different origins that were recognizably at the basis of the whole Brazilian civilization: African, Indian, and European. The fact that their melting had produced a new and original religious configuration was stressed by them as of the utmost importance. Thus, syncretism was the conspicuous quality which was elevated to the status of the primordial mark of the nation, its fundamental quality.

Yet, this does not explain why immigrants and their descendants were so quick to joint the new cult. There are not sufficient studies of this period to permit firm generalizations about it, but there are plenty of indications of what probably occurred. Just before the appearance of *umbanda, macumba*[13] was undergoing a major transformation in Rio de Janeiro: this old Afro-Brazilian cult had already been penetrated by immigrants, and even the priests were not always descendants of Africans. In fact, in some *terreiros*, Italians and even a Lebanese woman were exercising the highest functions (Bastide, 1961: 403, 415). The cult, with the apparently great magical power of its deities, was probably attracting the newcomers because they considered it useful as a means of helping them to be socially and economically upwardly mobile. The immigrants had been aware of magical practices in their countries of origin, so they had little difficulty in accepting the rituals of a religion that seemed to them full of good promises.

Before the birth of *umbanda*, therefore, immigrants and their descendants were already joining the existing Afro-Brazilian cults in Rio de Janeiro. At that time they were one of the meeting places where the first intimate contacts between black people and recently arrived immigrants took place. They must have witnessed an extraordinary mixing up of races and cultures. In the lower ranks of the social strata of Rio de Janeiro and São Paulo, where former slaves and their descendants lived in close proximity to white people who were strangers but also poor, the interpenetration of cultural complexes had the consequence of introducing new beliefs into the old cults, such as the notions of good and evil, and of integrating people of different ethnic groups in the *terreiros*.

The adaptation of immigrants has so far escaped serious study, but it is known that they underwent a very severe ordeal. They were exposed to the prejudices of the Brazilian-born population which were showed to them in informal but very effective ways. The autochthones manifested their uneasiness and displeasure in the face of what they saw as threats to their social position and even their political power.[14] The immigrants, living in very difficult conditions, tried all kinds of solutions to ease their suffering. Their recourse to the Afro-Brazilian cults could be seen as a search for relief and consolation. They did not appear to go there to establish spiritual communion with priests and adepts; they were asking for solutions to their personal problems and seeking simple consultations. Nevertheless, they contributed greatly to the 'whitening' of both the doctrine and the membership of the cults, and they contributed strongly to their internal evolution.

The aspirations of immigrants and former slaves were agreed on one point; that is, the desire to be upwardly mobile in the social and economic hierarchies. But mobility became a reality for only a very small number of them. In spite of this contradiction, the great hopes for a better life and the belief that it could one day be attained were widespread among the vast majority of lower-class citizens. The period was marked by optimistic views about the future, and euphoria could be observed in several manifestations and activities. Former slaves and freshly arrived immigrants shared the same desire for integration into a society that seemed to conceal inexhaustible possibilities for work and prosperity. This enthusiasm and confidence in the future were plain to see in *umbanda*.

In fact, its philosophy promised to those who were 'good' in this life an improvement of their social and economic conditions in a future life. This way of thinking was quite appropriate to the aspirations of the lower and middle strata of an urban society whose internal dynamics had always been governed by money, by unregulated, unbridled, ostentatious consumerism, and by aspirations for power. The ready acceptance of *umbanda* by the lower social strata of São Paulo and Rio de Janeiro can probably be explained as a direct consequence of the strong desire that they showed to ascend the social scale, although it contrasted with the rather low probability of their attaining it in real life. The extraordinarily rapid expansion of *umbanda*, beginning in the 1920s, seems to be a fruit of the imbalance between the deep desire of the Brazilian lower and lower-middle classes to be upwardly mobile and the difficulties that they met in their way. As a faith oriented towards the future and as a doctrine revolving around hope, *umbanda* brought to its believers a feeling of certainty that their hopes would be fulfilled in a future reincarnation.

However, a third phase in the expansion of *umbanda* occurred in the 1960s when it reached the middle and higher strata of the two cities. This phenomenon has not yet been adequately analysed, and valid explanations are still awaited. The expansion took place in classes quite opposite to those in which the first adepts were found, and it attracted to the *terreiros* people from the middle classes, including the upper-middle class as well as some intellectuals. *Umbanda* can now be said to be a Brazilian religion, drawing people from all social classes with neither ethnic nor economic limitations. And in all strata the importance of its syncretic origin is constantly reaffirmed by the adepts, priests, and 'sages'.

The economic and political circumstances that marked national life after 1960 can help to explain this new expansion. A new notion had been slowly gaining ground among individuals belonging to the middle and higher classes: Brazil was an underdeveloped country occupying a subordinate position in the community of nations. This was clearly confirmed by the military 'revolution' of 1964 which took place with the material aid and the overt blessing of the USA. The heavy military control of civilian life and the deterioration of economic conditions affected not only the lower strata but also the intermediate ones. The 'scientific' solutions preached by the government and by economists were tried one after the other but did not work: underdevelopment and misery were becoming unmistakably worse for the great majority of Brazilians.

The galloping inflation which began around 1970, along with the deterioration of modest as well as more fortunate budgets, was interpreted as a consequence of Brazil's underdeveloped and dependent situation in the world. The middle and higher classes were now quite well aware of the place occupied by their national society in the pecking order of the western world. And this realization dawned at the same time as inflation induced a strong feeling that things were out of balance.

The adherence of people from the middle and higher classes to the new Afro-Brazilian religion could be the consequence of the dissatisfaction that they experienced on two levels: (1) their deep desire to maintain the position that they had achieved and the fear that it was being threatened by many dangers, and (2) their deep desire that their country could rise to the first rank in the community of nations and the constant realization that this was a dream which could not come true as a result of normal measures. The difficulty of escaping from a situation of individual instability, the difficulty of freeing the country from economic and political servitude in a world context, and the discredit of 'scientifically' based solutions could all have strengthened the belief, in the higher classes, that only sacred solutions could bring salvation to individuals in Brazil and to Brazil in the community of nations.

Discussion

The transformations of Afro-Brazilian cults have been analysed here on different levels: (1) the level of the configuration of the cults, their relations to the groups of adepts and to the position that these adepts occupied in the social and economic hierarchy of Brazilian cities; and (2) the level of the groups of believers and their possible motives for joining the faith. The first stage of analysis was a diagnosis of the social and economic situation of the believers' groups in a society where positions were well defined in a somewhat rigid hierarchy, and whose culture was controlled in hegemonic manner by the higher strata. This was all set in a context of constant social and economic changes. The second level was concerned with analysing the changes in the cults and the changes in members' social and economic situations. Inferences were made about the motives that impelled the groups to display their adherence to the cults. The first stage of the analysis is supported by the findings of research which have shown how everything has progressed since the arrival of African slaves in Brazil. The second stage involves moving from these statements to propositions whose truth is believed to follow from that of the former. In other words, the second stage consists of making possibly explanatory hypotheses that are to lead to further research.

The analysis has dealt exclusively with the cults through the intermediary of groups, their composition, and their place in the social hierarchy at different historical moments. Religion as such – that is, an institutionalized system of attitudes, beliefs, and practices governing the relations between human and supernatural beings – was considered only when it became important to describe the cults' configurations and to clarify the changes that occurred in them. The opinions of the believers, the individual motives that attracted each of them to the *terreiros* were also left aside. The intention, in adopting this perspective, was to remain as far as possible on a sociological path with no interference from the science of religions or from social psychology.

The examination of various data and of the inferences that flow from them shows that the transformation of religious cults in Brazil follows the changes in the urban collectivities with which they are associated. To what extent can one speak of religious creation – that is, the act of producing something new in the realm of the sacred? To what extent can it be said that the mixture of different beliefs in Brazil generated a faith which differed from what had preceded it?

Candomblé might initially appear to suggest a positive answer, since it mingled with Catholicism. But more rigorous examination shows that Catholicism was only a mask behind which the African cult continued to exist. The contact between the two religions produced an ostensible mixture that concealed the reality which represented the continuity of tribal doctrines and rituals. That there was no profound blending was reflected in the fact that notions like sin or the distinction between good and evil were not transferred from Catholicism to the African cults of the past, as well as by the fact that the latter went on being associated with more or less small groups, that is, something akin to tribal groups. These ancient Afro-Brazilian cults retained the same form across the centuries until the beginning of the twentieth century, and during that long period Brazilian society remained a remarkably stable social and economic structure. Admittedly, syncretism did exist in Brazilian civilization at points where the fusion of elements from various cultural sources was actively at work. But the African religions seemed untouched by it and persisted very much in the forms in which they had existed in the mother country. They did not suffer a process of syncretism, if this concept is taken to mean a complete fusion of different forms of belief and the modification of their core; that is, their doctrine as well as their more general configuration, their organization in small independent units.

Only *umbanda*, among all the Afro-Brazilian cults, could really be characterized as a religious creation: it contained a set of beliefs which were different from the old tribal ones that lay at their roots. It was also widely different from Catholicism, spiritism, and the Indian cults. It was not only its faith but also its rituals which had characteristics that had not existed in the ancient religions. Even the features which persisted from ancient times were arranged in a different way. The doctrine, very much influenced by spiritism, became an adaptation of the faith preached by Alain Kardec with its notion of reincarnation and its opposition between good and evil. The connection with the ancient belief in vital forces, that did not disappear, produced a new understanding of the supernatural. From all points of view, *umbanda* was a new religious creation. The syncretism which had long been the mark of Brazilian civilization in everyday life finally reached into the depths of religious beliefs: doctrinal modifications finally accompanied ritual ones.

The creation of a new faith took place when urban society in Brazil was also undergoing a major change: some of its cities were losing their former shape as clusters of neighbouring groups and were becoming a metropolis. They contained large populations and were complex centres of many economic and political activities. Their inhabitants were distributed among numerous strata in a complicated social hierarchy. In the two largest cities, São Paulo and Rio de Janeiro, the shift from *candomblé* to *umbanda* paralleled these changes.

Incidentally, it is interesting to note that in Salvador (capital of the state of Bahia), where there were many more ancient Afro-Brazilian cults than in any other city of Brazil, and where the descendants of Africans were also more numerous than elsewhere, no transformations could be seen in *candomblé* groups. Instead, this city clung to its old social structure and organizations for many years, and any changes have been extremely recent. It seems, then, that the major modifications of urban society in Brazil favoured changes in the old cults and the creation of at least one new cult.

This parallelism takes on a new significance in the context of other observations by making it possible to see new meanings. For example, it now becomes clear that Afro-Brazilian cults in the ancient form, in which oral transmission was of utmost importance and in which very long periods of initiation required seclusion in the *terreiro*, were appropriate for illiterate people who did not have a wide choice of jobs. These cults represented chiefly the faith of Africans and their descendants and were therefore concerned with maintaining African ways of thinking, the commemoration of a distant country and the past. In the early days of *umbanda*, by contrast, written transmission became important, and faith was supported by 'scientific' reasoning. This was appropriate for urban agglomerations where industrialization required a different kind of education and took up most of people's time. As the lower urban ranks no longer consisted exclusively of the descendants of Africans only, *umbanda* opened its *terreiros* to people of all ethnic origins. All those who wanted consciously or unconsciously to rise in the social scale found that the faith supported their aspirations. The very gradual mobility that some of them managed to achieve confirmed them in the belief that the new religion was 'true'. The fact that only a very small minority could actually reach the top of the social scale paradoxically raised the hopes of the majority: social and economic advancement was possible, if not in this era, then in another reincarnation.

Candomblé and *umbanda* also differed in what they signified. They were both certainly symbols – that is, visible signs of something invisible – possessing a great internal power of representation so that they could immediately convey the perception of an idea or a feeling to a collectivity. *Candomblé*, with its small groups that clung to their independence, was oriented towards the maintenance of ancient African traditions and ways of thinking – in other words, the perpetuation of tribal behaviour. It went on being a concrete representation of its country of origin, that is, of the past. *Umbanda*, in its attempts to form federations, clearly showed its ambition to bring together all kinds of believers' groups and to become a national religion. It embodied 'Brazilianity' both to the autochthones and to the newcomers. It reunited the autochthones in their desire to protect their cultural distinctiveness against the continuous influx of alien elements into the country. But it linked them to the immigrants and their descendants who wanted to be assimilated into the society in which they had chosen to live. It represented to the lower classes a way of social and economic advancement to which they were always aspiring. And it permitted all strata, even the higher ones, to entertain the hope that their country could reach the top rank of nations. It is a cult oriented towards the future. Being the faith of a very complex society, *umbanda* lacked the uniformity of meaning displayed by *candomblé*. And being the faith of individuals who were unequally distributed among numerous social strata, its meanings varied according to, on the one hand, its members' social and economic origin, and, on the other, their ethnic ancestry.

Candomblé had a profusion of rites which varied with its ancient tribal origins: Nago, Yoruba, Bantu, and Dahomey. This variety was an obstacle to the grouping of the *terreiros* into federations, for each one jealously preserved its peculiarities, and their variety also prevented the cults from becoming a national faith. *Umbanda*, by contrast, tended from the beginning to bring its *terreiros* together and to form federations. All its religious groups have more or less the same form everywhere and the same pattern of structures, rituals, and doctrines (Ortiz, 1975a; Fry, 1978, 1986; Negrão, 1986). There is no doubt that this homogeneity makes it easier for *umbanda* to spread among all social strata and regions of the country. It also chimes with the impulse towards cultural uniformity that is evident nowadays not only in Brazil but in the whole world.

The fact that the believers' motives for joining the faith vary from one social stratum to another is not incompatible with the search for uniformity; it only shows that the level of individual motivation is not the same as that of collective representations. In spite of their different motives, individuals from very different backgrounds see in *umbanda* the embodiment of Brazilian civilization. The creation of *umbanda* suggests that symbolism pertains to a level of generalization that does not seem to exist at the level of socio-psychological motivation.

Candomblé and *umbanda* both sprang from contact between very different cultural heritages in Brazil, and they both have a strong bearing on the realm of symbolism – they are the visible sign of the invisible. But their deep significances are not the same. *Candomblé* continues to be the symbol of a clearly identified ethnic group in the wider Brazilian society. *Umbanda* has become the symbol of modern Brazilian society's singularity among the nations.

Notes

1 A good description of the various persecutions carried out by the Inquisition is found in Calasans (1952) and in Pereira de Queiroz (1965, 1968).

2 The slave trade finished officially in 1850 but went on secretly more or less until 1880. The abolition of slavery took place in 1888. But the links of the *terreiros* with Africa still exist, and the priests promote them to preserve the integrity of their faith.

3 There have always been free blacks and mulattos in Brazil. Many of them came voluntarily from Africa while others had been freed by their masters. They found work chiefly in crafts and trade. Their existence was important for the maintenance of the cults, since priesthood required a great deal of disposable time. Priests and priestesses were then mostly free men and women.

4 The Brazilian colonial period lasted from the sixteenth century until 1822; the imperial period from 1822 until the proclamation of the Republic in 1889.

5 Persecutions varied in intensity from one region to another. They became very strong in Rio de Janeiro around 1870 when the idea of abolition was taking shape and they lasted until the beginning of the twentieth century. But in Salvador (capital of Bahia), by contrast, where African people and their descendants were very numerous, persecution, even in its most severe form, met with resistance from the vast majority of believers and sympathizers who supported or helped priests and other cult agents.

6 *Umbanda*'s first Brazilian Congress of Spiritism took place in Rio de Janeiro in 1941; the Spiritist Federation of *Umbanda* then tried to standardize its ritual and doctrine. The process is still going on more or less slowly. Fry (1978) claims that it has stopped, but this opinion is contradicted by new research findings which show that it is still continuing.

7 It is difficult to gauge the real number of believers. The last attempt, by Peter Fry (1978: 30), estimated it at 20 million in a population of 110 million. The present estimate of 30 million includes only those adepts who openly confess their membership of the cult. Some people also attend the commemorations frequently and consult the priests without admitting it; they go on claiming that they are good Catholics.

8 This is true not only of descendants of European immigrants but also of those coming from the Middle East. Even the Japanese and their descendants have recently become habitués of the *terreiros*.

9 *Umbanda* is not the only religion that has recently shown spectacular development. The Pentecostal sects are now its greatest competitor and are also undergoing rapid expansion. See Teixeira Monteiro, 1977; Fry, 1978.

10 The campaign for the abolition of slavery was greatly intensified from 1870 onwards and ended with the 'Lei Aurea' (the Golden Law) of 1888. In all the works of the first Brazilian social scientists of that period the fear of Africans and their religions can be clearly perceived.

11 The demographic increase in São Paulo at the end of the nineteenth century was extremely rapid according to Morse (1970: 38):

1886	44,030 inhabitants
1890	64,934 inhabitants
1892	102,409 inhabitants

Morse adds that between 1908 and 1920, 340,000 immigrants through the port of Santos came to work in the city of São Paulo (1970: 301). Eva Blay (1985) has calculated the rate of the city's population growth as follows:

1872–1886	52%
1890–1900	168%
1900–1920	141%
1920–1934	83%

For this period, important sources are Monbeig, 1952; Morazé, 1954; and especially Martin, 1966.

12 A very interesting coincidence occurred in the 1920s in the city of São Paulo, where young intellectuals were then formulating a new theory about Brazilian identity, which they presented to the public during the Week of Modern Art in 1922, a week that began a revolution in all branches of art. They proclaimed that Brazilian identity had been constructed by mixing three cultural inheritances: the European, the African, and the Indian. See Pereira de Queiroz, 1980, 1981b, 1982; Ortiz, 1980, 1982.

13 The ancient Afro-Brazilian cults had different names in different regions even when they came from the same ethnic group: *xangô* in Pernambuco; *candomblé* in Bahia; *macumba* in Rio de Janeiro; *batuque* in Rio Grande do Sul; and *vodu* in S. Luiz do Maranhão.

14 The novels of Antonio Alcântara Machado, published in the 1920s, clearly reveal the prejudice against Italian immigrants in the city of São Paulo and all the obstacles that they found to their integration (Alcântara Machado, 1976; see also Martins, 1973, and Alvim, 1986).

References

Alcântara Machado, Antonio (1976) *Novelas paulistanas*. Rio de Janeiro: José Olympio Ed., 4th edn.

Alvim, Zuleika (1986) *Brava gente! (Os Italianos em S. Paulo: 1870–1920)* (Courageous People! – The Italians in S. Paulo: 1870–1920). São Paulo: Ed. Brasiliense.

Azevedo, Thales de (1953) *Les Elites de couleur dans une ville brésilienne*. Paris: UNESCO.

Bastide, Roger (1954) *Sociologie du Brésil*. Paris: CDU/Institut des Hautes Études de l'Amérique Latine.

Bastide, Roger (1958) *Le Candomblé de Bahia (rite nago)*. The Hague: Mouton.

Bastide, Roger (1961) *Les Religions africaines du Brésil*. Paris: Presses Universitaires de France.

Bastide, Roger (1978) *Images du nordest mystique en noir et blanc*. Nice: Pandora Ed.

Bastide, Roger and Florestan Fernandes (1955) *Relações raciais entre negros e brancos em S. Paulo* (Racial Relations among Black and White People in São Paulo). São Paulo: Ed. Anhembi.

Blay, Eva Alterman (1985) *Eu não tenho onde morar (vilas operarias na cidade de S. Paulo)* (I Don't Have a Place to Live in – Workers' Quarters in the City of São Paulo). São Paulo: Ed. Nobel.

Borges Pereira, João Baptista (1986) 'A presença de Roger Bastide nos estudos recentes sôbre relações raciais no Brasil' (Roger Bastide's presence in recent studies on racial relations in Brazil), pp. 21–7 in *Revisitando a terra de contrastes – a atualidade de Roger Bastide* (Revisiting the country of contrasts: actuality of Roger Bastide's studies in Brazil). São Paulo, CERU/FFLCH/USP.

Calasans, José (1952) *A Santidade de Jaguaripe* (Jaguaripe's sanctity). Salvador (Bahia).

Fernandes, Florestan (1978) *A Integraçao do negro na sociedade de classes* (Integration of Black People in a Class Society). São Paulo: Ed. Ática, 2nd edn.

Fry, Peter (1978) 'Manchester, sec. XIX: S. Paulo, sec. XX: dois movimentos religiosos' (Manchester, nineteenth century: S. Paulo, twentieth century: two religious movements) in *Religião e Sociedade*, 3 Oct.: 25–52.

Fry, Peter (1986) 'Gallus Africanus est, ou como Roger Bastide se tornou africano no Brasil' (Gallus Africanus Est, or How Roger Bastide in Brazil Became an African), pp. 31–45 in *Revisitando a terra de contrastes – a atualidade de Roger Bastide*. São Paulo: CERU/FFLCH/USP.

Martin, Jean-Marie (1966) *Processus d'industrialisation et développement énergetique du Brésil*. Paris: Institut des Hautes Études de l'Amérique Latine.

Martins, José de Souza (1973) *Conde Matarazzo: o empresario e a empresa (estudo de sociologia do desenvolvimento)* (Conde Matarazzo: the Businessman and Industry – Study in Sociology of Development). São Paulo: Hucitec, 2nd edn.

Monbeig, Pierre (1952) *Pionniers et planteurs de S. Paulo*. Paris: Librairie Armand Colin.

Morazé, Charles (1954) *Les trois âges du Brésil*. Paris: Librairie Armand Colin.

Morse, Richard M. (1970) *Formação historica de S. Paulo (de comunidade a metrópole)* (Historical Formation of S. Paulo – from Community to Metropolis). S. Paulo: Difusão Européia do Livro.

Negrão, Lísias Nogueira (1986) 'Roger Bastide: do Candomblé à Umbanda' (Roger

Bastide: from Candomblé to Umbanda), pp. 47–63 in *Revisitando a terra de contrastes: a atualidade da obra de Roger Bastide*. São Paulo: CERU/FFLCH/USP.

Ortiz, Renato (1975a) 'Du syncrétisme à la synthèse: Umbanda, une religion brésilienne', *Archives des Sciences Sociales des Religions*, 40: 89–97.

Ortiz, Renato (1975b) *La Mort blanche du sorcier noir*. Paris: Thèse de Doctorat du 3e cycle, École des Hautes Études en Sciences Sociales.

Ortiz, Renato (1979) 'La matrifocalité religieuse', *Diogène*, 105 (Jan–March: 38–56.

Ortiz, Renato (1980) 'Cultura Popular e Memória Nacional' (Popular Culture and National Memory), *Cadernos*, Centro de Estudos Rurais e Urbanos, 13 (Sept.): 9–22.

Ortiz, Renato (1982) 'Cultura brasileira e identidade nacional' (Brazilian Culture and National Identity), *Cadernos*, 17 (Sept.) 8–21.

Pereira de Queiroz, Maria Isaura (1965) 'Messiahs in Brazil', *Past and Present*, 31 (July): 62–86.

Pereira de Queiroz, Maria Isaura (1968) *Réforme et révolution dans les sociétés traditionnelles*. Paris: Ed. Anthropos.

Pereira de Queiroz, Maria Isaura (1972) *Images messianiques du Brésil*. Cuernavaca (Mexico): Centro Intercultural de Documentación.

Pereira de Queiroz, Maria Isaura (1974) 'Collectivités noires et montée socio-économique des noirs au Brésil', *Caravelle*, 22: 105–31.

Pereira de Queiroz, Maria Isaura (1976) *O Messianismo no Brasil e no mundo* (Messianism in Brazil and in the World). São Paulo: Ed. Alfa-Ômega, 2nd edn.

Pereira de Queiroz, Maria Isaura (1980) 'Cientistas sociais e o auto-conhecimento da cultura brasileira através do tempo' (Social Scientists and the Knowledge of Brazilian Culture through the Years), *Cadernos*, 13 (Sept.): 57–69.

Pereira de Queiroz, Maria Isaura (1981a) 'Évolution et création religieuse: les cultes Afro-Brésiliens', *Diogène*, 115 (July–Sept.): 3–24.

Pereira de Queiroz, Maria Isaura (1981b) 'Ainda uma definição do "ser brasileiro"?' (Another Definition of Brazilian Identity?) *Cadernos*, 14 (Dec.): 21–41.

Pereira de Queiroz, Maria Isaura (1982) 'Balanço da tradição do pensamento brasileiro sôbre Cultura e Sociedade, no sec. XIX' (Estimating Traditional Brazilian Thought on Culture and Society during the Nineteenth Century), *Cadernos*, 17 (Sept.): 5–14.

Teixeira Monteiro, Duglas (1977) 'Églises, sectes et agences: aspects d'un oecuménisme popularie', *Diogène*, 100 (Oct.–Dec.): 53–86.

6

The Emergence of Islamic Political Ideologies

Said Amir Arjomand

What is the relation between religion and politics? It depends on
the religion and on the politics in different times and different
places. Analytically, it does make sense to talk about the religious
and the political spheres of life provided we think of their degree
of overlap or distinctness as variable – that is, as varying from case
to case. This paper is about Islamic fundamentalists who contend
that there should be complete fusion between the religious and the
political spheres of life, and that the separation of religion and the
state is the result of a secularist plot to undermine and destroy
Islam. There are people – some of them respected Orientalists –
who say that Islam is essentially a theocracy or a divine monocracy:
rule of the Sacred Law; and that in Islam church and state are one.
I think all these assertions are misleading. It is true that the Prophet
of Islam was also the founder of the first Islamic state, and this
important fact of its sacred history distinguishes Islam from Judaism
and Christianity. Furthermore, it is highly relevant to the emergence of the contemporary Islamic ideologies. However, throughout Islamic history, we witness the development of differentiated
religious and political institutions and the prevalence of such distinct
conceptions as religion/politics and religion/the world. I should also
point out that the very outcry of the Islamic fundamentalists against
the separation of religion and politics clearly shows that they do not
have any difficulty in conceiving of religious and political activities
as distinct types of human endeavour. What they want is that the
latter be subjected to the former.

My subject is religion and politics in contemporary Islam, and I
have chosen to focus on what is to me the most interesting aspect
of this topic, namely, the construction of contemporary Islamic
ideologies.

The advocates of Islamic *ideology* understand it to be a
conception of Islam as a total unified socio-political system and a
total way of life based on the full unity of doctrine and practice.
Perhaps the most notable feature of this ideology is its commitment
to the establishment of Islamic government. Did Muslims hold this
conception of Islam during the past thousand or twelve hundred

years? I do not think so. Conceptions approximating the above view of Islam as a total ideology can be found in the Islamic revivalist movements, mostly on the frontiers of Islam – Africa and India – or when and where Islam was seriously threatened by an external force such as the invading Mongols or, more locally, by the Crusaders. I do not wish to deny that Islam, like other world religions, especially those of the ethical type, is and always has been a system of life regulation; nor that the ethical world religions are in a sense the prototypes for the later political ideologies. My point is that the explicit conception and formulation of Islam as a unified system of ideas and a total ideology – and above all the preoccupation with Islamic *government* (or Islamic state) – is a recent development. It has resulted from the spread of political ideologies from the First and the Second to the Third World; it presumes the existence of the modern nation state; it was preceded by Communism and Fascism and bears the imprint of these political ideologies. At the same time, however, the contemporary Islamic ideology is distinctively religious. It incorporates the ethical and legal prescriptions of Islam and bears a striking resemblance to earlier Islamic revivals.

On the religious front, periodic movements of revival are characteristic of Islam since its rise in the seventh century; and movements for orthodox reform – the purging of popular religious practices – have been especially conspicuous since the eighteenth century. On the political front, in the last two centuries, the Muslim world experienced either the establishment of direct western colonial rule, or attempts at the modernization of the state in imitation of the west. Since the Second World War, decolonization, far-reaching national political integration, incorporation of masses into the political society, and greatly increased political participation have all affected the Muslim world.

Historically, movement from the rural periphery into urban centres has been closely associated with the growth of congregational religions. This is true of Islam, as it was of early Christianity. Urbanization has entailed movement into cities with mosques and *madrasas* (seminaries) and thus increased religious orthodoxy and a more rigorous adherence to strict, legalistic Islam. Urbanization has therefore stimulated the movements for orthodox reform in this century. So has the spread of literacy. It has given rise to what Clifford Geertz describes as Islamic spiritualism and others have described as puritanical reformism. Now, it is essential to juxtapose this vitality of Islamic reformism and scripturalism, sustained by urbanization and the spread of literacy, to national political integration and increased political participation in order to understand the contemporary Islamic movements. (It is difficult for us to make this juxtaposition because in the west, the comparable national political integration occurred in the nineteenth and first half of the twentieth centuries when the religious question had been settled and against the background of far-reaching secularization of culture. But we must make the effort to see these two phenomena taking place simultaneously in the Muslim world.) I should also point out that for a long time these two processes were gradually evolving in the same society without being significantly interlinked. For at least a hundred years a variety of entrenched and aspiring political elites who were, and thought of themselves as, Muslims have produced political outlooks and ideologies which were termed Islamic but in which Islam played a subsidiary and sometimes only a decorative role: pan-Islam, Islamic nationalism, justifications of parliamentary democracy in Islamic terms, and finally, Islamic socialism. But the situation has changed in the last two decades, and the two phenomena have become interlinked. National political mobilization and integration have meant that the religious revival of the 1970s and 1980s has become politically conditioned. This political conditioning has entailed the harnessing of the spontaneous vitality of religious sentiment and activities in those settings into an Islamic ideology. The political conditioning of the contemporary religious revival has come about largely through the agency of a specific section of the intelligentsia. A group of lay publicists, journalists, and university students and graduates have created Islamic ideology in contradistinction to the secular political ideologies of liberalism, nationalism, and socialism. A passage from the leader of the Iraqi Muslim Brothers, Sawwaf, should suffice to illustrate the exclusivist intent of the new Islamic traditionalist ideologies:

> I declare frankly that there is no socialism in Islam, nor any Islam in socialism. If socialism is in agreement with Islam on one point, it diverges from it on a thousand. To attribute socialism or democracy or nationalism to Islam is to fool around with it. All these earthly notions are man-made whereas our Islamic Law is celestial and divine, made by the Lord of the human race. (Carré and Michaud 1983: 89)

Orthodox Islamic reformism and Islamic modernism – the attempt to justify western philosophy and political ideologies such as nationalism, democracy, and socialism in Islamic terms – form the immediate background of the emergence of Islamic ideology. Against this background, it would not be too much of an exaggeration to say that the creation of the prototype for all subsequent contemporary Islamic ideologies is the work of one man from the Indo-Pakistan subcontinent – Abu'l-A'la' Mawdudi – who died in 1979. He carried out the basic breakthroughs in the construction of a coherent Islamic political ideology in the period 1925–40 and moved into action in 1941. The Muslim Brotherhood in Egypt was groping in the same direction in that period as well as in the period after the Second World War but did not achieve anything like the same degree of ideological consistency until the 1960s, and under the heavy influence of Mawdudi. The Islamic ideology was then adopted, and given a heavy clericalist twist, by Khomeini's militant mullahs in Iran in the 1970s – incidentally, not only before but also during and after the Islamic revolution.

Both Mawdudi and al-Banna, the founder of the Muslim Brotherhood in Egypt, were deeply religious men, and their movements were fundamentally movements of religious revival. Under the conditions of modern politics, they would inevitably be highly political and increasingly politicized. Nevertheless, I would like to be old-fashioned and stress the primacy of religious motivation in the Islamic movements. It was the inconsistency between this religious motivation and the principles of political organization in the modern nation state which forced them to regard the traditional Islamic patterns of the institutional separation of the religious and political spheres as an aberration from the Prophet model, and to reject the modern idea of separation of religion and the state as a sinister plot by today's colonialist 'trinity': the Jews, Communism, and capitalism (Kepel, 1984: 115).

To demonstrate the primacy of the religious motive, let me quote al-Banna:

> If someone should say to you: This is politics! say; This is Islam, and we do not recognize such divisions. If someone should say to you: You are agents of revolution! say; We are the agents of truth . . . in which we believe and which we exact. . . .
> We summon you to Islam, the teaching of Islam, the laws of Islam and the guidance of Islam, and if this smacks of 'politics' in your eyes, that is our politics. (al-Banna, 1978: 36, 75; translation slightly modified)

Mawdudi conceived the modern world as the arena of the 'conflict between Islam and un-Islam', the latter term being equated with pre-Islamic Ignorance (*jahiliyya*) and polytheism. Modern creeds and political philosophies were assimilated to polytheism and ignorance. Their predominance necessitated the revival of Islam. For him, there was no question of reconciling modern secular philosophies and ideologies with Islam. In fact, Mawdudi considered the Islamic modernists a fifth column determined to corrupt Islam from within. After 1937, Mawdudi was alarmed that Muslims would be seduced away from Islam by nationalism, a false philosophy and a western phenomenon. He did not see, either in nationalism or in liberal democracy, a mechanism for bringing about an Islamic revival. He was equally hostile to Communism and Fascism; but he admired the ability of these movements to instil enthusiasm and commitment in their members, and he found in them an instrument which could be adopted by the Islamic revivalist movement. This instrument was ideology, and Mawdudi set out to create a coherent and consistently Islamic ideology. This new tool of ideology was to be used to affirm the eternal message and mission of Islam. This ideology is propounded in works that Mawdudi refers to as the 'Manifesto' of the Islamic movements (Mawdudi, 1960: 213). It is pervaded by 'Allah's absolute sovereignty' and is diametrically opposed to 'the spirit working at the root of un-Godly civilizations' – that is, 'man's autonomy, unbridled use of freedom and irresponsibility' (Mawdudi, 1963 [1940]: 21). The moral evil of the age consists in having accepted sovereigns other than God, namely, the will of the people (Adams, 1966: 382). From such Qur'anic verses as 'Verily His is the creation and His is the command' (7: 54) Mawdudi concludes that 'it has been definitely laid down in Islam that *de jure* sovereignty belongs to Allah whose *de facto* sovereignty is inherent in the working of the entire universe'; and further, 'that the acceptance and admission of the *de jure* sovereignty of God is *Islam* and its denial is *kufr* (infidelity)' (Mawdudi, 1960: 232–3).

The most novel feature of Mawdudi's ideology is his eventual contention that Islamic revival is impossible without the creation of an Islamic state. The most powerful embodiment of the spirit of un-Godly civilization is the secular state. Without its destruction and replacement by an Islamic state, it is impossible to bring about a revival of Islam; and it may be impossible to assure the survival of Islam – without it, Islam would succumb to the forces of secularization as Christianity had done in western and eastern Europe. It is therefore not surprising that Mawdudi writes a great deal about the Islamic state, consciously conceived as an alternative to the modern secular nation state. He tells us that the Islamic state, dedicated to the creation of the Kingdom of God on earth

> cannot evidently restrict the scope of its activities. Its approach is universal and all-embracing. . . . In such a state no one can regard any field of his affairs as personal and private. . . . Another characteristic of the Islamic state is that it is an ideological state. It is clear from a careful consideration of the Qur'an and the Sunna that the state in Islam is based on an ideology and its objective is to establish that ideology. (Mawdudi, 1960: 154–5)

Furthermore, given its divinely ordained purpose, there will be no oppositional political parties in the Islamic state. Mawdudi then searches for Islamic answers to about a dozen questions considered essential as the organizational principles of the Islamic state, which he infelicitously describes as a 'theo-democracy' (Mawdudi, 1960: 226–70). These include such modern political concepts as citizenship and elections. In the interest of economy, we cannot do better than to quote Mujeeb's (1967: 402–3) succinct summary of Mawdudi's political ideology.

> An Islamic state is not a matter of choice or expediency. It is fundamental to the Islamic way of life. This state, according to Maulana Mawdudi, has to be theo-democratic, with God as the sovereign, His law as the public and private law, with the individual citizen holding the position of His *khalifah* of earth, and helping equally with all other citizens in the maintenance of the *shari'ah*. The political ruler will be elected on the ground of his faith being purest and his conduct most righteous. But any canvassing for election will disqualify him. He will be advised by a Consultative Assembly which shall have no parties. It will make laws in matters not covered by the *shari'ah*, and all matters in which a doubt arises as to whether they are covered by the *shari'ah* or not will be referred to a sub-committee of the Consultative Assembly which shall consist only of *'ulama*. The judges will be appointed by the administration, but as their function will be to decide cases according to the law of God, they will not be subject to any authority after their appointment. Finally, the Islamic state cannot be delimited. It cannot have geographical frontiers. Any Muslim anywhere will be entitled to its citizenship.

Nor should we omit Mujeeb's equally succinct and very telling comment:

> This is a straightforward statement, of the kind that has a fatal attraction for those who are ignorant of political procedure and the facts of political life. (Mujeeb, 1967: 403)

What has not been adequately noted in the recent flood of writings on Islamic fundamentalism is the crucial importance of two factors: (1) the unspoken but assumed conditions of modern politics, especially of the western-inspired political paradigms of the nation state (Zubaida, 1982), and (2) the Marxist-inspired implicit assumption that society must be governed by a total ideology. The first factor is best reflected in Mawdudi's constitutional writings (1960) and in the Constitution of the Islamic Republic of Iran. The second factor is more pervasive and informs all the publicistic Islamic tracts of the new genre. This extensive implicit but unacknowledged western political input into the writings of Mawdudi and those of the subsequent Islamic ideologues in Egypt, Iran, and elsewhere accounts for the radical novelty of the contemporary Islamic ideologies within the Islamic tradition.

In Mawdudi's writings we also see the marriage of Islamic

revivalism and revolutionary ideology, and the appropriation of the modern myth of revolution. Already in 1926, in work which anticipates most of the ideological developments of the last two decades, the youthful Mawdudi had declared: 'Islam is a revolutionary ideology and a revolutionary practice, which aims at destroying the social order of the world totally and rebuilding it from scratch . . . and *jihad* (holy war) denotes the revolutionary struggle'. Furthermore,

> The call of Islam for the unity (*tawhid*) and the worship of God, the One, is not only a theological issue and principle . . . but is in fact a call (*da'wa*) for social revolution, aimed primarily at eradicating those who assumed the throne of divinity and enslaved people. . . .
> The expression 'Muslim' indicates the world revolutionary party established by Islam . . . and anyone believing in this call and truly accepting the responsibilities is a member of the Islamic community (*jama'at*) or the Islamic party . . . called the Party of God (*Hizb Allah*) in the Revelation. (Lerman, 1981: 500–1; translation modified slightly)

It is interesting to note that the method of the Islamic revolution is not domestic politics but the call to the unity of God. In its most perfect form, it has already occurred. It occurred in seventh-century Arabia under Muhammad's leadership. Nevertheless, because of the un-Godly forces threatening Islam, it is time for its renewal. The French revolution occurred under the influence of Rousseau and Voltaire, the Russian revolution under the influence of Marx, and the German National Social revolution under the influence of Nietzsche. 'Exactly in the same way, the Islamic Revolution can be brought about only when a mass movement is initiated on the theories and conceptions of the Qu'ran and the example and practice of Muhammad' (Mawdudi, 1947: 21).

In his account of the history of 'the revivalist movement in Islam', Mawdudi represents the replacement of the Rightly-guided Caliphate by Umayyad dynastic rule in 661 CE as a 'counter-revolution' which marked the return of ignorance, this time 'working its influence in the guise of Islam' (Mawdudi, 1963: 26–7). According to Mawdudi, it is the recurrent resurgence of ignorance which necessitates periodic renewal and underlies the need for successive *mujaddids* (renewers). Renewal (*tajdid*) is thus conceived as the fights against resurgent ignorance and the restoration of pristine Islam. Mawdudi sets the precedent for assimilating all contemporary and modern trends to a pre-Islamic world-view and thus conceiving them as ignorance, ignorance which can only be overcome by the renewal of pristine Islam. The result is a cyclical conception of history diametrically opposed to the western notion of unilinear progress. It incorporates the notion of unilinear progress in the history of religions (in the manner of David Hume) until the perfection of monotheism – that is, until the advent of Islam through the Messengership of Muhammad, the Seal of the Prophets. From then on, there can be no progress but only periodic renewal.

It is worth noting that this preemptive technique of appropriating a modern western political concept such as revolution is typical of the Islamic ideologues in other fields too. In a similar fashion, the philosophy of history implicit in the Qur'an is extracted and offered as the 'Islamic' philosophy of history (Haddad, 1982); evolutionism is admitted but is said to be typical both of the biological and the spiritual realm, with the spiritual evolution being said to complement biological evolution and to culminate in the coming of Islam (Taleghani, 1982: 155–76); freedom is reaffirmed but true freedom is said to be possible only in absolute submission to the will of God; alienation as the plight of modern man is to be overcome by the rediscovery of the true self as God's obedient servant (Asghari, 1984).

In the face of the aggressively secularist policies of the Middle Eastern states in the 1960s and 1970s, the Islamic ideologies elsewhere also appropriated the modern political myth of revolution and became revolutionary ideologies. At the same time, the Islamic revolutionary movements acquired some of the features of sectarian puritanism vowed to affirm Islam against its corrupt internal enemies. The most important figure in this new development is Sayyid Qutb, whose radical ideas were forged in Nasser's prisons and concentration camps. By this time, Fascism had long dropped out of the picture and Marxism had become predominant as the adversary ideology against which the Islamic ideology had to be constructed. This is clearly reflected in the substance of the writings of the Islamic ideologues in Egypt and in Iran. Interestingly, it often originated in the intense debates between the Marxists and the Islamic militants in the prisons of Nasser (Carré and Michaud, 1983: 75) and the Shah. Furthermore, in sharp contrast to the earlier grudging admiration for western political ideas, the new period was marked by the increasing conviction of the bankruptcy of east and west, of capitalism and socialism. Under these circumstances, it is not surprising that the God of Sayyid Qutb is truly a jealous God, even more so than Mawdudi's; jealous of the believers' submission to the autonomous secular state and its ruler, and jealous of this seduction by western cultural influences (Haddad, 1983: 26–8).

Qutb takes the contrast between Islam and un-Islam, conceived as ignorance, from Mawdudi and makes it the cornerstone of his radical Islamic ideology. He sharply diverges from the thought of his forerunner, the Supreme Guide of the Muslim Brothers, Hasan al-Banna, by branding contemporary Egyptian society as un-Islamic, as a society of ignorance (Kepel, 1984: 48). Furthermore, he diverges from the constitutional niceties of Mawdudi's thought, building a theory of an Islamic state almost exclusively on the stark contrast between Islam and ignorance.

Let us begin with a brief exposition of Qutb's idea of a society of ignorance. According to him, the true Islamic community of believers (*umma*) 'has ceased to exist since nowhere on the earth are men governed according to the Law of God'. Thus, 'in our times, the entire world lives in the state of Ignorance'. 'All society which is not *de facto* Muslim . . . , all society where men worship an object other than God and Him alone is in Ignorance. . . . Thus, we must include in this category all the societies which exist on earth in our time.' This is the case even with societies which recognize God but limit his jurisdiction to the heavens. Even though such a society allows individuals to worship God in synagogues, churches, and mosques, it forbids the proclamation that divine law regulates its existence. 'Thus, it denies or renders ineffective the divine quality of God on earth. . . . Owing to this, it is [still] a society of Ignorance' (Kepel, 1984: 46, 49, 53).

To extirpate ignorance from society, an Islamic government (*hakimiyya*; Mawdudi's neologism) has to be established and the Sacred Law applied:

> Society of Ignorance is all society other than Islamic society. . . . [Societies of Ignorance] do not believe in the divinity of God alone and confer divine attributes to others than Him by allowing the exercise of sovereignty (*hakimiyya*) to others than Him. . . . [It cannot be claimed:] this is the law of God except when the sovereignty of God is effectively declared and when the source of all public power is God Most High and He alone, and not 'the people' nor 'the party' nor any human being, and when, finally, this sovereignty refers to the Book of God and the Tradition of the Prophet so as to ascertain the will of God.

To establish Islamic government, Islamic revolution is necessary:

> The total revolution against sovereignty of human beings in all forms and all institutions, total rebellion everywhere on our earth, the hunting down of all usurpers of divine sovereignty who rule men by laws emanating from themselves; this means the destruction of the kingdom of man for the benefit of the kingdom of God on earth. . . . No more liberation of the Arab man by Islam, no more 'mission' for the Arabs, but man as such, the entire human race.
>   . . . Furthermore, the Muslim struggle is also a defensive war: defense of man against all that alienates his freedom and blocks his liberation, until such time that the kingdom of the Sacred Law (*shari'a*) upon the human race is installed. (Carré and Michaud, 1983: 94–7)

Qutb's prominent follower, Mrs Zaynab al-Ghazali, is more succinct:

> No Islam without the restoration of the Islamic Law and without government (*hukm*) according to the Book of God and the Tradition of His Prophet. (Carré and Michaud, 1983: 96)

The Party of God is to eradicate ignorance (*jahiliyya*) and to establish an Islamic society (Sivan, 1985). To this end, revolutionary armed struggle to overthrow un-Godly rule and to establish an Islamic government are preliminary steps. This last step, and the advocacy of Islamic government and Islamic revolution by Qutb, produced a split in the Islamic movement in Egypt in the late 1960s. It is interesting that the moderates who chose to continue their mission within the framework of existing states pointed out that the essential concepts of Qutb's and Mawdudi's political theories – terms such as sovereignty/government (*hakimiyya*) and *ubudiyya* (the state of the worshipper) – are neologisms not found in the Qur'an, and are used in a very different sense from terms from the same roots in the Qur'an and Traditions.

Whereas al-Banna had been careful to distinguish between laws and government, Qutb's key concept of the exclusive sovereignty (*hakimiyya*) of God is both judiciary and political. In 1969, in a tract significantly entitled *Preachers, Not Judges (du'ah la qudah)*, the Supreme Guide of the Muslim Brothers, Hudaybi, challenged this conflation without, however, naming Qutb. Speaking of individuals who, armed with the concept of *hakimiyya* of God and its alleged implications, maintain that whoever acts and thinks otherwise is opposed to God's sovereignty, Hudaybi stated:

> We are certain that the term *hakimiyya* cannot be found in any Verse of the Qur'an, and in the course of our research in the authentic Traditions of the Prophet we have found no mention of this term anywhere except to add to the absolute superiority and transcendence of our Lord God (Carré and Michaud, 1983)

This view of the sovereignty of God is therefore erroneous. *A fortiori*, it cannot be a part of the profession of faith. To be a Muslim, all that is needed is the utterance of the formula for the profession of faith – 'There is no God but God and Muhammad is His Messenger'. There are certainly Muslims who sin, but one cannot excommunicate a Muslim on that ground. Furthermore,

> What we need to know is what is permitted and what is forbidden. This we can know by consulting the texts. All this clearly has no relation to the existence or non-existence of an 'Islamic government'. (Carré and Michaud, 1983: 98–9).

Hudaybi is right. The root *h.k.m.* denotes justice and wisdom, and the term *hukuma* in classical Arabic refers to the administration of justice. In the medieval period the term, usually in its Persian form *hukumat*, came to be used in the sense of governorship. However, the use of the term in the sense of 'government' dates only from the nineteenth century (Lewis, 1982: 417). The advocates of Islamic revolution have played on the two senses of *hukm*, the old and the new, to arrive at their notion of Islamic government as the government and exclusive sovereignty of God. Such Qur'anic phrases as 'the judgement (*hukm*) is but God's' (6: 57; 12: 40, 67), 'His is the judgement (*hukm*)' (6: 62; 28: 70, 88), and 'He who does not judge (*yahkum*) by what God has revealed is an unbeliever' (5: 44), are taken to refer not to the judgement but to the 'government' of God as the absolute political sovereign.

That Qutb's condemnation of society at large fosters a sectarian attitude akin to that of the Kharijites – the earliest sectarians who broke away from the Muslim community in the mid-seventh century – should already be clear. Nevertheless, let me illustrate this tendency by one last direct quotation:

> When there are three believers touched by faith, the credo means this to them: 'Now you are a society, an Islamic society independent of and separate from the society of Ignorance which has no faith in the credo. . . .'
> What characterizes the Islamic credo and the society it inspires is being a movement (*haraka*) which does not allow anybody to keep apart . . . ; the struggle is continuous and the holy war lasts until the Day of Judgement. (Kepel, 1984: 55)

The sectarian attitude grew considerably stronger in the decades following Sayyid Qutb's execution in 1966. The Shah and Sadat were likened to the Pharaoh as the earthly claimants to divinity and opposed to Almighty God; and the Ba'ath – the ruling party in Syria and Iraq – has been likened to the Mongols. This sectarian spirit is nicely captured by the name given to one Egyptian Islamic revolutionary group *Takfir wa'l-hijra* – excommunication [of society at large] and withdrawal [from corrupt society on the model of the Prophet].

The new sectarians conceive themselves as the Party of God engaged in revolutionary struggle against the Party of Satan. Here is an Islamic ideologue writing in 1977:

> Some people today divide the world into democratic or fascist [systems], labor or liberal parties. Islam does not recognize any parties except two: the Party of God and the Party of Satan. The Party of God are those who act as His agents on earth and govern by His laws. The others are the Party of Satan – whatever variation there may be in their system of

government and regardless of the conflict among them. In the end, they are one coalition formed to oppose God the Mighty, the Omnipotent. (Haddad, 1983: 28)

The spirit of sectarian militancy, neo-Kharijism, reaches its culmination in a work by the engineer M.A.S. Faraj, *The Hidden Obligation*, which inspired Sadat's assassins:

One thing is certain: the tyrants of this world do not disappear except by the force of the sword. . . . The establishment of Islamic government is an obligation denied by some Muslims and neglected by others; nevertheless, proofs on the topic of the obligation to establish [Islamic] government are multiple. . . . And if [Islamic] government cannot be installed except through fighting (*qital*), then the latter is our duty. . . .

In our time, the rulers modify what God has revealed. They apply impious legislations, legal systems conceived by impious infidels. [Reference to Qur'an, 5: 44] After the definitive abolition of the Caliphate in 1924 and the suppression of the Islamic legal system in its entirety – which system is replaced by the positive laws of the infidels – the situation resembles the Tartar period. The present rulers of the Muslims are in a state of apostasy. . . . They pretend to be Muslims, and the Sunna insists that the fact and legal consequences of apostasy are different from those of infidelity by birth. The apostate must be killed, even if he is not in a state to wage war. . . .

To want to begin by fighting imperialism is useless and futile, a complete waste of time. We must concentrate on our Muslim problem, namely to establish the Law of God in our own countries before all else, and to subordinate everything in them to the cause of God. (Carré and Michaud, 1983: 102)

Surprising as it may seem, the wave of revolutionary Islamic ideologizing did not reach Iran until the early 1970s. Until then, the field had been dominated by orthodox reformism – represented, notably, by the late Ayatollah Taleqani – and Islamic modernism – represented by Bazargan. In a work entitled *The Evolutionary Revolution of Islam (Enqelab-e Takamoli-ye Eslam)* published in 1970, the lay Islamic ideologue Jalal al-Din Farsi attempted to appropriate the modern political myth of revolution in a manner entirely derivative from Mawdudi. The rise of Islam is described as a 'religio-ethical', 'political-economic', and military revolution. The term *counter-revolution* is predictably used to refer to the Umayyad opposition to ʿAli, and the method of analysis is contrasted to dialectical materialism. Nevertheless, Farsi uses the term *nation* (*mellat*) rather than the *community of believers* (*ummat*), and characterizes the new political regime installed by the Islamic Revolution as a 'constitutional republic' (Farsi, 1970: 116–53). The distinctively clericalist Iranian (Shiite) idea of Islamic government, to be realized by the Revolution of 1979, was the work not of lay publicists but of a religious leader, Ayatollah Khomeini.

In or about 1970, Khomeini began to lecture on Islamic government. The term he used, *hukumat*, was not a neologism like Qutb's *hakimiyya*. To the ordinary speakers of Persian it simply meant *government*, and only the learned knew its older judiciary connotations. Khomeini's argument, though a radical innovation in Shiite history, was nevertheless stated in the traditional Shiite frame of reference and did not betray any influence of the ideological innovations of Mawdudi and Qutb. It simply extended the general judiciary authority of the jurist (*faqih*), as well as some of his very specific rights of gerency, to comprehend the right to rule (Calder, 1982; Arjomand, 1988: ch. 8).

Nevertheless, Mawdudi and Qutb were read avidly, in Persian translation and/or in Arabic, by Khomeini's militant followers; and their influence is unmistakable in the revolutionary slogans and pamphleteering, most notably in the application of the term *taghut* (earthly idol or false god) to the Pahlavi political order. This influence has become more pronounced since the elimination of the moderates and Islamic modernists in 1980–1, and is easily noticeable in the speeches of the political elite of the Islamic Republic of Iran.

Khomeini's 'sovereignty of the jurist' is on some crucial points in sharp contrast to Mawdudi's 'theo-democracy'. Nevertheless, it is at least equally Islamic; and is all the more easily accepted as such because it is so proclaimed by the Shiite hierocracy. In fact, Ayatollah Safi (1982) has no difficulty whatsoever in combining the advantages of the ideologies of Mawdudi and Qutb with the clericalist ideas of Khomeini. The government of the jurist on behalf of the Hidden Imam is the true government of God on earth, vowed to the implementation of His Law. All other political regimes are un-godly orders, regimes of ignorance, and of *taghut*. The Islamic revolution will continue until the overthrow of all these regimes (Safi, 1982: 16–18). Meanwhile,

> The refusal to associate others with God (*shirk*) means this: that [the believer] should not accept political regimes and rulers other than the regime of Imamate, which is the divine political order, and should not posit partners for the Imams who are the leaders of this order and have authority in affairs on behalf of God. (p. 19)

This argument assumes that the supreme jurist who rules on behalf of the last of the Imams, the Hidden Imam, and who has assumed the title of Imam himself, can somehow do all this without being posited as a partner for God. Not so a secular ruler, who is inevitably made a partner to God by anyone who accepts the non-theocratic regime over which he presides.

Conclusion

My opening remarks were intended to suggest that we would not go very far in our understanding of contemporary Islamic movements by looking for essential and unchanging relationships between religion and politics in Islam. The ensuing analysis accordingly highlighted the novel aspects of contemporary Islamic ideologies. In conclusion, let us sketch this changing face of Islam in broader strokes.

The distinctiveness of the contemporary movements in Islamic history is due to the centrality of *ideology* and to their preoccupation with the Islamic state, or more accurately, with the definition of the state in Islamic terms. This novelty is the result of the process of national integration and the enlargement of political society, and consists in the adaptation of the ideological form and the substantive appropriation of such modern political notions as democratic government, constitution and revolution. These new political ideas are grafted on to the old Islamic dichotomies of (monotheistic) Islam/(polytheistic) Ignorance and the community of believers/infidels to form distinctively Islamic total ideologies.

Contemporary Islamic ideologies vary according to the relative salience of constitutional government versus revolution, and according to the definition of un-Islam and the corresponding identification of the infidel enemies. The radicalization of Islamic movements in the past two decades has meant a shift of emphasis to revolution at the expense of constitutional government, hand in hand with the broadening of the definition of the infidels and apostates to include internal Muslim enemies. The Islamic activists have become more revolutionary and more sectarian. This makes the occurrence of Islamic revolutions possible but not inevitable. In Iran, the Shah's regime collapsed, and the Islamic movement could destroy the secular political order that it rejected, replacing it by an Islamic theocracy. Where this has not been possible but where the Islamic groups have nevertheless gained a strong voice in government, as in Pakistan and the Sudan, they have de-emphasized the sectarian rejection of the larger society and the necessity of revolution, and have reached mutual political accommodation with de-secularizing states. By contrast, where the Islamic groups have been denied access to political power, as in Egypt, they have maintained their sectarian rejection of the existing society and their revolutionary commitment to the overthrow of the secular state.

Note

An expanded version of this chapter will appear as Chapter 14 of the author's

Tradition, Millenarianism and Revolution in Islam. London: Oxford University Press (forthcoming).

References

Adams, C.J. (1966) 'The Ideology of Mawlana Mawdudi', in D.E. Smith (ed.), *South Asian Politics and Religion.* Princeton, NJ: Princeton University Press, pp. 371–97.
al-Banna, H. (1978) *Five Tracts of Hasan Al-Banna (1906–1949)*, C. Wendell (trans.), University of California Publications, Near Eastern Studies, vol. 20. Berkeley, CA: University of California Press.
Arjomand, S.A. (ed.) (1988) *Authority and Political Culture in Shi'ism.* Albany, NY: SUNY Press.
Asghari, M. (1984) 'Azadi chist?' *Ettela'at*, Bahman 1, 1362.
Calder, N. (1982) 'Accommodation and Revolution in Imam Shi'i Jurisprudence; Khumayni and the Classical Tradition', *Middle Eastern Studies*, 18(1): 3–20.
Carré, O. and G. Michaud (1983) *Les Frères Musulmans.* Paris: Gallimard/Julliard.
Farsi, J. (1970/1349) *Enqelab-e Takamoli-ye Eslam.* Tehran: Asia.
Haddad, Y.Y. (1982) *Contemporary Islam and the Challenge of History.* Albany, NY: SUNY Press.
Haddad, Y.Y. (1983) 'The Qur'anic Justification for Revolution: the View of Sayyid Qutb', *The Middle Eastern Journal*, 37 (1): 14–29.
Kepel, G. (1984) *Le Prophète et Pharaon.* Paris: La Découverte.
Lerman, E. (1981) 'Mawdudi's Concept of Islam', *Middle Eastern Studies*, 17(4): 492–509.
Lewis, B. (1982) 'Hukûmet and Devlet', *Belleten*, C.XLVI. Ankara: Turk Tarih Kurumu Basimevi), 415–21.
Mawdudi, A.A. (1947) *Process of Islamic Revolution.* Pathankdt, Punjab: Maktab-e Jamaat-e Islami.
Mawdudi, A.A. (1960) *Islamic Law and Constitution*, Kh. Ahmad (trans.), 2nd edn. Karachi, Lahore, Dacca: Islamic Publications Ltd.
Mawdudi, A.A. (1963) *A Short History of the Revivalist Movement in Islam*, Al-Ash'ari (trans.). Lahore: Islamic Publications Ltd, 1st edn, 1940.
Mujeeb, M. (1967) *The Indian Muslims.* London: Allen & Unwin.
Safi, L. (1982) *Nezam-e Emamat va Rahbari.* Tehran: Bonyad-e Be'that.
Sivan, E. (1985) *Radical Islam: Medieval Theology and Modern Politics.* New Haven and London: Yale University Press.
Taleghani, S.M. (1982) *Society and Economics in Islam: Writings and Declarations of Ayatullah Sayyid Mahmud Taleqani*, R. Campbell (trans.). Berkeley, CA: Mizan Press.
Zubaida, S. (1982) 'The Ideological Conditions for Khomeini's Doctrine of Government', *Economy and Society*, 11(2): 138–72.

7

Islam as a New Religious Movement in Malaysia

Daniel Regan

This chapter takes shape around a simple, but hopefully not simplistic, question: how might the more 'cult-like' segments of Islamic resurgence in Malaysia be distinguishable from, say, the Hare Krishna movement in the United States? It is avowedly a western, and non-Muslim, question, although one, I hope to show, with social scientific implications for the study of new religious movements (NRMs). An 'insider' to Malaysia or to Islam would be unlikely to raise, or care about raising, a question with such a putatively 'obvious' answer; as a well-known Malay-Muslim philosopher once said to me, why should he bother spending his time, even part of his time, as an Occidentalist, and thus doing the Judaeo-Christian west's work for itself? And if raised, the Muslim answer to our comparative question would most likely point to the advantages of an Islamic system said to constitute its natural superiority, and hence its appeal.

To a comparative problem such as this one, however, an adequate social scientific answer – at least a western social scientific answer[1] – must be more relativistic; it cannot remain satisfied with an explanation grounded in the valuation of a particular belief system, however complete and satisfying a life plan or blueprint Islam provides those who embrace it. The major thesis of this chapter is that the movement of Islamic resurgence in Malaysia differs from other religious movements less in terms of the doctrinal distinctiveness of Islam – although it certainly exists – or in terms of the characteristics of the movement itself (actually, it exhibits some striking similarities to other religious movements) than in its specific 'mode of insertion' (Beckford, 1985) in Malaysian society. In a real sense, it is the society within which the movement is embedded, and specifically the apparatus of the state, perhaps more than the particular activities of movement members themselves, which 'makes' Islamic resurgence what it is, and gives it its meaning. The implication is that analyses of new religious movements might well focus less on the mechanisms of recruitment, 'conversion', and the like than on the wider society which facilitates, then decries, a movement's existence.

This chapter contains a secondary analysis of Islamic resurgence in Malaysia. No new empirical information is uncovered or reported in these pages;[2] nor is the attempt here to break new ground by promulgating a novel conceptual scheme to analyse the many varieties of new religious movements, including Islamic ones, which have become a matter of intense scrutiny among sociologists of religion. This chapter does seek to gain insight into religious developments in predominantly Muslim, but multi-ethnic and multi-religious, Malaysia by applying a conceptual framework – the analysis of NRMs, as developed by Beckford (especially 1985) and others – which is new to the study of Islamic resurgence in South-east Asia. In addition, the attempt is to extend and test the utility of NRM analysis by bringing a new case, that of Malaysian Islam, beneath its conceptual umbrella. Thus the strategy is to examine available information in a slightly different light by merging two bodies of heretofore disparate literature: one, on NRMs, which is analytic and focused, if anywhere, on North American and western European cases of religious movements of Asian provenance, and the other, on resurgent Islam in Malaysia, which is descriptive, at times even atheoretical, and specific to South-east Asia.

Islam as an NRM in Malaysia and ISKCON/USA

If one is willing to grant for the moment that comparing ISKCON (International Society for Krishna Consciousness) in America to segments of the Islamic movement in Malaysia might be valid, then what sorts of resemblances might be detected between these otherwise dissimilar movements? Certainly the experiences of movement members – one is tempted to say 'converts' even in the Islamic case since the thrust of the *dakwah* movement has been to return somewhat lapsed members, by strict standards, to the fold – bear similarities with respect to the variety of religious practices and life-style restrictions which unite them with fellow 'devotees' and separate them, to varying degrees both within and between movements, from the society at large.

Do's and don'ts: take, for instance, the statement of eight vows, quoted by Rochford (1985: 12–13), which is posited for new male recruits in the Los Angeles ISKCON community. The first and sixth enjoin specific prayer rituals, the centrality and intensity of which are certainly matched by Malaysia's new–old Muslims. Two more (numbers 2 and 8) refer to food prohibitions; besides the usual Islamic taboos, revitalized Islam in Malaysia is marked by a thoroughgoing concern for extremely rigorous standards of ritual purity when it comes to food. The third vow forbids illicit sexual relations, while, in the Islamic case, the totality of restrictions upon heterosexual contact, much less 'illicit sex', is one of the most frequently noted aspects of the contemporary resurgence.

ISKCON's early members, only a small minority of whom report no prior drug use, came disproportionately from drug-infused segments of western counter-culture (Rochford, 1985: 60–8); for them, adherence to the ban against intoxicants (vow number 4) represents a renunciation of their former life style as well as a symbolic break with the immediate world around them. Although many of Malaysia's newly fervent Muslims, like Krishna devotees, appear to be 'God-intoxicated', orthodox Islam has always frowned upon foreign, intoxicating substances. Koranically, the idea of being a Muslim (that is, 'one who submits [to God]') can only follow from lucidity: that is, from a clear-headed examination of the 'evidence' followed by a conscious decision, re-enacted each day through prayer, to declare one's faith. Hence anything which clouds the senses and robs one of the capacity to make such a decision must be abjured. All this is well known, but the Islamic movement goes further in its emphasis on an environment which is free from drugs. Segments of it, especially the retreatist, communal Darul Arqam, like ISKCON, attempt particularly to rehabilitate and recruit Malay urban youth with drug dependencies (Nagata, 1984: 110). This is intended to demonstrate the practical superiority of an Islamically-based way of life over the state's on-again, off-again version of establishment Islam. Such a demonstration compels attention in a society for which drugs have been defined officially as the number one security problem, followed (interestingly) by 'religious extremism', and only then by the threat of Communist subversion.

As for other intoxicants, such as alcoholic ones, which are banned by the Krishna movement, Islamic resurgents also denounce their consumption, as part of a campaign against the alleged laxity of modern urban life. Alcohol, seen as alien and western, also serves as one convenient symbol for the charges of corruption levelled at Malay-Muslim, especially governmental, elites. These accusations are of two kinds and are substantiated by different forms of evidence: one alleges economic corruption and pursues its claims by pointing to self-aggrandizing behaviour on the part of administrators and National Front (the ruling coalition), especially UMNO (United Malays National Organization, the coalition's leading party) politicians; the other condemns moral 'corruption' and pursues its claims by exposing elements of elite life styles seen as immoral and un-Islamic. The very availability of alcohol at government functions, in deference to the tastes of non-Muslims in attendance, has also become a target. For the resurgents, alcohol in that setting conveniently epitomizes not only the willingness of authorities in the secular government to consort with non-Muslim elites but also, more significantly, their lack of commitment to an Islamic way of life, much less an Islamic state juridically regulated by the *syariah*.

That leaves Hare Krishna vows number 5, proscribing gambling, and number 7, prescribing certain religiously inspired garments as part of an overall dress code, to be compared with the behavioural forms of Islamic resurgence in Malaysia. Gambling, especially that which goes on under government auspices, and even lotteries have come under fire for encouraging, one supposes, the view that certain social institutions obey the laws of chance, not of God, and work through fate rather than divine plan. (On the other hand, arguing that certain big winners had been divinely selected might be more objectionable still!)

As for dress, members of the three major, non-governmental religious organizations associated with a *dakwah* or evangelical orientation, as well as many who are more loosely aligned with the 'movement', place considerable stock in outward symbols of inner commitments. For them, as for their ISKCON counterparts, religion is not solely a personal, inner commitment, but one which also requires external rituals and other behaviours, including boundary markers which identify members as belonging to a religious community. In both instances, obviously, adopting a unique style of dress also serves to set that community apart from the, as yet, less enlightened.

The particular styles of clothing adopted – Arab-inspired in the Malaysian case and Indian in the other – also point up a similarity between the two movements. Both freely borrow cultural items, imagined or real, from their respective religious centres. And elements of the Krishna Consciousness movement, like some Arabist elements of Islamic resurgence, seem even more clearly removed from their cultural origins. Of course this is not to deny the immeasurably deeper roots that Islam has in Malaysia compared to Hinduism in the United States. The point is only that both movements share a predilection for importing selected cultural items, such as dress and eating styles, into the spiritual 'periphery' which their respective societies represent. Each movement, that is, possesses elements which are far from autochthonous and which, in fact, represent a rejection of traditional, indigenous roots – in the Malaysian case, of a peasant, pre-Islamic, and Indic past in favour of a purer, less syncretic Islamic future.

Like most centre–periphery relations, the Arab–Malaysian connection which Islamic resurgence has highlighted may be difficult to sustain at times. It is fraught with tension, despite well-established ties dating back several centuries, via the pilgrimage and other means which have linked Malaysia to West Asian centres of Islam. The tension is injected by temporal matters – the ideological, religious, not to mention military disputes of West Asian states tend to be reflected in the divided external sympathies of Malaysia's faithful – and by the ambivalence of Malay-Muslims outside the movement proper towards the Arab world in general. Arabs are revered for their proximity and longstanding connection to the sacred centre of universal Islam. Their struggle against Israel strikes a chord among Malaysia's Muslims; just as earlier defeats had brought sorrow, so the 1973 Egyptian victory brought joy and pride to Malay-Muslim circles. On the other hand, Arabs are sometimes resented for their apparent domination of Islamic civilization, at least in the eyes of outsiders to it, despite forming only a small minority of Muslims world-wide. On occasion, as well, they are reviled for what is perceived as arrogance and worse.[3] One doubts that such sentiments, although much attenuated and decidedly out of fashion in the current climate of resurgence, have vanished entirely.

The ambivalence is akin to that which Rochford (1985) reports for members of the American Krishna movement towards Indians resident in the United States who are aligned, often rather loosely, with Hare Krishna. They are looked to for financial support, but occasionally denounced for their material involvement and success in American society which makes possible those monetary contributions. They are admired for their connection to the larger Hindu tradition with which ISKCON seeks increasingly to align itself, but are criticized for their greater allegiance to Hinduism than to ISKCON as an organization.

Other similarities: so far the comparison between Islam as an NRM in Malaysia and ISKCON/USA, with respect to their members' practices and life-style restrictions, has yielded an analytic draw. Are there other salient points of comparison? Members of both groups – the more 'cult-like' segments of the movement for Islamic resurgence in Malaysia and the Society for Krishna Consciousness in the United States (and elsewhere)[4] – are youthful and tend to be products of what the novelist Salman Rushdie calls hybrid cultures. As such, in each case the search for purity is a way out of an unsatisfying experience with hybridity. It is not a return to long-submerged roots, since in neither case is the religious style which members adopt particularly 'authentic'. That is, the apparently 'traditional' character of each religious movement is, for its members, far from traditional; it is something new, conscious, deliberate – part of the culture of modernity which participants in both movements decry.

To focus on the Malaysian case, Malay-Muslim culture has always been hybrid and highly cosmopolitan, a crucible which fuses a varied set of cultural elements – the 'great' traditions of Islam and parts of the Judaeo-Christian west along with the 'little' tradition of South-east Asia's peasantry. Because Malaysia is located at the crossroads of important trade routes, it has for centuries been open to a wide array of cultural influences. What is noteworthy is that, now, a mostly youthful generation of Malay-Muslims has come to experience hybridity as unsatisfying, unrewarding, and constricting, not liberating. As migrants from village to city, or as students living an enclave existence, their exposure to western culture may have been too partial to reap its fruits; besides, such an act of cultural borrowing is replete with overtones of intellectual and cultural dependency. The immersion in Islam has similarly seemed too incomplete and, as for their 'own', peasant-based culture, it carries little weight in a national or international arena. So, for intellectuals and youth, greater immersion in Islam has provided a satisfying solution to problems of identity and dependence. Through Islam, Malay-Muslims can participate in a universal tradition without paying the price of a nagging intellectual or cultural dependency upon the west.

Before linking their personal futures to a collective Islamic 'movement', they may have found their own lives, and western models for changing them, wanting in several respects. Precisely because of the shortcomings that they sense and act to redress, their participation in the resurgence is born of choice, and not solely of anxiety. This is a point some observers have found difficult, if not vexing. V.S. Naipaul (1981), for instance, meets Muslim after newly strengthened Muslim to whom he imputes extreme anxiety as the factor which explains their renewed fervour. But the anxiety is much more the author's than his informants'; he cannot fathom the choice they have made. As we have seen, however, their choice, while not inevitable, does make sense in terms of providing solutions for problems of spiritual and cultural identity. In this sense too, young Muslim resurgents resemble their Hare Krishna counterparts. Unlike Hare Krishna, however, or so I shall argue, the movement for Islamic resurgence in Malaysia, although severely hemmed in by the primarily identity aspirations of many ordinary members and by state attempts to constrain it and instead co-opt the cause of Islam as its own, possesses much greater political power. By this, following Beckford (1987: 27) via Lukes, I mean the power 'to define situations, to affect the course of events, and, above all, to gain a hearing for religious testimony, declarations, and directions': in short, 'the capacity to set the agenda, i.e., to decide what will, and what will not, count as relevant topics for consideration or criteria for evaluation'.

These differences remain to be addressed. For now, however, it is worth noting that, in attaining their individual and collective aspirations, both organized Islam and the Hare Krishna movement benefit from their links to world-transforming, 'parent' movements of a global or at least supra-national nature. This is another major point of similarity between them. Islamic resurgence (like ISKCON) is not at all the same from one country to another. It is home-grown, with its global themes and emphases refracted according to the possibilities (and constraints) of particular cultural contexts, and with the realization of especially local aspirations in mind.

But the foregoing is not at all incompatible with a complex set of international connections from which various wings of the movement draw considerable strength. Different versions of radical Islam vie for Malaysian supporters. Khomeini's Iran provides a model of Islamic totalism. Qadhdhafi's Libya proffers an alternative model (and sometimes much else) which is no less appealing to some resurgents. And the state, attempting to diffuse the potential impact of such ties, cements its own state-to-state relations with Iran and with Libya, and taps the financial resources of conservative Saudi Arabia for assistance. Much attention has been paid to these connections (for example, Gunn, 1986) and to the embeddedness of contemporary Malaysian Islam in an international, and not exclusively domestic, context, so that little more needs to be added here. Clearly, participants in Malaysia's Islamic resurgence situate their activities, as do ISKCON members, within the context of a global movement.[5]

With their international ties to bolster them, organized Islam as well as ISKCON/USA become more potent 'weapons of the weak' (Scott, 1985; also, Buttel, 1987, and Nagata, 1987). Other versions of Hinduism and of Islam serve more clearly as instruments of economic and ideological domination; resurgent Islam, Hare Krishna, and other NRMs do not appear to do so in the eyes of most of their members who, in some way and for whatever reason, feel themselves to be marginal. If movement leaders are busy contending for power, generally their rank-and-file members pursue more modest goals of self-esteem and recognition. But resurgent Islam in Malaysia has another, incompletely realized constituency, which makes its potential highly significant: besides appealing to those whose sense of disadvantage may be a matter of relative deprivation, though no less real for that, this multivoiced Islamic movement carries with it the possibility of forging links, through connections with the party of Islamic opposition (PAS), to the objectively marginalized of Malaysian society.

State responses to NRMs

Despite differences in their belief systems, their geographical locations and the length of time they have been there, the outward appearance of their members, and their respective civilizational underpinnings, Islam as an NRM in contemporary Malaysia and ISKCON/USA possess several underlying similarities – and more might be noted[6] – which make it possible to discuss them in one analytic breath. At some point, however, their commonalities end and the Islamic movement acquires a more public and political meaning.

Why? To answer this it would be easy to take the movement's own overarching religious philosophy as descriptive of the path it comes to take: Islam always seeks to realize itself institutionally, contains no distinction between the sacred and the secular, is ultimately political, and so on. Although there is obviously truth in the identification of these as Islamic principles, it would be misleading to pinpoint them as the core reasons for the different trajectory that this movement assumes, compared to ISKCON and other NRMs. In our search for an answer, it is one thing to weigh the effect of the Word upon believers; to consider it determinative, however, would be going too far and would ignore the multiplicity of ways such general dicta have been implemented by Muslims throughout Islamic history. It would be similarly misleading to assume that movement leaders successfully translate the public goals they proclaim into programmatic initiatives which energize the membership as a whole. More likely there is considerable slippage in implementing the goals which are articulated by the leadership, and even foot-dragging on the part of members in such a loosely structured movement. This suggests that the reasons behind the political meaning of Islamic resurgence in Malaysia cannot be sought primarily in the rhetoric of its leaders.

Rather than seek a political theory of Islam which would apply, or assume a smooth translation of leadership goals into movement actions, here we focus upon the societal – and intertwined with it the state – response to Islam as an NRM in contemporary Malaysia.[7] It is primarily in this response that we locate the political character of resurgent Islam, and hence its divergence from other NRMs such as Hare Krishna.

In doing so, a few reservations are in order. First of all, even when it comes to the response accorded them, there are some surprising similarities between the Islamic and Krishna movements. Each, for instance, has been the subject of a major legal inquiry investigating the behaviour of its members. Accusations of drug trafficking, copyright infringement, child neglect and molestation have been levelled against members of the large Krishna community at New Vrindaban, West Virginia (*Pittsburgh Post-Gazette*, 20 March (1987), and its powerful leader, Kirtanananda Swami Bhaktipada, stands accused of complicity in the murder of a former devotee and ex-resident of the commune who was his most outspoken critic (*New York Times*, 17 June 1987). In Malaysia, meanwhile, Darul Arqam has been investigated on charges of improperly conducting Islamic marriage rites and thereby sanctioning illicit unions (*Utusan Malaysia*, 16–18 May 1985). The most celebrated case involved the questionable marriage of a well-known singer, Sahara Yaacob, to an Arqam member and her difficulties in securing an official divorce although her former spouse had by then pronounced the required declarations. In the religiously charged atmosphere of present-day Malaysia, these allegations involving the improper assumption of religious authority are serious ones indeed; they made front-page headlines in the national press, just as *Rolling Stone* magazine (9 April 1987) and the *New York Times*, among others, carried exposés of ISKCON which reached a national readership. In addition, the revelations were similar in that each sought to impugn movement members on moral grounds as violators of important mores, thus standing outside the mainstream of their respective societies. Along these lines, besides the criminal charges which I cited previously, the Krishnas have also been accused of 'brainwashing' and the abuse of female devotees. Significantly, it is not the role of the Krishnas in various local economies or political systems which is played up and comes under fire, at least in the press at the national level. Sahara Yaacob, meanwhile, in the Malaysian Arqam case, charged male group members with routinely taking more than one wife, causing the interruption of studies for female students with whom they became involved, and continuing to sleep with women against whom they had already uttered the divorce formulas; her allegations received wide publicity. To a point, therefore, ISKCON and segments of the Islamic movement garner comparable responses: campaigns to delegitimate them are similarly conducted on primarily moral, and not explicitly political, grounds.

The second reservation to our line of argument is that, although the Malaysian government's response has generally been critical, at times even denunciatory, recognizing the Islamic movement as a whole as generally oppositional in character and a major political threat, the relationship between that movement and the state is by no means exhausted or captured by depicting one as condemner and the other as condemned. At times, elements of genuine respect are displayed towards the movement, for the fervour, activism, and dedication of its members. More pragmatically, representatives of the state know they cannot press their criticism too far; it must be measured lest their own commitment to the cause of Islam be questioned by the faithful. Beyond this, through a variety of gestures, the state claims the cause of Islam as its own (Mahathir, 1985; Mauzy and Milne, 1983–4; Mohamad Abu Bakar, 1981; Nagata, 1980b, 1984). Most dramatic (but far from unique) in this regard has been the successful co-optation – some might say 'infiltration' – of Anwar Ibrahim, the erstwhile leader of ABIM, the most influential wing of the Islamic movement, into the ruling coalition's leadership, as UMNO youth leader, now one of the party's three vice-presidents, and into the Cabinet where he now sits as Education Minister.[8]

Thus in several ways resurgent Islam needs the society which it rejects, as well as the state which it hopes to reform and, ultimately, take over. Although not quite the great Satan, as the United States is to Iran, the Malaysian state is rather useful to resurgent, fundamentalist Islam, which needs its ogres, of elite corruption, the opulence of conspicuous consumption counterposed to widespread poverty, moral laxity, and the like (see Chandra Muzaffar, 1986), to contrast to its own claims of high-minded superiority. The regime, too, as has been shown, bears a somewhat contradictory relationship to the movement. Its representatives spawn, yet question it, and permit, yet limit, its activities; and although they are sharply critical of the *dakwah* movement, they also 'need' the threat that that movement presents, to justify the consolidation of their position through a series of increasingly repressive measures (Barraclough, 1984). The Islamic challenge also provides a convenient justification for enacting, in response, several discriminatory policies against non-Malay-Muslims. There has been nothing inevitable or necessarily enduring about the relationship between the Islamic movement and the Malaysian state up to now; but that relationship has been complex, interactive, and dialectical, and not exclusively oppositional.

In spite of these two reservations, there remains a critical divergence from Hare Krishna and other western NRMs in the political character of Malaysia's Islamic movement. Leaving aside the complexities discussed above, there remains an undeniable element of challenge which the movement poses, and hence of criticism and tension in the response of the state. Resurgent Islam cannot be denied a political dimension in the Malaysian context. To put it bluntly, in a stable, low-threat political environment, both internal and external (Noordin Sopiee, 1984), the Islamic movement represents virtually the only realistic political threat.

In the following section, after citing several brief examples of critical responses on the part of the state to the movement for Islamic resurgence, I analyse why, rightly or wrongly, that movement is perceived as a threat.

Consociationalism and the Islamic challenge

The year 1984 was a trying one for the Islamic movement in Malaysia. By the second half of the year, cover stories in Asia-based news weeklies were highlighting 'Malaysia's Islamic Battle' (*Asiaweek*, 14 Sept. 1984). The government had launched its own religious counter-movement in earnest, seeking to contest who would define the intent and methods of Islamic evangelism. Who would be the rightful bearer of the Islamic message and successful wielder of Islamic symbols? As part of the attempt to assure a monopoly for the state-sponsored programme of Islam, various officials levelled a barrage of criticism which, although most often directed explicitly at the opposition PAS, did not fail to implicate, either directly or indirectly, other parts of the movement as well. Although less directly political, they could not escape their ties to PAS or at least sympathies with a portion of PAS's Islamic agenda.

On 1 Syawal, the first of two feast days marking the end of the fasting month, the Prime Minister exhorted Muslims in the country 'to reject extremists and deviationists and to hold fast to the true teachings and spirit of Islam' (*New Straits Times*, 30 June 1984). He went on to describe these 'extremists and deviationists' as 'guided by their arrogance and lustful wishes and not by Islamic rules or doctrine'. By 19 July the Prime Minister, in front-page news, was awaiting a police report on an apparent display of Khomeini's photograph at an Islamic-oriented seminar (*Utusan Malaysia*). Although their participation was later denied by the organizer, members of ABIM, Arqam, and Jemaat Tabligh, the three major non-governmental organizations of the *dakwah* movement, were specifically mentioned as being among the seminar participants. Revelations soon surfaced concerning secondary students, under the influence of the Islamic opposition, who refused to mix with members of other ethno-religious groups, participate in athletics, or sing the national anthem which they regarded as un-Islamic

(*Utusan Malaysia*, 7 Aug. 1984). As the end of August neared, and hence the climactic end-of-month anniversary of independence, the King – standing above politics as symbol of the state and not just of a particular regime or government – used the occasion of an investiture ceremony marking his fifty-second birthday to warn 'against an overzealous interpretation of Islamic values in society, reminding religious groups that coercion and intimidation in the name of Islam are forbidden' (*New Straits Times*, 29 Aug. 1984).

Shortly thereafter, on National Day itself, the King's themes were echoed and developed by the Prime Minister. In a live message on radio and television, Datuk Seri Dr Mahathir Mohamad decried those 'who want to bring an administrative system like that practised in an oligarchy, in communism or in the rule by *mullahs* which they try to portray as the Islamic system. Actually, the rule by *mullahs* is not Islamic. It is in fact anti-Islamic' (*New Straits Times*, 31 Aug. 1984). Mahathir followed this message with a well-publicized speech to hundreds of invited guests who had participated in the nationalist, anti-Malayan Union movement of the late 1940s. Aware of the symbolic value of an audience composed of elderly nationalists, he used the opportunity to criticize PAS supporters who 'exploited Islam as a political instrument, degraded the victory of independence, preaching that the pride of being Malay contradicted Islamic principles'[9] (*New Straits Times*, 1 Sept. 1984).

The new Muslim year of 1405 was rung in with the acting Prime Minister, Datuk Musa Hitam, calling for unity among the *umat*, noting that disunity and internal squabbling would be self-defeating and would even incur 'the curse (*kutukan*) of God' (*Utusan Malaysia*, 26 Sept. 1984). On 29 September claims were aired, again making the front page, that an erroneous and extreme conception of Islamic *jihad* was being conveyed to Malaysian students and youth through their contacts, first-hand and otherwise, overseas (*Utusan Malaysia*, 29 Sept. 1984). And a month or so later the government issued a White Paper on the religious 'threat to Muslim unity and national security'. This remarkable document, published separately, printed in full in the newspapers, and presented to the Malaysian Lower House, is a kind of primer of tactics for the state-sponsored Islamic counter-movement. In it, ABIM, Arqam, and Tabligh are not mentioned explicitly, but PAS 'supporters' and a wide variety of Islamic groups are assailed for helping, directly or indirectly, the banned Communist party of Malaya to achieve its goal of domination.

The White Paper having been tabled in Parliament, the state continued to campaign against religious zealotry. On the occasion of his installation as Malaysia's eighth Yang di-Pertuan Agong, the new King spoke out against extremism and for unity and moderation as the true Islamic way (*Utusan Malaysia*, 16 Nov. 1984). Less than two weeks later the campaign was pushed a step further by 'revelations' that a new Communist wing – the National Malay Revolutionary Party of Malaya (NMRPM) – was using deviationist Islamic teachings spread by extremists to gain power. 'The objective of the NMRPM is to identify itself with groups propagating teachings that seem to champion the Islamic cause', said a front-page article in the government-owned and -controlled press (*New Straits Times*, 28 Nov. 1984). Efforts to discredit non-official Islamic activities did not stop there. The year 1985 began with a blistering, ministerial-level attack on certain 'anti-social' and 'chauvinistic' elements among the overwhelmingly Malay-Muslim student body of the UKM (*Universiti Kebangsaan Malaysia*, the Malaysian National University), a hotbed of Islamic resurgent activity (*Utusan Malaysia*, 23 Jan. 1985). At a mid-year Qur'an reading competition, the theme of which was Muslim unity, there was a verbal barrage aimed by the Deputy Prime Minister at new Islamic groups who were said to isolate themselves arrogantly and to assume that only they were true Muslims so as to divide the ranks of believers (*Utusan Malaysia*, 6 May 1985). Subsequent criticism of Malaysian students overseas (*Utusan Malaysia*, 15 May 1985), who had been influenced by the fundamentalist movement and were then denounced for using Islam to justify only half-hearted attention to their (secular) studies, showed that the campaign against Islam as an NRM was not to abate easily.

To understand the rationale behind such sustained efforts to discredit non-governmental resurgent Islam, and not just the opposition party PAS, one cannot rely too heavily on ministers' statements which offer justifications for each twist and turn of state policy. The reasons for opposition to Islam as an NRM are far from exhausted by official claims of a state duty to quell religious deviationism or stem the potential for civil disorder brought on by Muslim extremists. Instead, it is the political system itself which necessitates attention, to outline the contours of the Islamic challenge to it. And even if whole segments of the Islamic movement largely disavow politics, they cannot escape the political meaning which a nervous state attributes to their activities, nested as they are within an overall loosely structured and multivocal movement.

That political system is 'a version of "consociationalism"' (Milne and Mauzy, 1978: 354), the basic pattern of which is described by Lijphart (1968, 1969), Nordlinger (1972), and others, and its evolution, as has been observed numerous times (for example, von Vorys, 1975), has accommodated the nation's deeply hewn ethno-religious and class cleavages. A formal democracy at a kind of political crossroads, the political system oscillates along the borders of democracy, with authoritarian overtones, and incipient authoritarianism, with a democratic face; as political developments after the lower-class Malay–Chinese violence of 1969 showed, there is a more fluid boundary between the two systems than some theorists have claimed. The state's preoccupation with order and fear of open political wrangling shapes a clear preference for a less competitive and politicized variant of democracy: as one Malaysian said to me when the conversation turned to the subject of parliamentary democracy, 'We took the flour from the English but we'll make the bread *our* way' (*Ambil gandum dari Inggeris, kita buat roti cara kita*). In 1972 a national 'front' emerged out of an agreement between the dominant party and several 'opposition' parties. Opposition strength in Parliament, always weak, further declined as the newly formed 'grand coalition' served to mute the competitive aspects of politics. More recent developments have, if anything, strengthened and sharpened these trends. Despite leadership changes and successions, the top ministers and other officials remain convinced that an intercommunal consensus forged in secrecy among ethnic leaders, and not the open articulation of competing interests, will reduce the threat of violent conflict, ensure political stability, and speed development.

The 'consociation' is formed by a series of carefully planned linkages between and within each of the several vertical blocs which correspond to the major religious and/or ethnic divisions in Malaysia's population. Of these, the blocs of Malay-Muslims and of Malaysian Chinese are politically the most consequential. Although certain state resources go disproportionately to Malay-Muslims, overall, resources are supposed to be allocated by a roughly proportional rather than majoritarian (or 'winner take all') system. This makes unity within an ethno-religious bloc of unusual and paramount importance, and, to this extent, the repeated harping upon this theme in the ministers' statements referred to previously makes good political sense. To achieve the degree of communal unity deemed desirable, leaders must (according to the consociational formula) lead, and followers must follow. In other words, the non-elite members of each bloc are faced with a demand to defer to their respective communal leaders.

The basic blocs or pillars are vertical rather than horizontal because, for this system to work, communal loyalties must transcend social class lines. And according to the thinking of the

National Front, that vertical structure, emphasizing unity, loyalty, hierarchy, and deference, is ideally reproduced within a communally based political party which is a constituent member of the overall coalition. Mass mobilization across ethno-religious lines is strongly discouraged. Instead, decisions are reached by bloc leaders who hammer out intercommunal agreements behind closed doors while the public arena for political association and expression is strictly limited.

Indeed, because this is a 'democracy without consensus' (von Vorys, 1975), additional safeguards are deemed necessary to assure compliance with the informal rules of the political game. These include the superimposition of certain supra-political, national symbols plus repressive measures to restrain the free play of competitive politics. A cloud of uncertainty over what can be said or done with impunity helps keep the citizenry on narrow, safe courses. Finally, the system keeps itself afloat and moving, albeit slowly, by producing certain outputs. Through them – the provision of infrastructure and services, business opportunities, licences, places in land schemes, educational opportunities, and many others – a consociational solution is made palatable to the mass clients of this patronage system writ large.

From this somewhat schematic description of the Malaysian version of consociationalism, several fault lines in its structure may be discerned. When pressure is applied along these fault lines, the frailties of the structure are exposed, and the consociational system may be threatened. That system has been strained and modified, but not fundamentally altered in the last thirty years. The rules of its game are still jeopardized *if: with respect to the leadership*, (1) communal leaders refuse to bargain in good faith across ethno-religious lines; (2) elites transgress the accepted boundaries for 'washing dirty linen in public'; (3) intercommunal collusion at the elite level becomes too blatant, and is perceived as too exploitative; or (4) heightened chauvinism extinguishes the proportionality formula in favour of more complete Malay-Muslim dominance; *with respect to the membership*, (5) rank-and-file members refuse to defer to their bloc leaders; (6) intra-communal class loyalties supplement ethno-religious ones; or (7) intercommunal communication and cooperation supplant ethno-religious ties (and in the extreme case, intercommunal class loyalties supplant ethno-religious ones); *with respect to the narrow national consensus*, (8) nationalism is denigrated and the acceptance of national symbols is undermined; and if, *with respect to the system*, (9) political party allegiances transcend communal lines; (10) the ethno-religious blocs become blurred and social cleavages between them lose their clarity; or (11) the system tends toward immobilism and paralysis rather than the production of minimal outputs necessary for it to survive.

Islam as an NRM deepens the fault lines of Malaysia's political system. It threatens to undermine the consociational arrangement by creating several of the eleven conditions which would destabilize it. In particular, however circumspectly its major figures may actually behave, the non-governmental Islamic movement creates the impression that it neither respects nor feels compelled to heed the accepted limitations upon public political discourse and criticism (number 2, above). Its more politicized wings attack elite corruption (number 3), and in general the movement releases dynamic and somewhat unpredictable forces – compounded, as Bedlington (1979: 16) observes, of 'nativism and pan-Islamism' – which the state finds difficult to control (number 4). Resurgent Islam vaults into prominence new leaders who compete with established religious authorities and with political elites for a popular following (number 5). Along with them comes a new set of considerations which makes it possible to rate the performance of ruling elites according to Islamic criteria, and not their adherence to the consociational formula. The resurgence also portends at least the possibility of restructuring Malaysian society along the lines of class, rather than communal group (numbers 6 and 7), but not perhaps to the same extent as the Marxist-Leninist challenge which, however, is now distant. The dominant trend of the movement builds upon Malaysia's 'all-pervasive culture of ethnicity' (Chandra Muzaffar, 1986: 12), and dresses it in new, Islamic garb: as Chandra Muzaffar contends (1986: 7), compared to neighouring Indonesia, Islamic resurgence in Malaysia 'seems to be more involved in the question of identity and the symbols and rituals which help define it'.

But there are also elements of a subordinate theme (Chandra Muzaffar, 1986: 11) emphasizing Islamic universalism, social justice, and the elimination of great inequalities in an overall programme of social and economic reconstruction. Although no Khomeini-style revolution is in the offing for Malaysia, the new Islamic ethos rather obviously challenges a nationalist one (number 8), as demonstrated by some of the newspaper reports cited previously. Most but not all of the efforts to propagate Islam seek to strengthen an Islamic spirit among Malay-Muslims; attempts at conversion outside their ranks, however, have the potential of blurring existing communal lines (number 10), by substituting religious markers for those based upon the intersection of religion and ethnicity. And most of all perhaps, Islam as an NRM appears threatening by insistently questioning the worth of government programmes and of the development and modernization philosophies upon which they are based (number 11).

Quite apart from issues of political right or wrong, the state has an expedient interest in ensuring that these conditions do not occur to destabilize the longstanding consociational system. It is implied that other threats to the longevity of those arrangements would garner an equally, if not more, severe response. For now, however, resurgent, militant, fundamentalist Islam is the major realistic threat, and one which is difficult to control. The prolonged and critical response from the state, detailed in a previous section, is a measure of the threat that it perceives in Islam as an NRM. Although as yet unrealized, the potential opposition posed by the forces of resurgent Islam was summed up to me by one of the heroes of the movement, who commented, 'For Muslims the state is not the emblem of justice. What is important is justice to one's self, and to God . . . God is the ultimate value, not the state.'

What's new, what's old about Malaysia's Islamic movement?

Everyone agrees on the new religious 'feel' which has come to characterize Malaysian society in the 1980s. Commentator after commentator who heretofore had ignored the 'religious factor' now feels compelled to recognize it. Milne's earlier work (1967) on Malaysian politics, for instance, makes rather few mentions of Islam and plays down its significance in the political process. But his later book (1986, with Diane K. Mauzy) incorporates a sense of the importance of Islam into the work's very title.

The average Malaysian has also become more attuned to Islam both within and outside the nation. The newspapers, especially the increasingly popular Malay-language ones, are full of Islamic news. Along with coffee and perhaps a Malaysian breakfast speciality, Islam has now become standard fare in the morning paper. On the day of Yasser Arafat's arrival in Kuala Lumpur (23 July 1984), for example, *Utusan Malaysia* readers learned about: a state religious department investigation of an allegedly deviationist Muslim group; an example of the Prophet's good works as a thought for the day; an Indian family's conversion to Islam, with an accompanying photograph of the ceremony; a government warning to members of the Islamic opposition who 'threaten national security'; a proposal from a former PAS president for an agreement to be forged on steps to Islamize the polity; Iran's receipt of advanced weaponry and plans to launch an attack against Iraq; the hijacking of a Middle East Airlines jet as a protest against Israel; the arrival of pilgrims in Jeddah; health in Mecca; UMNO measures to counter Islamic interpretations that it considers erroneous; a state official's exhortation to parents to attend carefully to the religious education of their children; an increase in the number of government officials with academic qualifications from the Islamic religious stream; former paratroopers with a picture of them at prayer; and about an apparently PAS *imam* whose Friday sermon the government found inappropriate (plus an editorial commentary about this), besides the lead story about Arafat's arrival with its own Islamic overtones. This summarizes only the stories with specifically Islamic content, and those found only in the eight news pages of the newspaper. The feature pages included much more Islamica, with a special focus on the international context. The share market news, classifieds, and sports pages were virtually the only sections without Islamic content. And this example of the preoccupation with matters Islamic, although perhaps intensified because of the state visitor, is not all that atypical.

The widespread and heightened concern about Islam as a measure of one's modernity is also new. To a substantial degree, a preoccupation with Islam has become part of modern Malay-Muslim youth culture.[10] The outward manifestations of this development are far-flung. On an American university campus such as my own, for example, Malaysian women are the only student group to be clad in conservative Muslim garb. They and their fellow Malay-Muslims search for a kind of Islamic purity uncommon – but not unprecedented – in South-east Asian Islam which has been characterized more by tolerance and syncretism than by rigour and purity. The new, militant, fundamentalist turn is a response to much, including modernization and globality, that is, 'the fact and the perception of ever-increasing interdependence at the global level, the rising concern about the fate of the world as a whole and of the human species . . ., and the "colonization" of local by global life' (Robertson, 1987: 35). Perhaps because an 'emergent global culture of modernization' (Robertson, 1987) is most evident in the urban areas, it is the cities which these resurgents contest.

Having acknowledged what is new, it is well not to overstate it. In some ways Malaysia's Islamic movement *is* genuinely novel; but in some ways it is the latest phase of a very old religious movement which has always spread in waves and has taken its strength 'from an irregular series of pulses over centuries' (Johns, 1984: 117). Although it may seem wholly new to participants and to outside observers, the historian of South-east Asian Islam may yawn with a sense of *déjà vu*. In fact, to 'resurge' means to rise again, forcefully, with the swelling or billowing action of a wave.

Therefore, the Islamic movement in Malaysia draws attention not only to the emergence and perhaps eventual decline of new religious movements but also to the persistence of old ones.

The contemporary resurgence did not arise from an atmosphere of hostility to religion or from a climate of atheism. A crisis of belief or of faith is not what spurred participation in the first place. Concerning the period prior to and during the Islamic efflorescence, there is as much religious continuity from one to the other as there is disjunction between them. In the early 1970s, before the resurgence had hit its stride, I surveyed, among other themes, the religious orientations of Malaysia's leading intellectuals and discovered a very high level of claimed religiosity and practice among Malay-Muslims, compared to their American counterparts; and the public arena for discourse, via the media, public meetings, and other activities, was almost as full of religious talk as it is today. Inevitably, a movement such as Malaysia's 'new' Islamic one is in part a reflection, albeit a selective and heightened one, of the wider society from which it springs, all the while its self-depiction is as a radical alternative to that society. Thus the analysis of Islam as an NRM also compels attention to the surrounding society, and to the interactive relationship between that society, the movement inserted within it, and the state.

There are other continuities as well. In terms of life style, conservative restrictions upon male–female interaction, 'female roles and comportment' (Nagata, 1984: 74), and upon acceptable styles of dress are hardly new to Malay-Muslim society. Organizationally, ABIM is a direct descendant of the earlier National Muslim Students' Association of Malaysia (PKPIM), founded in 1961, and was formed to accommodate non-students and former students as well as sympathizers on campus (Nagata, 1984). The possibilities for variegated contacts with the wider Muslim world are much greater now; but the fact of overseas connections, such as those upon which the main *dakwah* organizations are often accused of leaning, is far from unprecedented in the world of archipelagic South-east Asian Islam. Even the wildly divergent colourations of resurgent Islam have been seen many times before, at other moments of religious ferment when revitalizing movements of orthodox purity have surfaced alongside other, fringe and extremist, groups.

Without discounting what is new, the resurgence appears to highlight and intensify religious features which already exist, rather than to fill in what is lacking. Thus, to a substantial degree, Malaysian Islam remains characterized less by wide religious scope, in terms of the 'range of social contexts within which religious considerations are regarded as having more or less direct relevance', than by considerable force, in terms of the passion, intensity, or 'thoroughness with which such a [religious] pattern is internalized in the personalities of the individuals who adopt it' (Geertz, 1968: 111–12). This is so despite the pronouncements and aspirations of movement leaders, and despite the tactical responses of the state which often give political meaning to, at times, a politically recalcitrant movement whose members may be more interested in identity considerations than in raw power.

In short, when it comes to writing about Islam in contemporary Malaysia, the 'changing face' of religion may not be the most appropriate organizing title – unless, of course, we mean by the use of that term the changing surface characteristics which mask deeper continuities and regularities.

Notes

1 *Pace* Ali Shari'ati (1979), who posits an 'Islamic sociology', based upon the Qu'ran and Islam, and not merely a sociology *of* Islam.

2 For a comprehensive account, Judith Nagata's *The Reflowering of Malaysian Islam* (1984) is an especially rich source.

3 A minor, stock character of South-east Asian fiction has been the greedy or corrupt trader who is a 'foreign' Muslim. In *Atheis* (Atheist) by the Indonesian Muslim Achdiat K. Mihardja, he is an Arab, and in *Sungai Mengalir Lesu* (Lazy River) by Malaysia's A. Samad Said, he is an Indian Muslim merchant.

4 Note the similarities between Chandra Muzaffar's (1986) enumeration of the causes of Islamic resurgence in Malaysia and the reasons Rochford gives (1985: 280) for Hare Krishna expansion in the Third World generally.

5 Almost any issue of ABIM's (*Angkatan Belia Islam Malaysia* [Malaysian Muslim Youth League], the most important organization of the revival movement) regular publication *Risalah* confirms this point. The bulk of most issues is devoted to the cause of Islam world-wide.

6 Besides a common reliance upon renowned spiritual masters, and perhaps a certain drift towards authoritarianism, both groups share a fascinating similarity – their non-observance and non-celebration of certain significant national holidays – which has been noted for other religious movements as well (see Davidman, 1986: 114, and Kanter, 1972: 84). Take, for example, Memorial Day (25 May), 1987 in New Vrindaban, a commune in the hills of rural West Virginia, USA, where the Hare Krishna movement maintains a temple complex and an extensive settlement of devotees. Far from the movement of Islamic resurgents in distant Malaysia, and even from the American society which immediately surrounds it, this ISKCON centre marks the national holiday in isolation from, not contestation with, its host society. No creative re-interpretation of the holiday's major theme is evident. The movement makes no attempt to particularize the observance by, for instance, stressing the 'sacrifices' of its founder, Srila Prabhupada, for the good of humankind. Instead, when I asked a senior member, resident in the community for more than a decade, about Memorial Day in New Vrindaban, he said, 'No, devotees do nothing special. We worship God *every* day'. When I enquired as to why, atypically, so few

devotees were to be seen at work – whether beautifying the temple gardens or continuing the community's many half-finished construction projects – the answer was that they were resting that day, not working.

Their day of rest, however, had only indirectly to do with the American holiday and nothing at all to do with its core meaning; rather, the long Memorial Day weekend had been a big one for overnight guests to New Vrindaban, staying at the Palace of Gold lodges, and the community was recovering from holding a festival for them and from serving their visitors' various needs. Memorial Day weekend was transformed into an opportunity for a new category of 'fringe' devotees to go on retreat – to 'recharge their spiritual batteries', said our informant – as well as, incidentally, an opportunity for the community to make a considerable profit. Thus, where the values of American society are reflected, the reflection has nothing to do with the core religious values of the movement; where the movement poses an alternative, its criticism of the mainstream goes uncommunicated, and the alternative has little to do with the reality of life for, or the issues confronted by, most in the surrounding society.

Although extensive first-hand evidence – mine or anybody else's – is lacking on the way in which Muslim revivalists in Malaysia celebrate their King's Birthday and National Day, the two most important national holidays, the indications are that the same inattention characterizes their observance. Probably that is especially, but not exclusively, true for the wings of the movement which seek refuge from the wider society rather than a more explicit revitalization of it. The inattention of organized resurgent Muslims to the ritual calendar of the nation state makes all the more noteworthy the state's quite considerable attention to them on such occasions: for example, the Prime Minister's denunciation of 'religious fanatics who were trying to topple the government' (*Asiaweek*, 14 Sept.) on the occasion of National Day, 1984. See below for a discussion of some reasons behind the occasionally sharp and condemnatory responses to Islam as an NRM in Malaysia.

7 For this theme, too, Nagata's book (1984) merits special mention.

8 Sometimes the official efforts to outflank everybody else when it comes to the cause of Islam seem almost humorous, as in the temporary ban on the American television series *Fame* during Ramadhan, 1985, when its contents were deemed inappropriate for the fasting month.

9 A feeling of shame has been planted in their hearts, because our race is supposedly contradictory to the teachings of Islam. They have been influenced by a political party purportedly Islamic but willing to use Islam in ways that are not *halal* (permissible.) (*New Straits Times*, 1 Sept. 1984)

10 It is much more than that, of course, as this chapter has attempted to show in its emphasis on the political role that Islam as an NRM has come to play.

References

Ali Shari'ati (1979) *On the Sociology of Islam*. Berkeley, CA: Mizan Press.
Barraclough, Simon (1984) 'Political Participation and its Regulation in Malaysia: Opposition to the Societies (Amendment) Act 1981', *Pacific Affairs*, 57(3) (Fall): 450–61.
Beckford, James A. (1985) *Cult Controversies: the Societal Response to New Religious Movements*. London and New York: Tavistock.
Beckford, James A. (1987) 'The Restoration of "power" to the Sociology of Religion', pp. 13–37 in T. Robbins and R. Robertson (eds), *Church–State*

Relations: Tensions and Transitions. New Brunswick, NJ, and Oxford: Transaction Books.

Bedlington, Stanley S. (1979) 'Comparative Aspects of Islam in Malaysia and Indonesia: Some Desultory Comments', Paper presented at the Symposium on the Malay World, Ohio University, 3–5 May.

Buttel, Frederick H. (1987) Review of James C. Scott, *Weapons of the Weak: Everyday Forms of Peasant Resistance*. *Contemporary Sociology*, 16(3) (May): 301–4.

Chandra Muzaffar (1986) 'Islamic Resurgence: a global view', pp. 5–39 in Taufik Abdullah and S. Siddique (eds), *Islam and Society in Southeast Asia*. Singapore: Institute of Southeast Asian Studies.

Davidman, Lynn R. (1986) 'Strength of Tradition in a Chaotic World: Women Turn to Orthodox Judaism', Unpublished PhD dissertation, Department of Sociology, Brandeis University.

Federspiel, Howard M. (1985) 'Islam and Development in the Nations of ASEAN', *Asian Survey*, 25(8) (Aug.): 805–21.

Funston, N. John (1985) 'The Politics of Islamic Reassertion: Malaysia', pp. 171–9 in Ahmad Ibrahim et al. (eds), *Readings on Islam in Southeast Asia*. Singapore: Institute of Southeast Asian Studies, first published, 1981.

Geertz, Clifford (1968) *Islam Observed: Religious Development in Morocco and Indonesia*. Chicago and London: University of Chicago Press.

Gunn, Geoffrey C. (1986) 'Radical Islam in Southeast Asia: Rhetoric and Reality in the Middle Eastern Connection', *Journal of Contemporary Asia*, 16(1):30–54.

Hammond, Phillip E. (ed.) (1985) *The Sacred in a Secular Age: Toward Revision in the Scientific Study of Religion*. Berkeley: University of California Press.

Hubner, John and Lindsey Gruson (1987) 'Dial Om for murder', *Rolling Stone*, 9 April.

Israeli, Raphael and Anthony H. Johns (eds) (1984) *Islam in Asia II: Southeast and East Asia*. Boulder, CO: Westview Press.

Johns, Anthony H. (1984) 'Islam in the Malay World: an Exploratory Survey with Some Reference to Quranic Exegesis', pp. 115–61 in R. Israeli and A.H. Johns (eds), *Islam in Asia II: Southeast and East Asia*. Boulder, CO: Westview Press.

Kanter, Rosabeth Moss (1972) *Commitment and Community: Communes and Utopias in Sociological Perspective*. Cambridge, MA: Harvard University Press.

King, Roger (1986) *The State in Modern Society: New Directions in Political Sociology*. Chatham, NJ: Chatham House Publishers.

Landon, Kenneth Perry (1949) *Southeast Asia: Crossroad of Religions*. Chicago and London: University of Chicago Press.

Lijphart, Arend (1968) *The Politics of Accommodation: Pluralism and Democracy in the Netherlands*. Berkeley and Los Angeles: University of California Press.

Lijphart, Arend (1969) 'Consociational Democracy', *World Politics*, 21(2): 207–25.

Mahathir Mohamad, Datuk Seri, Dr (1985) 'We Are Islamic Fundamentalists', *Islamic Herald*, 9(3): 40–1.

Mauzy, Diane K. and R.S. Milne (1983–4) 'The Mahathir Administration in Malaysia: Discipline through Islam', *Pacific Affairs*, 56(4) (Winter): 617–48.

Milne, R.S. (1967) *Government and Politics in Malaysia*. Boston: Houghton Mifflin.

Milne, R.S. and Diane K. Mauzy (1978) *Politics and Government in Malaysia*. Vancouver: University of British Columbia Press.

Milne, R.S. and Diane K. Mauzy (1986) *Malaysia: Tradition, Modernity, and Islam*. Boulder, CO: Westview Press.

Mohamad Abu Bakar (1981) 'Islamic Revivalism and the Political Process in Malaysia', *Asian Survey*, 21(10) (Oct.): 1040–59.

Nagata, Judith (1980a) 'The New Fundamentalism: Islam in Contemporary Malaysia', *Asian Thought and Society*, 5(15) (Sept.): 128–41.

Nagata, Judith (1980b) 'Religious Ideology and Social Change: the Islamic Revival in Malaysia', *Pacific Affairs* 53(3) (Fall): 405–39.

Nagata, Judith (1984) *The Reflowering of Malaysian Islam: Modern Religious Radicals and Their Roots*. Vancouver: University of British Columbia Press.

Nagata, Judith (1987) Review of James C. Scott, *Weapons of the Weak: Everday Forms of Peasant Resistance*. *American Journal of Sociology*, 92(5) (March).

Naipaul, V.S. (1981) *Among the Believers: an Islamic Journey*. New York: Vintage Books.

Noordin Sopiee (1984) 'Malaysia's Strategic Environment: One Perspective on the Present and the Future', paper presented at a Conference on Malaysia, The Fletcher School, 18–20 November.

Nordlinger, Eric A. (1972) *Conflict Regulation in Divided Societies*. Cambridge, MA: Center for International Affairs, Harvard University.

Obaid ul Haq (1986) 'Islamic Resurgence: the Challenge of Change', pp. 332–48 in Taufik Abdullah and S. Siddique (eds), *Islam and Society in Southeast Asia*. Singapore: Institute of Southeast Asian Studies.

Pipes, Daniel (1983) *In the Path of God: Islam and Political Power*. New York: Basic Books.

Robertson, Roland (1987) 'Globalization and Societal Modernization: a Note on Japan and Japanese Religion', *Sociological Analysis*, 47(S): 35–42.

Rochford, E. Burke, Jr. (1985) *Hare Krishna in America*. New Brunswick, NJ: Rutgers University Press.

Roff, William R. (1985) 'Islam Obscured? Some Reflections on Studies of Islam and Society in Southeast Asia', *Archipel*, 29: 7–34.

Scott, James C. (1985) *Weapons of the Weak: Everyday Forms of Peasant Resistance*. New Haven, CT, and London: Yale University Press.

Von der Mehden, Fred R. (1980) 'Islamic Resurgence in Malaysia', pp. 163–80 in J.L. Esposito (ed.), *Islam and Development: Religion and Sociopolitical Change*. Syracuse, NY: Syracuse University Press.

Von der Mehden, Fred R. (1987) 'Malaysia: Islam and Multiethnic Politics', pp. 177–201 in John L. Esposito (ed.), *Islam in Asia: Religion, Politics, and Society*. New York and Oxford: Oxford University Press.

Von Vorys, Karl (1975) *Democracy Without Consensus: Communalism and Political Stability in Malaysia*. Princeton, NJ: Princeton University Press.

8

The Sacred in African New Religions

Bennetta Jules-Rosette

There are currently more new religions in non-western nations than during any previous historical period. Many new African religious movements (whether they are separatist break-offs or independent developments) are influenced by contact with diverse 'unorthodox' western movements. Additionally, fragmentation and schism are internal characteristics of many of these movements. Government persecution creates further external pressures towards schism. Internally, conditions of plural culture contact and the failure to stabilize leadership roles and patterns of succession promote schism and fragmentation. This development is a byproduct of the decline of customary religious authority and the transposition of many of the functions of religion into the secular domain. It suggests that 'subjective secularization', or the manifestation of secularization as a psychological orientation, may be less prevalent in the African context than structural changes resulting in new tensions in the relationship between religion and society.

Africa's dramatic social upheavals over the past two decades have been accompanied by the rise of a variety of new religious movements that are characterized by symbolic protest and search for cultural continuity. These movements involve a symbolic re-definition of what is perceived to be sacred in society. In this discussion, I shall explore the types and dynamics of new African religious movements as sources for re-defining concepts of the sacred and the secular and examine the implications of these conclusions for the present and future state of research in the field.

Africa's new religions: major types and sources

Over 7,000 new religious movements exist in sub-Saharan Africa. Together they claim more than 32 million adherents (Barrett, 1982: 782 and 791). These movements have arisen primarily in areas where there has been intensive contact with Christian missionary efforts. However, prophetic and revitalistic movements existed in Africa prior to extensive European contact. Many movements originated as early as the 1880s. The period from 1914 to 1925 marked a second peak in the emergence of new religions in Africa. A final period may be demarcated from the early 1930s to the present. It is the groups that have emerged during this most recent period which are generally referred to as the new religious movements of sub-Saharan Africa. Some of these movements actually began earlier but did not gain momentum until the 1930s. Many have persisted in largely the same form that they took over fifty years ago. Others have gone underground and re-surfaced, often retaining their initial doctrinal and membership requirements.

With reference to doctrinal base, organizational structure, and geographic distribution, three major types of new religious movements in sub-Saharan Africa may be designated: (1) indigenous, or independent, churches; (2) separatist churches; and (3) neo-traditional movements. These groups have taken different forms in West, Central, Southern, and East Africa. They blend elements of traditional religion with the influence of historical and modern churches. Many of these groups arose as a result of the political and social domination of colonialism and the sense of psychological dependency that it created. However, in the contemporary period, other sources have stimulated the continued growth of these movements.

Historically speaking, the impetus for the growth of new African religious movements may be traced to five basic sources. (1) The disappointment of local converts with the premises and outcomes of Christianity led to the growth of prophetic, Messianic, and millenarian groups. (2) The translation of the Bible into local African vernaculars stimulated a reinterpretation of scripture and a spiritual renewal in Christian groups. (3) The perceived divisions in denominational Christianity and its failure to meet local needs influenced the rise of separatist churches and community-based indigenous churches. (4) The impotence of western medicine in the face of personal problems, psychological disorders, epidemics, and natural disasters was a catalyst for concerns with spiritual healing in the new African religious movements. (5) The failure of mission Christianity to break down social and cultural barriers and generate a sense of community has led to the strengthening of social ties in small, sectarian groups. In general, the new African churches have tried to create a sense of community in the new urban environment and in the changing context of rural life.

Among the three groups of new religious movements designated, indigenous churches are the most rapidly growing local responses to Christianity. These churches are groups that started under the initiative of African leaders outside the immediate context of missions, or historic religions. Their membership is estimated to comprise nearly 15 per cent of the Christian population of sub-Saharan Africa. Also termed 'independent' churches, these groups have devised unique forms of social and political organization and have developed their own doctrines. Groups as diverse as the Harrist Church in Côte d'Ivoire, the Aladura Church in Nigeria, Kimbanguism in Zaïre, and the Apostolic movements of Zimbabwe may be classified as indigenous churches. Nevertheless, the specific doctrines and the response to government control in each of these churches is distinctive. These groups also vary on the organizational level depending on the extent of their local appeal and the demographic and cultural composition of their membership. Indigenous churches may be divided into three specific sub-types: prophetic, Messianic, and millenarian groups. All of these types evidence doctrinal innovation, efforts at spiritual renewal, and a reaction to the presence of mission churches.

Re-envisaging the sacred and the secular

New African religious movements provide an innovative way of re-envisaging the sacred, and challenge conventional sociological theories of secularization and the decline of religiosity in contemporary society. Emile Durkheim (1915: 52) stated that 'all known religious beliefs, whether simple or complex' presuppose the classification of the world into 'sacred and profane' domains. For Durkheim, no particular entity, object, or event is considered sacred. Instead, the sacred consists of collective moral and symbolic expressions projected and reinforced by the social group. Social processes are treated as the source for generating and sustaining a sense of the sacred.[1] Durkheim's definition of the sacred refers to ways of seeing and thinking about the world as much as it does to a set of social institutions.

This approach contrasts with Max Weber's view that the sacred is embodied in specific religious institutions and must be studied in terms of their relationship to the rest of society (Weber, 1963: 207–8). It is from the latter perspective that the opposition between the sacred and the secular as a source of social change has developed as a tool for analysing historic and contemporary religions. The much-debated problems of secularization and the decline of religiosity, which became major scholarly and popular concerns for western researchers and theologians in the 1960s and are still a source of controversy, were partially set in motion by Weber's approach.[2]

Recent research has both debated and refined Weber's initial assumptions. In his introduction to the English translation of

Weber's *The Sociology of Religion,* Talcott Parsons (1963: lxii) argues that the rise of interdenominationalism and liberal Protestantism in the United States seriously challenges Weber's view of how the secularization process would unfold in contemporary western societies. In his master plan for the comparative study of religion, Weber never envisaged the processes of rapid social change and cultural contact resulting from decolonization in the Third World. The notion that the people of modern Africa would have a voice in re-directing the course of religion and institutional change in Europe did not appear as an empirical possibility at the beginning of the twentieth century. As movements of protest, many new African religious groups have become vehicles for the creation, exercise, and legitimation of power by their adherents. Those who were formerly powerless have found in religion a means of altering their situation and even reversing their status in both symbolic and social terms. The adherents of these new movements have created and manipulated sacred symbols to attain secular goals. Therefore, the existence of these movements necessarily modifies conceptualizations of the relationship between the sacred and the secular.

A fundamental question lingers when assessing US and European research on African religious movements. This concerns the comparative lens through which such studies are conceived and developed. The church–denomination–sect typology, which has been widely debated since Troeltsch and Weber, probably reached its peak as an analytical tool in the United States by 1970 (Eister, 1967: 85–90; Demerath and Hammond, 1969; Johnson, 1971: 124–37; Martin, 1978). This typology has done much to obscure research on new religious movements in Africa and elsewhere. This distinction grew out of historical studies of European Christianity. The effects of this typology for research in Africa have been particularly misleading because it has promoted a tendency to view new religious developments as 'sectarian' responses rather than as autonomous developments with different cultural and historical roots than those of more established churches and denominations. The wide range of cultural combinations and socio-political goals in African groups renders the church–sect typology a relatively weak descriptive device.

Much of the research conducted on African religious movements during the 1950s and 1960s examined them as responses and challenges to colonialism (Balandier, 1955: 417–19). In his study of African and other Third World religious movements, Vittorio Lanternari (1963: 19) labelled these movements 'religions of the oppressed', which he considered to result from 'the spontaneous impact of the white man's presence on the native society'. The 'sacred', in this case, is defined in terms of passive resistance to, and rebellion against, symbols of political and religious domination.

Ten years after Lanternari's book was published in English, Bryan Wilson (1973) developed a typology that compressed African religious movements into two empirical and doctrinal types: the thaumaturgical and the revolutionist, or the magical and the millennial. Although this distinction refers to both world views and specific movements, a concern with supernatural powers – magic, healing, and purification – is, for Wilson, the major thrust of *all* religions emerging in pre-industrial societies. What the sociologist considers 'magical' in this context, of course, may be viewed by movement followers as a set of rational alternatives logically derived from tradition or from innovative doctrinal combinations. Wilson's 'magic' is actually a description of a wide variety of indigenous customs, beliefs, and new conceptions of symbolic action and protest.

For Wilson, millenarian movements contain much that is 'magical' and, therefore, have little broad, lasting political or social impact. He cites the case of West African groups such as the Cherubim and Seraphim movement of Nigeria (Peel, 1968: 2–9) and of some American Indian movements in support of this tendency of millenarian movements to be temporary and localized. When such movements of protest do arise, in Wilson's opinion, they are often so replete with supernatural and other worldly elements as to be marginally effective as instrumental movements of protest. However, I would argue that a challenge to the existing social order is implicit in many African religious movements, regardless of the specific traditional cultural or 'magical' elements that are present. In this regard, the meanings and uses of new religious movements for their own group members become central issues for study. One must ask how these group members envisage the sacred and the secular and what symbolic challenge they perceive themselves as making.

This point reinforces the methodological concern in some recent studies with defining the cosmology and belief systems in new African religions (Fernandez, 1982; MacGaffey, 1983). On the ethnographic level, this process is essential in order to assess the larger influence of new movements on the societies in which they appear. Building upon a semantic anthropological approach to religion, this line of research suggests that the comparative study of new African religions must be preceded by a schematic interpretive and descriptive treatment of the content of religious doctrines and practice. This suggestion raises key issues of both theological and sociological import. Specifically, how do members of new religious movements conceive of the sacred, of categories of religious belief and practice, and of the distribution of ecclesiastical authority within these groups? Beyond simply noting that these categories challenge or differ from those of western religious belief and practice, it is necessary to examine the new terms in their own right. I adopted this approach in my own ethnographic and sociolinguistic studies of Apostolic churches in Zaïre, Zambia, and Zimbabwe (Jules-Rosette, 1975: 21–56).

A western model of 'church' and 'state' that neatly separates the sacred and secular domains often does not apply to the history and cultural context of new African religions. For example Larry Shiner (1966: 218) states: 'When we apply this spiritual–temporal polarity to non-Western situations where such differentiations did not originally exist, we falsify the data.' Yet, if we return to the Lanternari and Wilson theses, we are plagued by the possibility that new religious adherents have used their beliefs as meaningful coping mechanisms and survival strategies. What were previously religions of the oppressed, however, have now become religions of opportunity and channels of upward mobility (Glazier, 1983: 16). The sacred vision has been transformed into the secular opportunity.

This latter view builds upon a Weberian model of the emergence of an instrumental rationality that accompanies modernity and change. Indeed, this model has been applied to ethnographic studies of new African religions. A landmark study in this regard is Norman Long's (1968) monograph on the religious and social responses to modernity among the Jehovah's Witnesses of Kapepa village in Zambia. The Weberian view holds that modernity is accompanied by the structuring of religious activities according to secular ideals. Religious motivations for action are rechannelled into the secular domain. Long found a classic version of the Protestant ethic operative among the Witnesses of Kapepa. Most of them were relatively young villagers with little urban experience. They equated hard work and economic success with the process of preparing themselves for the millennium and entry into the 'New Kingdom' (Long, 1968: 214). Relative to their fellow villagers, the Witnesses made a rapid transition from hoe to plough agriculture with notable commercial success. Long (1968: 239–40) remarks: 'I . . . concluded that like the correlation that Weber suggested between the Protestant ethic and "the spirit of capitalism", there existed in Kapepa a close correspondence between Jehovah's Witnesses and their social and economic behavior. . . . But social, economic, and cultural factors also play their part.'

Religion, in this case, helped the Witnesses of Kapepa to adapt to change. They did so by re-defining their social world in millenarian religious terms and acting upon these beliefs in their economic lives. Long's study might be used to exemplify the secularization thesis in Africa. However, it also demonstrates the opposite: an increase in religiosity through the involvement of the African Witnesses in a spiritual re-definition of every aspect of their daily lives. Moreover, Long's data on the Kapepa Witnesses is atypical of many Central African groups that developed as offshoots of the Watch Tower movement during the colonial period (Biebuyck, 1957: 7–40).[3] These movements tended to exhibit extreme millenarian religious and political responses to European domination without specific social programmes for their members or with ephemeral political protest as a result.

The problem of secularization in the African context

Just as the interpretation of the sacred takes a unique form in new African religions, so too does the process of secularization. Peter Berger (1967: 171) argues that the world-wide spread of the structures of the modern industrial state triggers religious change in non-western societies and is an important stimulus for the secularization process.[4] On the other hand, Wilson (1973: 499) points to the decline of traditional authority structures and religious beliefs in the face of colonial domination and 'westernization'. The implication of both assertions is that tendencies towards secularization are introduced to changing African societies from the outside as a by-product of the eventual movement of all societies towards industrial and post-industrial socio-economic structures (cf. Parsons, 1966: 109–14). These changes are accompanied by cultural pluralization, more frequent contact of diverse social groups, and an increase in bureaucratic forms of organization with impersonal social relationships.

Similarly, Shiner (1966: 209–17) has noted three important characteristics of secularization that may be associated with this transition to modernity: (1) de-sacralization, or a decline in the role of religion in defining the social world; (2) the process of structural differentiation by which religious and secular institutions become distinct and autonomous; and (3) the transposition of religious knowledge and activities into the secular domain. This process of transposition is distinct from the decline of the social influence of religion (Wilson, 1982: 149). When applied to new African religious groups, it suggests that followers of these movements retain aspects of customary religion and newly introduced cultural elements without exclusively associating themselves with either alternative. As a result of all three of the processes outlined by Shiner, individuals re-order their religious beliefs in a new way to meet the demands of modern society – a society that western theologians and social scientists have argued has become increasingly secular.

The combination of the sacred and secular domains in many new African religious movements creates thorny problems when analysing the process of secularization (Turner, 1974: 697–705). In these groups, the political domain had traditionally been defined and reinforced by sacred symbols and beliefs that are fundamental to the communities involved. African movements that draw upon customary religious and political symbolism have often been regarded with a mixture of alarm and suspicion by both colonial governments and new regimes. When these cultural combinations are aggravated by millenarian tendencies in the new groups, the issue becomes even more complex. It is, therefore, difficult to disentangle a nostalgic return to traditional notions of the sacred from new conceptions of the sacred developing from changing political and social demands. The decline of old concepts of the sacred and re-sacralization, or the re-definition of the sacred, in this context, may actually constitute two complementary poles of a single phenomenon. Hence, the concept of secularization offers an incomplete framework for analysing what actually takes place when old and new symbolic categories are combined.

In defining secularization in the African context, one must also consider the problem of symbolic realism (Bellah, 1970: 89–96). How do members of these groups see their own religious claims *vis-à-vis* the emerging secular society? Peter Berger (1966: 8) suggests that recent research on religion often takes for granted the predominance of a universal 'secularized consciousness', or total acceptance of a scientific reality, without considering the possibility that, for some people, the standard for cognitive validity may be the sacred, or a non-scientific reality. The quest to regain a sense of the sacred through religious, cultural, and national identity is a common response to social and cultural change in African nations.

Secularization is often assumed to be a linear and uniform process (Lalive d'Epinay, 1981: 406). Accordingly, the predictable economic and social changes accompanying industrialization are viewed as making religion marginal in contemporary society. In fact, however, many new religious movements in Africa react to industrial change and the new social orders that accompany it by seeking to create a sense of religious unity and group identity characteristic of pre-industrial communities. Elsewhere, I have referred to this process as the impossible arcadian wish to return to old values and a simpler form of life (Jules-Rosette, 1979: 219–29). In this case, the growth of modern social and economic institutions results in an effort to 're-sacralize' African societies through new religious groups and nationalistic political movements.

Liberation theology is another product of, and reaction to, the world-wide process of secularization and the spread of modern industrial structures to all corners of the globe (Brown, 1974: 269–82; Berryman, 1987: 136–8.). Through this approach, theologians operating within established Catholic and Protestant traditions view the Bible as a revolutionary book which documents the processes of religious and political liberation and the goal of freedom. Their objective is to redefine the sacred as a set of moral principles which can be invoked in the wider society to reduce social inequities and injustice. Although liberation theology in Africa and Latin America shares some features with millenarian movements, it differs in its direct equation of secular goals such as social justice with religious ideals.

The example of liberation theology suggests that secular, political goals directly influence the formation and growth of new religious movements. Consequently, it is important to analyse how tendencies towards secularization have actually shaped new religious movements. One method for exploring this problem is to examine tensions in the relationships between church and state in African nations. In many African nations such as Zaïre, Zambia, and Malawi, the growth of new religions takes place under close government scrutiny, and many movements (such as the Watch Tower spin-offs) are outlawed as threats to nation building. In these cases, new religions are seen as potential sources for weakening civic political commitments by virtue of their ability to mobilize masses of people in activities which are not directly supervised or controlled by the state. Political control attempts to restrict the sphere of influence of the new religious movements in a secularizing society.

A counterbalancing tendency in this secularization process is one towards ecumenical cooperation across the new religious groups. Martin West (1975: 142–70) analyses the rise of ecumenism among South Africa's indigenous churches based upon two large-scale surveys of these movements. He notes efforts towards cooperation among these groups, particularly in education and financial programmes but not on the level of doctrine and ritual. Similar tendencies have appeared among indigenous churches in Zambia and East Africa. Some scholars have argued that this process of cooperation ultimately results in the secularization of doctrine and leadership structures within new religious movements. In describing the Apostles of John Maranke, an African prophetic movement which I also studied, Angela Cheater (1981: 45) has argued that pragmatic concerns of economic success and secular social and family ties have actually altered the interpretation of the sacred within the group and diminished its scope. She sees cooperation with other groups in the larger society as a major force in modifying the doctrinal and organizational structure of the religious group. This controversial argument suggests that social differentiation and change may eventually cause subjective secularization, or a personal decline in religiosity.

Cultural responses to secularization

African religious movements and movement types have adopted a variety of cultural and psychological responses to the process of secularization. These responses may be summarized in terms of at least four basic tendencies, according to which several movements types may be classified:

1 *Neotraditionalism*: retains the myth of an ideal past and is often accompanied by an attempt to reconstruct an authoritative religious tradition. The persistence of traditional religious forms in Africa within the contemporary context is a case in point.
2 *Revitalization*: introduces new concepts to regenerate the old. On the psychological level, this response is perceived as *comprehensive* and seeks an explanation of the sacred in both old and new terms. African indigenous churches and prophetic revitalization movements are examples.
3 *Syncretism*: is the process through which former definitions of the sacred are combined with innovative patterns to produce a satisfying definition of the whole and an expression of core values which is both in line with the past and adaptive to new institutions. Santeria, Latin American Pentecostalism, and many African movements exhibit this process.
4 *Millenarism*: creates a myth of the ideal future which attempts to construct a new definition of the sacred and a new social order in ways that yield pragmatically effective results for members of new movements. New African movements and, to a lesser extent liberation theologies, use this approach. Messianic movements may be included in this category.

Although these four options do not exhaust the cultural and symbolic responses to secularization, they point to ways in which new religious movements in Africa have attempted to re-define the sacred in a secularizing society. In some instances, a direct re-definition of political and social values is involved, as in the case of millenarism and liberation theology. In other instances, the sacred is re-validated through efforts to preserve customary notions of community and conventional expressive symbols, as evidenced in revitalistic, evangelical, and spirit-type movements. In the latter case, a re-sacralization of dominant traditional symbols occurs, often in reaction to the decline of religious values and institutions in the rest of the society. In spite of the re-sacralization process, some scholars like Robin Horton (1971: 107) have argued that religion in modern Africa will ultimately move in an increasingly secular direction in terms of its doctrine and organization and will survive primarily 'as a way of communion but not as a system of explanation, prediction, and control'. At present, however, a more prevalent trend in African religious movements is the attempt to create cohesive forms of community in which religious values are more coherent and exercise a larger, direct influence on social life. Dynamic religious movements throughout Africa are re-defining the psychological, religious, political, social, and cultural aspects of life that interweave the sacred and the secular.

The future of the new African religions

An important concern in the field of African religious studies centres on the extent to which new movements may be considered stable over time. It has been argued that the new religions develop through a process of schism and renewal. They break away from the influence of both missions and newly established churches to develop bonds of family and community that are particularly strong at the local level. Utopian ideals and fundamentalist interpretations of scriptures reinforce the initial break and the sense of spiritual renewal in these groups. Schism may be regarded as a sign of doctrinal ambivalence and organizational weakness. At the same time, it is the hallmark of spiritual experimentation and renewal. There is a combination of customary symbols and the new values characteristic of cultural pluralism. Many newer groups stress that their religions form inter-ethnic and transcultural associative networks.

Although some of the new Christian groups of Africa originate in ethnically homogeneous areas, most emphasize the potential and even the necessity for cultural sharing through overarching symbols and doctrine. This sharing does not mean that an external system is imposed on, or destroys, old cultural forms. These processes of cultural combination and symbolic protest allow the members of new religious movements to acquire a reflective stance towards their immediate problems and to preserve past cultural ideas. The types of religious responses vary widely with respect to a group's attitudes towards tradition and to the degree of change which individuals consider to be possible in a particular society. The four types of movement responses mentioned above resolve social and cultural clashes through blending old and new interpretations of the sacred.

At the same time, a question of stable leadership and its institutionalization arises. The death or demise of a leader creates an important challenge to the viability of a group. Often several branches of an indigenous church or separatist movement exist in a single area because of the inability of members to resolve a crisis in leadership succession or to integrate competing doctrinal variations. Thus, schism continues to threaten the stability and survival of new religious movements after they have established autonomy from missions or historic churches. This problem has led some scholars to speculate that the new African religions are unstable and highly mutable and that their appearance merely marks one phase of social, political, or religious protest in the emergence of Africa's new nation states. Nevertheless, historical evidence suggests that these groups have considerable longevity in spite of their shifting leadership structures, new membership, and fluctuations in popular appeal. The persistence of groups like the Bwiti cult in Gabon and the Kitawala movement in Zaïre and Zambia from the turn of the century to the present follows this trend.

Another important tendency contributing to the eventual stability of the new religious movements is the shift towards ecumenism. Churches such as the Kimbanguists and the Aladura, which have endured for practically half a century, have made attempts to become international in outlook and to associate themselves with world-wide ecumenical movements. Several indigenous churches affiliated themselves with the World Council of Churches between 1969 and 1981. They include: The Church of the Lord Aladura in Nigeria, the Kimbanguist Church in Zaïre, the African Israel Ninevah Church in Kenya, and the African Church of the Holy Spirit in Kenya (cf. Perrin Jassy, 1970: 86–8). Other indigenous churches and cults have made efforts to join together in local, national, and all-African cooperative associations which represent them as united political and cultural groups.

Local voluntary associations formed by these churches attempt to retain the doctrinal autonomy of each group while developing joint fundraising, educational, and cultural efforts. This type of cooperation is evident in the African Independent Churches' Association formed in 1965 in South Africa and in similar ecumenical councils and associations that have formed in Zambia and Kenya (West, 1974: 121–9). Although such associations do not solve the problem of internal group conflict and leadership succession, they appear to reinforce cooperation and political stability within the independent church movement.

The cultural and social contribution of Africa's new religions

Many of Africa's new religious movements arising from the 1920s to the present have started as religions of the oppressed and later have become movements of protest, opportunity and mobility. Their protest has often been expressed as a challenge to the authority and liturgy of mission churches. Several of these groups, including the early Watch Tower movement inspired by Kamwana in Nyasaland, Kimbanguism in Zaïre, and the Harrist Church in Côte d'Ivoire, have also led to, or supported, movements of political liberation and national independence. The close relationship between political and religious conceptions of freedom and human rights has contributed to this development.

The social influence of Africa's new religions, however, is not limited to the political sphere. The new images and ideals of community promoted by these groups offer alternative life styles to their members and to others who come into contact with the new movements. Through tightly knit communities and internal support structures, Africa's new religions establish claims to loyalty. Culturally, they promise a popular religion that is not alien to the 'masses'. Nevertheless, some of the contemporary groups emphasize the ultimate attainment of rewards promised in orthodox doctrines. This goal is accomplished through social insulation, withdrawal, and strict personal adherence to the Bible or to the Qur'an. The literal interpretation of sacred writings serves to develop a new fabric of ideas through which individuals attempt to create alternative types of social relationships. In some instances, this return to fundamentalist doctrines within the African context has had the effect of triggering charismatic renewals and new forms of proselytizing within established mission churches.

The more insulated religious movements still adamantly retain a radical separation from some aspects of the contemporary societies in which they appear. Nevertheless, their attitudes towards work, towards the role of women, and towards new forms of cultural expression, such as discourse and dress, permeate other sectors of social life that are not directly associated with their religious origins. Religious language and imagery, such as the Jamaa teachings and Apostolic or Zionist sermons and rituals, have now entered common parlance as aspects of urban popular culture (Fabian,

1971: 202). The study of Africa's new religious movements, therefore, leads to a broader exploration of new cultural forms.

Conclusions

Because religion involves a high concentration of innovative and restorative symbols, it is a well-spring from which these new expressions are transmitted to a wider society. Through Africa's new religious movements, conventional cultural and symbolic forms are revived and reinterpreted. Taken from their original source, some of these religious beliefs have been applied to secular life. The ultimate viability of these new religions may, in fact, reside in the capacity of their beliefs and practices to beome more fully integrated into the mainstream of modern Africa's social and cultural life. The greatest impact of these groups may, thus, take place through cultural diffusion and sharing rather than through the spread and historical evolution of any particular movement.

The processes of fragmentation and re-definition of leadership roles and goals in Africa's new religions take place under unique cultural conditions (cf. Sinda, 1972: 111). Often, these processes involve re-defining the sacred as part of a new search for collective identity and reinterpretation of tradition. Paradoxically, these re-definitions may challenge conceptions of the sacred in western religious traditions. Heterodoxy, however, is not always synony-mous with secularization (Berger, 1980: 23–38). By suggesting novel ways in which the sacred may be integrated into contemporary life, Africa's new religions offer an empirical challenge to sociological theories that propose that secularization is an essential feature of the incorporation of Third World communities into the industrial and post-industrial social orders.

Notes

1 Durkheim considered the concept of the sacred to refer to the symbolic, categorical, and moral aspects of social life. His view has been refined and re-emphasized in contemporary studies of the social institutions that support religious world-views and concepts of the sacred (cf. Berger, 1967: 33–4; Douglas, 1966: 21).

2 Peter Berger's presidential address to the Society for the Scientific Study of Religion in Boston (1966: 3–16) summarizes the influence of the secularization thesis on contemporary theology before the impact of new religious movements and the rise of the new evangelical Christianity in the United States had been fully assessed by researchers. Larry Shiner (1966: 207–20) presents an excellent overview of the problems of using the concept of secularization in empirical research. Although many new empirical developments have taken place since Shiner's article was published, the methodological issues that he proposes are still important contribu-tions to the discussion of secularization.

3 Norman Long's example of the Zambian Jehovah's Witnesses who, according to him, fit neatly into a Weberian model of social change is atypical. For example, the Watch Tower movement that began in 1908 under Elliot Kamwana may be viewed as a powerful millenarian response to the colonial regime of Nyasaland (Barrett, 1968: 29). Although this movement re-surfaced later in other forms, it never assumed the characteristics of the Zambian group described by Long.

4 Along these lines, Ted Solomon (1977: 1–14) suggests that the transposition of concepts of the sacred into the secular domain and the bureaucratization of religious movements may be productively analysed through the new religions of Japan including Sokka Gakkai, Rissho Kosei-kai, and PL Kyodan. These groups have been politically active and have used Nichiren Shoshu Buddhism to reshape the expression of Japanese nationalism.

References

Balandier, Georges (1955) *Sociologie actuelle de l'Afrique noire*. Paris: Presses Universitaires.

Barrett, David B. (1968) *Schism and Renewal in Africa: an Analysis of Six Thousand Contemporary Religious Movements*. Nairobi, Kenya: Oxford University Press.

Barrett, David B. (ed.) (1982) *World Christian Encyclopedia: a Comparative Study of Churches and Religions in the Modern World, AD 1900–2000*. New York: Oxford University Press.

Bellah, Robert (1970) 'Christianity and Symbolic Realism', *Journal for the Scientific Study of Religion*, 9 (Summer): 89–96.

Berger, Peter L. (1966) 'A Sociological View of the Secularization of Theology', *Journal for the Scientific Study of Religion*, 6 (Spring): 3–16.

Berger, Peter L. (1967) *The Sacred Canopy: Elements of a Sociological Theory of Religion*. Garden City, New York: Anchor Books.

Berger, Peter L. (1980) *The Heretical Imperative: Contemporary Possibilities of Religious Affirmation*. Garden City, New York: Anchor Books.

Berryman, Phillip (1987) *Liberation Theology*. New York: Pantheon Books.

Biebuyck, M.O. (1957) 'La société Kuma face au Kitawala', *Zaire*, 11: 7–40.

Brown, Robert McAfee (1974) 'Reflections on "Liberation Theology"', *Religion in Life*, 43 (Fall): 269–82.

Cheater, Angela (1981) 'The Social Organisation of Religious Difference among the Vapostori weMaranke', *Social Analysis*, 7: 24–49.

Demerath, N.J., III and Phillip E. Hammond (1969) *Religion in Social Context*. New York: Random House.

Douglas, Mary (1966) *Purity and Danger: an Analysis of Concepts of Pollution and Taboo*. New York: Praeger Publishers.

Durkheim, Emile (1915) *The Elementary Forms of the Religious Life*. Joseph Ward Swain (trans.). London: Allen & Unwin.

Eister, Allan W. (1967) 'Toward a Radical Critique of Church–Sect Typologizing: Comment on "Some Critical Observations on the Church–Sect Dimension"', *Journal for the Scientific Study of Religion*, 6 (Spring): 85–90.

Fabian, Johannes (1971) *Jamaa: a Charismatic Movement in Katanga*. Evanston, IL: Northwestern University Press.

Fernandez, James W. (1982) *Bwiti: an Ethnography of the Religious Imagination in Africa*. Princeton, NJ: Princeton University Press.

Glazier, Stephen (1983) *Marchin' the Pilgrims Home: Leadership and Decision-Making in an Afro-Caribbean Faith*. Westport, CT: Greenwood Press.

Horton, Robin (1971) 'African Conversion', *Africa*, 41 (April): 85–108.

Johnson, Benton (1971) 'Church and Sect Revisited', *Journal for the Scientific Study of Religion*, 10 (Summer): 124–37.

Jules-Rosette, Bennetta (1975) *African Apostles: Ritual and Conversion in the Church of John Maranke*. Ithaca, NY: Cornell University Press.

Jules-Rosette, Bennetta (ed.) (1979) *The New Religions of Africa*. Norwood, NJ: Ablex Publishing Corporation.

Lalive d'Epinay, Christian (1981) 'Popular Culture, Religion, and Everyday Life', *Social Compass*, 28, 4: 405–24.

Lanternari, Vittorio (1963) *Religions of the Oppressed: a Study of Modern Messianic Cults*. Lisa Sergio (trans.). New York: Alfred A. Knopf.

Long, Norman (1968) *Social Change and the Individual: a Study of the Social and Religious Responses to Innovation in a Zambian Rural Community*. Manchester: Manchester University Press.

MacGaffey, Wyatt (1983) *Modern Kongo Prophets: Religion in a Plural Society*. Bloomington, IN: Indiana University Press.

Martin, David (1978) *A General Theory of Secularization*. New York: Harper & Row.

Parsons, Talcott (1963) 'Introduction', in Max Weber, *The Sociology of Religion*. Ephraim Fischoff (trans.). Boston: Beacon Press, pp. xix–lxvii.

Parsons, Talcott (1966) *Societies: Evolutionary and Comparative Perspectives*. Englewood Cliffs, NJ: Prentice-Hall.

Peel, John D.Y. (1968) *Aladura: a Religious Movement Among the Yoruba*. London: International African Institute.

Perrin Jassy, Marie France (1970) *La Communanté de Base dans les Églises Africaines*. Bandundu, Zaïre: Centre d'Etudes Ethnologiques, série II, vol. 3.

Shiner, Larry (1966) 'The Concept of Secularization in Empirical Research', *Journal for the Scientific Study of Religion*, 6 (Spring): 207–20.

Sinda, Martial (1972) *Le Messianisme Congolais et ses Incidences Politiques*.Paris: Payot.

Solomon, Ted J. (1977) 'The Response of Three New Religions to the Crisis in the Japanese Value System', *Journal for the Scientific Study of Religion*, 16 (Spring): 1–14.

Turner, Harold (1974) 'Tribal Religious Movements, New', *The New Encyclopaedia Britannica*, XVIII: 697–705.

Weber, Max (1963) *The Sociology of Religion*. Ephraim Fischoff (trans.). Boston: Beacon Press.

West, Martin (1974) 'Independence and Unity: Problems of Co-operation Between African Independent Church Leaders in Soweto', *African Studies*, 33: 121–9.

West, Martin (1975) *Bishops and Prophets in a Black City: African Independent Churches in Soweto, Johannesburg*. Cape Town, South Africa: David Philip.

Wilson, Bryan R. (1973) *Magic and the Millennium: a Sociological Study of Religious Movements Among Tribal and Third-World Peoples*. New York: Harper & Row.

Wilson, Bryan R. (1982) *Religion in Sociological Perspective*. Oxford: Oxford University Press.

9

The Changing Face of Khasi Religion

Soumen Sen

The Khasis are a matrilineal tribe inhabiting the Khasi Hills of Meghalaya, a state in the north-eastern region of India. They are principally shifting cultivators. Physical anthropologists are more or less certain about their Indo-Mongoloid racial identity, but a puzzle remains about how they speak a language that beongs to the Monkhmer group of Austric languages. This puzzle has also raised a controversy about their racial identity. A tentative solution has been sought in describing them as palaeo-Mongoloids, being an intermediate or mixed type between Indo-Mongoloid and Austro-Asiatic populations (Guha, 1944: 8). Current research, however, puts them in the Indo-Mongoloid population group (Das, 1978), although many Austric elements have been traced in their religion (Chowdhury, 1978: 183–223).

From a sociological point of view Khasi religion is to be described as 'objective' since it involves a recurring performance of certain human activities which regulate the experiences of psychic life. The objective and subjective aspects of religion are thus intertwined. The psychic becomes secondary since it is a reflection of the practical aspect of life. In this sense the Khasi religion is to be taken more as a communal than as a personal religion.

Though there are some universals in all religious systems, including what is called magic and the supernormal, some degree of differentiation is to be traced between essentially ritualistic and essentially non-ritualistic types. The ritualistic religions are primarily concerned with group experience and with the integration of religious faiths into a unified world-view. What can be said generally about non-literate cultures is also true of ritualistic religion, namely, that gods have many preoccupations in addition to the support of an ethical system, as they are to see to it that the crops grow, that children thrive, that their worshippers prosper, that wars are won and evils are suppressed (Herskovits, 1969: 216). It is unlikely that such a religion will be monotheistic.

An analysis of the Khasi ritualistic system will show (as is usual with a religion which aims more at group solidarity for group achievement) that it acts as a binding force for the group by renewing and strengthening shared convictions. This system is composed of certain rules designed to initiate an individual into a communal life with a sense of communal well-being combined with responsibilities to clan and community. Significantly, the Khasi religion based on such a system is designated as *Ka Niam Khasi*, meaning 'Khasi rules of conduct'. A Khasi is bound by these rules of conduct to his or her religion by almost the same ties that bind him or her to his or her family.

Rituals

The rituals both at family and group level indicate ancestor worship, nature worship, spirit worship and divination, with a preponderance of sacrifices and wine libations. Even if there is a concept of a Creator God, he is merely propitiated along with other gods, especially goddesses, among whom the principal position is occupied by the Mother Earth.

Ancestor worship permeates every sphere of life of a Khasi, from birth to death. At the level of individuals it starts with ceremonies and rites before and after childbirth and ends with a funeral. Marriage ceremonies come in between. The most essential part of their communal life, in all community rites and festivals, is ancestor worship, and it fits in with their practice of erecting monoliths. It is a common belief among ancestor worshippers that dead ancestors freed from earthly bondage (in Khasi language, *Ka ruh shong bynda*) are elevated to a supernatural status capable of lending material aid to mortals in times of crisis. The Khasis do not accept death, do not mourn death with outward signs, preserve the bones of the dead in the clan ossuary (*mawbah*), and bid farewell to the departed souls only with the words: *Khublei khie leit bamkwai sha iing U Blei ho* ('Good bye, go and chew betelnut in the house of God'). Life and fertility, not death, occupy the centre of interest, and the dead ancestor's wish is supposed to be for the eternal continuation of life power.

For similar reasons, the Khasis have had to evolve the idea of nature worship in order to bring the forces of nature to their aid. It was an essential part of their struggle for existence. It has arisen from the practical necessity for hazardous activities and dangerous undertakings in the conflict between human goals and the realities that confront a people inhabiting a mountainous country and struggling for subsistence by means of shifting cultivation.

The same principle is at work in spirit worship and divination. An element of luck is always present in the hard struggle for existence. As good and ill luck were attributed to superior powers, benevolent and malevolent spirits, the principle of worshipping occult power and of being dependent on divination is only natural.

Every ritual is preceded by a divination of which the two most common forms are hepatoscopy and egg-breaking. This is followed by libation and sacrifice. When the priest scatters wine from a gourd on to the soil, he and his people expect more fertility from the soil. When they sacrifice a goat or a pig they expect a magical occurrence which would be to their benefit. The purpose remains the same when they invoke their ancestors. Rituals inspire them to action.

The rituals of Khasi religion, as is usual with such types of religion, are observed at both family and community level. Family rites are performed at different stages in the life cycle from birth to death, but they cannot be described as *rites of passage* which introduce an individual to a way of life. In fact, initiation rites are significantly lacking in the Khasi Hills. The ceremonies at birth and death can be regarded as parts of a composite ritual system which is mainly associated with ancestor worship. If rituals are taken as the implementation of a belief, the Khasi rituals implement the belief that the ancestors, who have been elevated to a supernatural status, will materially aid mortals in times of crisis. Sacrifice and libations are thus the integral parts of these rituals. Goats are sacrificed in consideration of their virility – blood flows to earth, and wine is likened to blood. Both are used with two ends in mind: overcoming death and ensuring birth – they amount to a life-giving principle, for it is believed that the fertility of the soil is thereby enhanced, thus fulfilling a dream which is dear to agriculturists.

Pomblang

Of all the community rituals, the *Pomblang* is the most important Khasi ritual organized under the patronage of the ruler (*syiem*) of the state (*hima*) of Khyrim which was carved out of the old state of Shillong (*Ka Hima Shillong*). Since the ritual takes place at Smit, near Nongkrem, the official residence of the *Syiem* of Khyrim and since dances form an important part of the five-day festival, *Pomblang* is now more popularly known as *Shad Nongkrem* or the Nongkrem Dance Festival. *Pomblang* means goat killing, and this indicates the significance of goat sacrifice in the ritual.

According to tradition, *U Blei Shillong* (the God of Shillong) was the founder of the state of Shillong. The *syiem* clan (the ruling clan) are the descendants of *Ka Pah-Syntiew*, the first ancestress known as *Lei Long Syiem*. The matrilineal system demands that the nephew of the present *syiem* should be the next *syiem*, and as such the rites are performed by both the sister of the *syiem* (*Ka Syiem*

Sad) and the *syiem* himself. Libations and sacrifices are offered to
U Blei Shillong, Lei Long Syiem, and *U Suidnia,* the first maternal
uncle. The ancestors are invoked to ensure rain, a good harvest,
and eradication of epidemics and famine. The *syiem* prays for
guidance from the ancestor.

The ritual part of this ritual-cum-dance festival begins in the
evening of the first day when the chief priest (*soh blei*) enters the
main hall of the *iing sad* (the residence of the *syiem* family) and
takes his seat near a hearth. The sister of the *syiem* then gives him
a gourd of rice-beer (*Ka kiad*) which he pours in libation to *U Blei
Shillong,* the God of the state of Shillong. The second gourd of rice-
beer is then given and poured for the sake of the blessing of *Lei
Long Syiem,* the ancestral mother of the *syiem* clan, and the third
is poured in libation to *U Suidnia,* the first maternal uncle.

This ritual over, the *syiem,* his ministers, and others called
bakhraw (nobles) enter the main hall. There is a holy oak pillar
called *Rishot Blei* in front of the hearth. The *syiem,* members of his
family and the ministers worship this pillar. Tradition has it that this
tree trunk dates from the time of the establishment of the state and
is considered as the living god.

On the second day the villagers clean the compound in front of
iing sad and the path to a hilltop from the *iing sad* where a goat is
to be sacrificed on the third day to propitiate *U Blei Shillong. Ka
Blei Synshar,* the reigning goddess of prosperity and justice, is also
worshipped. The headmen of different administrative units bring
goats to offer to the *syiem* at night as an indication of their
solidarity. These goats are to be sacrificed next day, the fourth day
of the festival, along with the goats to be offered by the *syiem* to
twelve different goddesses.

The elaborate ritual of the goat sacrifice on the fourth evening is
observed in three stages. In the first, the headmen of different
administrative units sit in a line in the compound of *iing sad* with
metal plates in front of them containing *pan* (betel leaves), rice, rice
powder, and betelnuts. Libation is done from the metal pitchers
seemingly to invoke the corn spirits. The next stage is divination.
The chief priest (*soh blei*) kills the cocks brought by the headmen
and takes out the entrails to examine them. It would be a bad omen
if there are holes in the entrails. But if they are found in order, then
the priest throws rice on the ground and on the goat to be sacrificed
and prays to *U Blei Shillong* with the sword in his hand, which he
passes on to the *syiem* after the prayer. The *syiem* then prays to the
god of the state (*U Blei Shillong*) holding the sword in his hand.
After the prayer, the sword is given to a person of the *nengnong*
clan who is to perform the sacrifice.

Deities

The principle of communal well-being is also operative in the conception of Khasi deities. The deities are conceived in role-specific terms which are influenced by social forces. A matrilineal society, by its own logic, conceives of female deities as agents of human well-being. A goddess *Ka Sngi* (the Sun) reigns, and a supreme goddess *Ka Blei Synshar* ensures prosperity and justice. By the same logic Mother Earth (*bei rymmaw*) is conceived of as only next to god almighty or the supreme god (*U Blei Nongthaw*), the creator of the universe. *U Blei Nongthaw*, however, is never worshipped directly and has no place in the rituals. The supreme god can only be propitiated by libation to *Bei Rymmaw*. This reflects the importance of the feminine or mother principle in a matrilineal society engaged in agriculture. Other deities associated with communal well-being are also female.

The idea of male deities presumably came later than state formation since they are all associated with administration and territorial defence. It is to be remembered that in Khasi society women are forbidden to take part in state activities. The *durbars* (councils) at all levels from the village (*shnong*) to the state (*hima*) are all-male institutions. Thus the gods associated with administration and territorial defence are male (Sen, 1985: 96–7).

The Seng Khasi movement

Christian missionaries came to the Khasi Hills almost simultaneously with the establishment of British colonial hegemony. But the progress of Christianity was considered as a challenge to the national culture of the Khasis and so a small group of educated social reformers formed a sociocultural association in 1899 called *Seng Khasi*. The formation of this association has been described by one of its leaders in the following words:

> Urged by a deep concern for the future of their race whose social structure was being eroded, whose moral fibre weakened and whose bond of unity disintegrating by the inroad of foreigners, especially the Welsh Calvinistic Mission, who mercilessly attacked, denigrated and maligned their religion, condemned their culture, sixteen Khasi non-Christian young men met together on the 23rd November, 1899 in the Brahmo Samaj Hall at Mawkhar in Shillong to form an association to forge and mould again its people and to revive the moral teaching and tenets passed on from generation to generation. (Singh, 1982: 7)

Thus it appears that the immediate cause for the formation of *Seng Khasi* was the challenge posed by the Christian missions with the active support of the colonial government. The challenge was

real. In addition to Christian proselytization, a campaign had been
launched against traditional institutions and practices. The principal
objective of the *Seng Khasi* was, therefore, to work for the retention
of their sociocultural and religious heritage. Since the tribe was at
the stage of development when social institutions were bound to be
interwined with kinship and religion, the *Seng Khasi* leaders
emphasized the importance of religion for retaining social cohesion
and fellowship. The constitution of the *Seng Khasi* states that it is
an organization of all the Khasis who adhere to the traditional
religion. These Khasis are described as *Khasi Khasis* to differentiate
them from the Christian Khasis. A Khasi is declared to be a Khasi
only because of his religion; to understand him, one has to go deep
down into the very roots of his religion.

The *Seng Khasi* has recently been admitted to the International
Association of Religious Freedom (IARF) as an associate member,
and two of its delegates attended the 24th IARF Congress in
Holland in 1981. They declared in the Congress that according to
the Khasi religion there is but one God, the God Universal, the
Creator of Mankind, and that religion is a way to God as well as
to man and is known as *Ka Niam Tipbriew Ka Niam Tipblei* – the
man-knowing and God-knowing religion (Mawrie, 1982: 70).

In this sense Khasi religion is claimed to be monotheistic. One
important objective of the *Seng Khasi* is to create consciousness of
God, the Sovereign Lord, the Almighty, the Creator, the Omnipotent, the Omniscient. It is to be remembered that in the formative
stage the *Seng Khasi* worked in close cooperation with the Unitarian
church and the *Brahmo Samaj*, both of which preach the existence
of only one single God as the Sovereign Creator, the Almighty.

There is also an attempt at adjusting an ethical system to the
matrilineal kinship system. It is claimed that the Khasi religion has
two parts; the first is knowledge of God as the supreme Creator –
Ka Niam Tip Blei – and the second is knowledge of communal
solidarity or knowing one's fellow men and accepting the matrilineal
system – *Ka Niam Tip Briew, Tip Kur, Tip Kha* (Singh, 1979: 96).
Accordingly, the tenets of the religion were written down, of which
the following are basic:

1 Earn righteousness (*Kamai ia ka hok*);
2 Know man, know God (*Tip briew tip blei*);
3 Know your maternal and paternal kin (*Tip kur, tip kha*).

In the *Seng Khasi* interpretation, the Khasi religion is monotheistic and God is conceived as a personal God with whom an individual
can have direct communion. He can be worshipped alone in one's
own house or in the open, in fact anywhere. There is no established

priesthood (Rymbai, 1979: 115). This is distinctly different from the ritualistic system which permits only communal propitiation conducted by a priest with libation and sacrifice as carried out by *soh blei* (the chief priest) in *Pomblang*. Moreover, *lyngdohship* in the Khasi Hills is nothing but an established priesthood.

It is also said that *U Blei*, the name given to God, is He and only He, signifying his masculinity. At the same time, this Creator God is understood to be above gender, called *Ka Blei U Blei*, as well as above number and called *Ki Blei U Blei* (Mawrie, 1979: 83). Thus, while in one interpretation God is masculine (*He and only He*), in another version it is said that God is addressed in prayers as either *A Blei* or *Ko Blei* without using the masculine prefix *U* or the feminine prefix *Ka*. God is also addressed as *Ka Blei U Blei* with the feminine prefix *Ka* having precedence (Rymbai, 1979: 112).

Whatever the manner of addressing this divinity, the *Seng Khasi* interpretation is that God is one and that the religion is monotheistic. With regard to worship, however, the Khasi religion, as propagated by the *Seng Khasi*, constitutes God in three aspects: God Universal, the Creator of mankind; God Localized, the guardian of the land and the people of the Khasi Hills; and God at home, a Being right inside the house and family. This supreme God known as *U Blei Nongthaw Nongbuh* also takes different identities at the different levels of universe, locality, and home. While at the levels of universe and locality He has all male identities, at the family level He takes on a feminine character and is called *Ka Blei ha iing* (Mawrie, 1982: 70).

The identities of God that are propagated by the *Seng Khasi* leaders seem to have been superimposed on the earlier concept of religion with mostly female deities.

Religion idealized

Keenly feeling the twin challenge of the modern age and Christianity, the leaders of the *Seng Khasi* set out to revive, reform, and codify their version of Khasi religion. With this end in view, U Jeebon Roy, the architect of the *Seng Khasi*, brought out a book, *Ka Niam Jong Ki Khasi*, in 1897 followed by another, *Ka Kitab ba Batai Pynshynna Shaphang Uwei U Blei*, in 1900. In these books, U Jeebon Roy dwelled upon the universality of God and conceptualized Khasi religion. Since then other writers have also made similar contributions. The *Seng Khasi* leaders maintain that Khasi religion is not animistic in the sense of being based on ancestor-, spirit- and nature-worship but is spiritual and monotheistic. It has now assumed the character of a distinct faith with an ethical system appropriate to both the age-old ritualistic system and matrilineal social order.

Thus, the *Seng Khasi* leaders proceeded in a highly selective fashion, and the selections operated in the direction of both modernity and monotheism. This enterprise, which canonized some elements of the old religion and preserved others, was certainly creative and idealized. It also seems to have met with a certain measure of success.

References

Chowdhury, J.N. (1978) *The Khasi Canvas*. Shillong: Chapala Book Stall.

Das, B.M. (1978) *Variations in Physical Characteristics in the Khasi Population of North-East India*. Guwahati: Datta Barua & Co.

Guha, B.S. (1944) 'Racial Elements in the Population', *Oxford Pamphlets on Indian Affairs*, no. 22.

Herskovits, M.J. (1969) *Cultural Anthropology*. New Delhi: Oxford and IBH.

Mawrie, H.O. (1979) 'God and Man', *Khasi Heritage*, H. Roy (ed.). Shillong: Seng Khasi, pp. 83–90.

Mawrie, H.O. (1982) 'A Short View of Khasi Religion', *Where Lies the Soul of Our Race?* H. Roy (ed.). Shillong: Seng Khasi, pp. 66–71.

Rymbai, R.T. (1979) 'Some Aspects of the Religion of the Khasi-Pnar', *Khasi Heritage*. Shillong: Seng Khasi, pp. 110–18.

Sen, Soumen (1985) *Social and State Formation in Khasi-Jaintia Hills: a Study of Folklore*. New Delhi: B.R. Publishing Corporation.

Singh, Kynpham (1979) 'Khasi and Jaintia Religion', *Khasi Heritage*. Shillong: Seng Khasi, pp. 91–109.

Singh, Kynpham (1982) 'Seng Khasi', *Where Lies the Soul of Our Race?* Shillong: Seng Khasi, pp. 7–19.

Notes on Contributors

Said Amir Arjomand is Professor of Sociology at the State University of New York at Stony Brook. He has written extensively on Iran, Shiism, and religion and politics in Islam and is currently working on a comparative study of revolution. His publications include *The Shadow of God and the Hidden Imam* (University of Chicago Press, 1984) and *The Turban for the Crown* (Oxford University Press, 1988).

James A. Beckford is Professor of Sociology at the University of Warwick. His main publications include *The Trumpet of Prophecy* (1975), *Cult Controversies* (1985) and *Religion and Advanced Industrial Societies* (1989). He is the editor of *New Religious Movements and Rapid Social Change* (1986) and was President of the Association for the Sociology of Religion, 1988–9.

Roberto Cipriani is Professor of Sociology of Knowledge at the University of Rome and Secretary of the International Sociological Association's Research Committee for the Sociology of Religion. His main publications include *The Sociology of Legitimation* (1987) and *La religione diffusa* (1988).

Michael Hill studied and later taught at the London School of Economics until his appointment in 1975 to the Chair of Sociology at Victoria University, Wellington, New Zealand. He is the author of *A Sociology of Religion* (1973) and *The Religious Order* (1973).

Bennetta Jules-Rosette is Professor of Sociology at the University of California, San Diego. Her research interests include semiotic studies of religious discourse, tourist art, and new technologies in Africa, and since 1969 she has conducted a series of field studies in Zaïre, Zambia, Côte d'Ivoire and Kenya. Her main publications include *Symbols of Change* (1981) and *The Messages of Tourist Art* (1984).

Yves Lambert is Director of Research in Rural Sociology at the National Institute of Agronomic Research and Lecturer in the Sociology of Religions at the University of Rennes in France. His study of the religious evolution of a Breton village, in collaboration with the National Centre for Scientific Research, resulted in *Dieu Change en Bretagne* (1985). He is currently studying the value systems of rural youth and comparative religions.

Thomas Luckmann is Professor of Sociology at the University of Konstanz in the Federal Republic of Germany. His main publications include *The Social Construction of Reality* (with Peter Berger, 1966), *The Invisible Religion* (1970) and *Life-World and Social Realities* (1983).

Maria Isaura Pereira de Queiroz is Director of the Centro de Estudos Rurais e Urbanos and Professor of Sociology at the University of São Paulo in Brazil. She has published numerous books and articles, including *Réforme et Révolution dans les Sociétés traditionnelles* (1968) and *Os Cangaceiros: les Bandits d'Honneur brésiliens* (1968).

Daniel Regan is Associate Professor of Sociology and International Affairs at the University of Pittsburgh, USA. He is the author of a work on freedom of speech and expression in Malaysia and is also conducting (with John Markoff) a study of the religious contents of the world's constitutions. He is the author of numerous articles on Southeast Asian intellectuals (including their religious orientations), civil religion, and medical professionals in the Third World.

Roland Robertson is Professor of Sociology and Religious Studies at the University of Pittsburgh, USA. He is the author or co-author of a number of books, including *International Systems and the Modernization of Societies, The Sociological Interpretation of Religion* and *Meaning and Change*. His current empirical work centres on East Asian religion, modernization and globalization.

Soumen Sen is Head of the Centre for Literary and Cultural Studies at the North-Eastern Hill University in Shillong, India. He has written extensively on Khasi-Jaintia society and culture, and his numerous articles and books include *Social and State Formation in the Khasi-Jaintia Hills: a Study of Folklore* and an edited volume, *Folklore in North-East India.*

Wiebe Zwaga is a Graduate Assistant in the Department of Sociology, Massey University, Palmerston North, New Zealand. His undergraduate studies were completed at Tilburg University in the Netherlands, and he is now engaged on postgraduate research on mass-media and religion.

Index

Index compiled by Peva Keane